— Mapping the Beat —

— Mapping the Beat —

Popular Music and Contemporary Theory

*Edited by
Thomas Swiss,
John Sloop,
and Andrew Herman*

First published 1998

Blackwell Publishers Inc.
350 Main Street
Malden, MA
02148

Blackwell Publishers Ltd.
108 Cowley Road
Oxford OK4 1JF
UK

Library of Congress Cataloging-in-Publication Data

Swiss, Thomas
    Mapping the beat : popular music and contemporary theory / Thomas Swiss, John Sloop, and Andrew Herman.
        p. cm.
    Includes bibliographical references and index.
    ISBN 1-57718-077-1. – ISBN 1-57718-078-X (pbk.)
    1. Popular music – Social aspects. 2. Music and society. 3. Popular culture. I. Sloop, John M. II. Herman, Andrew. III. Title
ML3470.S96 1998
781.64--dc21   96-39868
                                                                             CIP
British Library of Congress Cataloging-in-Publication Data

Compositon by Megan H. Zuckerman

Manufactured in the U.S.A.

Contents

Contributors

Norma Coates writes on gender and popular music. Her recent work includes an essay in *Sexing the Groove* (Routledge), and a piece on Courtney Love and the construction of "bad mothers."

Cynthia Fuchs is Associate Professor of English, Film & Media Studies at George Mason University. Her most recent published work has focused on Michael Jackson and the Artist Formerly Known As Prince. She is co-editor, with Chris Holmlund, of *Between the Sheets, In the Streets: Queer/Lesbian/Gay Documentary* (Minnesota).

Andrew Goodwin is the author of *Dancing in the Distraction Factory: Music Television and Popular Culture* (Minnesota), and he has co-edited a number of books on music and television, including *Sound and Vision* (Routledge). He is Professor of Communication at the University of San Francisco.

Robert Hanke's work has appeared in many journals, including *Public Culture*, *Critical Studies in Mass Communication*, and *Public*, as well as in the book *Men, Masculinity and the Media* (Sage). His most recent contribution to multicultural media criticism appears in *Television Criticism* (Houghton Mifflin).

Andrew Herman has taught courses in popular music at Boston College and Drake University, and has published essays in journals such as *Option* and *Postmodern Culture*. He has a book forthcoming from Westview in 1998: *The "Better Angels" of Capitalism*. He is Assistant Professor of Sociology at Drake University.

Tony Kirschner is a doctoral candidate in Communications and Cultural Studies at the University of Illinois at Urbana-Champaign. His work focuses on critical theory, qualitative research methods, and popular culture.

Holly Kruse teaches in the Department of Communication at La Salle University in Philadelphia. She has published essays on such topics as audio and domestic space, subcultural identities, and college music in *Stanford Humanities Review*, *Popular Music*, and other journals.

Ramona Liera-Schwichtenberg is Associate Professor of Women's Studies at the Center for Women's Studies, Wichita State University. She teaches courses in popular culture, Chicana feminism, and feminist film theory. She has published widely on postmodernism, feminist theory, and the media. She is editor of *The Madonna Connection* (Westview).

Mark J. V. Olson is a graduate student in the Department of Communication Studies and is affiliated with the University Program in Cultural Studies, University of North Carolina at Chapel Hill.

Russell A. Potter teaches at Rhode Island College in Providence, Rhode Island. He is the author of *Spectacular Vernaculars: Hip-Hop and the Politics of Postmodernism* (SUNY), and writes a regular column, "Roots 'n' Rap," for *Headz Up!*, an on-line magazine of hip-hop music and culture.

David Sanjek is the Director of Archives for Broadcast Music Inc. In addition to publications on popular music and film, he is the U.S. Chair of the International Association for the Study of Popular Music. He also serves on the Archives and Preservation Committee of the National Academy of Performing Arts and Sciences.

John Sloop is Assistant Professor of Communication Studies at Vanderbilt University and author of *The Cultural Prison: Discourse, Prisoners, and Punishment* (Alabama). He has published essays on the intersections of ideology, race, rap, and autobiography in *Communication Studies* and the *Journal of Film and Video*.

Thomas Swiss has published criticism in such journals as *Postmodern Culture*, *Popular Music*, and *The New England Review*. His books include *Measure* (Alabama) and *Rough Cut*, a collection of poems (Illinois). He is Center for the Humanities Professor of English at Drake University where he teaches courses on music and contemporary culture.

Steve Waksman is writing a cultural history of the electric guitar. He is currently working in the American Studies program at the University of Minnesota.

Deena Weinstein, professor at DePaul University, specializes in cultural sociology and has taught a Sociology of Rock course for over a dozen years. Her many publications include the contemporary classic *Heavy Metal: A Cultural Sociology* (Macmillan).

Sheila Whiteley is head of Research and Postgraduate Studies in the Department of Popular Music, Salford University, England. She is author of *The Space between the Notes* (Routledge) and is currently editing and contributing to *Sexing the Groove* (Routledge), a collection of articles on gender and popular music.

Acknowledgments

Our commitment to the project of *Mapping the Beat* began as shared work on a conference on popular music held at Drake University in 1996. We're grateful to the presenters and participants at that conference as well as to our assistant, Jen Smith, and the Center for the Humanities for its material support.

Collaborating across our respective disciplines – English, Communication Studies, and Sociology – turned out to be engaging and illuminating work. So did the pleasurable task of working with the contributors to this book – we owe them our thanks. The many individuals who contributed to this project include the anonymous readers of an early draft of the collection, Susan Rabinowitz, our enthusiastic editor at Blackwell, and both Donna Jones and Nancy Smith who kept us on track.

The editors also wish to thank Marvin and Kitwoolsey (fibs), Heidi Henson for grace under pressure, Cynthia Lewis, the English and Sociology Departments at Drake, the Department of Communication Studies at Vanderbilt, Kent Ono, Jacob and Alley for their music, "Peabod," and Simon Frith.

Part I

NOISE,
PERFORMANCE,
AND THE POLITICS OF SOUND

1

Mapping the Beat

Spaces of Noise
and Places of Music

Andrew Herman, Thomas Swiss, and John Sloop

I t is no exaggeration to say that one of the most vibrant areas of scholarship and teaching over the past decade has been the interdisciplinary field of cultural studies. One of the consequences of cultural studies as an approach to the analysis of social dynamics of cultural production and consumption has been the reinvigoration of popular music studies. This collection of essays is intended as both a general contribution to current thinking in the field and a site for debating various current models for the analysis of popular music.

In particular, a number of essays engage what we describe in this introduction as a spatialized analysis of popular music, an analysis that explores the promises and possibilities of a cartography of sound as a territory of power. For these contributors, "mapping the beat" often denotes a critical approach that works from the assumption that relations of social power are located on the shifting boundaries between "noise" and "music." Jacques Attali's work, especially *Noise: The Political Economy of Music* (1985), serves as a kind of touchstone for many of these contributors. Other essays, however, embark from other positions; equally focused and theorized, they trace the ways in which popular music is represented and imagined, experienced and used. All of the essays offer in their various ways *stories* about popular music and the study of popular music: stories that involve reflection and critique, narration and exposition, and that chart more than a few new routes through a remarkably rich terrain.

Although popular music studies is a diverse field and while many studies cover a broad range of interests, scholarship has tended to emphasize one of three different categories of analysis. First, there are works primarily concerned with the *institutional* analysis of the production of popular music and its political economy. Work in this area includes political-economic and organizational analyses of the music industry, as well as considerations of the technologies of musical production, government policies towards musical production, and the practices of musicianship itself. This approach is evinced in books such as Negus (1992), Jones (1992), Bennett et al. (1993), and Cohen (1991). Second, there are works devoted to the *textual* analysis of the representations and symbolic meanings of popular musical forms. Such works tend to offer musicological analysis of the structure of popular music, interpretation of lyrical content, or the examination of the visual iconography of music in the form of music video. Key works in this area include Shepherd (1991), Walser (1993), Whiteley (1992), and Brackett (1995). Third, there are works that concentrate on the *ethnographic* analysis of rituals of everyday life through which popular music is interpreted and used. Here, the focus is upon fans in general, and musical scenes or subcultures in particular, as they actively create cultural meaning and identity. Works in this area include classics such as Hebdige (1979) and Willis (1978), and more recent works such as Lewis (1992) and Thornton (1995).

Taken as a whole, these three approaches comprise the dominant framework for investigating popular music from a cultural studies perspective. Indeed, over the years, this tripartite division of labor has developed into a well-defined logic of analysis. According to this logic, popular musical texts can be analyzed as institutionally produced commercial commodities that function as cultural artifacts inscribed with meanings which are then consumed and interpreted by fans and audiences. This logic has roots in the critical analysis of popular culture, specifically in the work of Theodor Adorno and the Frankfurt school. For Adorno (1990), the holistic critical analysis of popular music as it moved through the circuits of production, textualization, and audience reception was central to understanding the politics of mass culture in modern capitalism. Popular music was a rationalized, standardized, and pseudo-individualized artifact that produced rationalized and standardized responses of emotional sentimentality and "false consciousness" in the consuming audience.

In contemporary popular music studies, Adorno's monolithic view of the culture industry, his high-culture dismissal of the aesthetics of popular music, and his pessimistic account of the pleasures and uses of popular music have all been soundly criticized. Within cultural studies, the theoretical counterpoint to Adorno has been the Gramscian emphasis on the resistance to hegemony among the "people" and their capacity to produce their own meanings of popular texts and artifacts through ritual, recontextualization, and alternate readings.[1] Certainly, it has been the emphasis on the potential among consumers of popular culture to be creatively active readers and users, and thus evade being sewn up into dominant ideology, that has energized most of the ethnographic work on musical subcultures and fandom from Hebdige (1979) to Fiske (1989, 1993).[2] Nonetheless, both Adorno and Antonio Gramsci, and the work derived from each, share a common desire to connect production-text-audience at the core of a political economy of culture in capitalist society. This logic has been implicitly accepted as the basis for much work on popular music from cultural studies.[3]

Two recently published textbooks for popular music studies, Longhurst (1995) and Shuker (1995), explicitly embrace versions of the production-text-consumption framework as *the* organizing principle for popular music study and pedagogy. Of course, this model has the distinct appeal of being able to conceptualize certain undeniably salient features of popular music in contemporary culture. Popular music is, after all, primarily produced within the institutional and organizational contexts of media corporations whose primary intent is to make money. Thus the music industry has important (if not easily determined) effects on the ways in which musicians work, how styles and genres are formed and marketed, the technological means through which music is recorded, broadcast, and circulated, and the aesthetic form and meaning of popular music.

There is still much to be to be learned from these three modes of analysis and the logic that links them. Indeed, some of the contributions to this volume can be located most comfortably within this framework. Our project in this introduction, then, is not to argue with the work generated from within this framework; rather, it is to deepen it and, beyond that, create a

space of interdisciplinary conversation between such work and an alternative, yet complementary, framework for conceptualizing and understanding
popular music. This approach attempts to cut across the division and links
between institution, text, and consumption by focusing on how popular
music constitutes a terrain of social and cultural identity that can be mapped
in terms of its spatiality or, more precisely, as spaces of noise and places of
music.[4]

TOWARDS A MAPPING OF THE BEAT

> Everything in the world of pop music is a commodity, whether
> sound, image, word, or act – that tells us both everything and
> nothing about how it works.
>
> –Jody Berland, "Sound, Image, and Social Space," 25

> The project of mapping spaces of power inevitably will raise dif-
> ferent and other questions: questions about mobilities rather
> than change, about lines of intensities rather than identities. Spa-
> tial power is a matter of orientations and directions, of entries
> and exits.
>
> –Lawrence Grossberg,
> "Cultural Studies and/in New Worlds," 7–8

Why engage in a cartography of music and noise, or what we call the
process of "mapping the beat"? Part of the rationale for situating the study
of popular music within the cultural analysis of spatiality is expressed by
Jody Berland in the quotation above. Indeed, the concern with the politics
of music and culture as commodity form tells us everything and nothing.
Popular music is an ubiquitous quotidian commodity in the capitalist world
system, whether one is in Los Angeles, London, or Lagos. But what, asks
Berland, does this incorrigible social fact of capitalist culture tell us about
how popular music operates in everyday life? For Berland, unlike cultural
populists like Fiske, this is a not a issue that leads to a valorization of the
moment of consumption as the arbiter of meaning and power. Rather,
Berland's strategy is to reconceptualize the moments of production-text-
consumption as a part of a broader "cultural technology."

Building upon the work of Colin Mercer (1988) and Teresa de Lauretis
(1987), Berland argues that popular music as cultural technology can be

understood as "a mediation between a mode of address, the occasion of its reception, and its social and material consolidation as technique" (1993: 27). Take, for example, the cultural form of the popular song. Berland argues that the commodification of the song is only the beginning of the story, for we must understand the processes through which the song is insinuated into the fabric of people's lives. The fuller story involves the displacement of live performance as the primary mode of address and occasion of reception of popular music; the separation of singer from song and from the listener through sound recording; and the mobile privatization of the site and occasion of listening through technologies of electronic reproduction. Consideration of popular music as cultural technology, in turn, raises the issue of spatiality. As Berland argues: "In theoretical terms, we need to situate cultural forms with the production and reproduction of capitalist spatiality. How does one produce the other: the song, the car, the radio station, the road, the town, the listener?…Why is the literature on pop music…so often empty of cars, not to mention elevators, offices, shopping malls, hotels, sidewalks, airplanes, buses, urban landscapes, small towns, northern settlements or satellite broadcasts?" (Berland, 1992: 39).

Berland's analysis locates the meanings and effects of cultural commodities within the material context of spatiality, the interrelated locales in which the moments of production-text-consumption are instantiated, rather than within the hermetic logic of the moments themselves.

Berland's call for a spatialized approach to cultural studies, and popular music studies in particular, has been extended by Lawrence Grossberg in his more recent writings (1994, 1996). One of the many nuances of Grossberg's critique of the production-text-consumption model is that, in terms of understanding the effect of cultural forms and practices such as popular music, "sometimes the production of meaning can be little more than a distraction" (1992: 52). That is, the most important effects of popular music in everyday life involve economic, bodily, libidinal, emotional, and political effects, some of which are material and some of which are ineffable, effects that cannot be reduced to the meaning of a cultural text and how that meaning is inscribed in production or interpreted in consumption. Moreover, such effects are articulated in and through concrete situations such as work, play, shopping, family life, and so on. Thus, Grossberg argues that space must be understood materially before it can be understood phenomenologically or hermeneutically.

Finally, Henri Lefebvre (1991) offers a somewhat different conceptualization of mapping and spatial power that moves us closer to understanding
spaces of noise and places of music. He distinguishes between two forms
that mapping and spatiality in capitalist society can take: *representations of space*
or *spaces of representation*. Representations of space embody the ways in which
spaces and places are conceived by dominant groups in society and through
which the dominant order of society is materially inscribed. This refers to
the spatial imaginary of architects, urban planners, engineers, politicians,
zoning boards, and land use experts who seek to rationally order concrete
space according to an abstract *vision* of the spatial requirement of capitalist
rationality. This regime of mapping embodies what Derek Gregory calls the
"eye of power," an eye that "soars up into the abstract space of the visible and
the geometric. The architect who designs, the planner who draws up master
places, see their 'objects,' buildings and neighborhoods from afar....They
pass from the 'lived' to the abstract in order to project that abstraction onto
the level of the lived" (Lefebvre quoted in Gregory, 1995: 404).

In contrast, "spaces of representation" are rooted, not in the abstract eye
of planners, police or corporate locators, but in the concrete spaces and
places of everyday life. For Lefebvre, spaces of representations are coun-
termappings, "linked to the clandestine or underground side of social life,
and also to art." They are literally *embodied* in spatial practices through which
space is lived in and used in ways quite different from those imagined and
desired by the powerful. "It is in this space that the 'private' realm asserts
itself, albeit more vigorously, and always in a conflictual way, against the
public one.... Any mobilization of 'private life' would be accompanied by a
restoration of the body, and the contradictions of space would have to be
brought out into the open....The restoration of the body means, first and
foremost, the restoration of the sensory-sensual-of speech, the voice, of
smell, of hearing. In short, of the non-visual" (Lefebvre, 1991: 362–3).

Like those of Berland and of Grossberg, Lefebvre's insights into the
embodied politics of the conflict between public and private, strategies of
power and tactics of resistance, representations of space and spaces of representation are central to a spatialized analysis of popular music. They direct
attention away from the realm of visuality to that of aurality. Although
Lefebvre's arguments about the "restoration of the body" to cultural politics

may be no more than, as he says, "suggestions" or "pointers," they point in the right direction, which is towards a mapping of the beat.

But first, a story.

STORY SPACES

[T]he very idea of a map, with its implicit dependence upon the survey of a stable terrain, fixed references and measurement, seems to contradict the palpable flux and fluidity of metropolitan life and cosmopolitan movement. Maps are full of references and indications, but they are not peopled.
　　　　　　　　 –Ian Chambers, "Cities without Maps," 188–9

An unseen ruler defines with geometry
an unruleable expanse of geography
straining eyes try to understand
the works incessantly in hand
the carving and the paring of the land
the quarter square the graph divides,
beneath the rule, a country hides.
　　　　　　　　　　 –Wire, "Map Ref. 41° N 93° W"

What follows is a spatial story, an exploration and a cartography, a story of maps and mappings of both the legible and the audible. It is also a story of the noises and hybrid musics of the city that spill over the edges of certain maps in a festival of sound. Here, certain spaces of noise and places of music converge in order to make a difference in a landscape of indifference.

The story: I am sitting in my home office, looking at a series of maps.[5] They represent an area of the city in which I live, Des Moines, called the Carpenter/Drake Park Neighborhood. The maps were given to me by the city's Community Development Department and are part of an "Action Plan" for "neighborhood redevelopment." There is a map of the city as a whole; a smaller map of the Drake Neighborhood whose territory encompasses the Carpenter/Drake Park Neighborhood; a detailed map of the streets and individual buildings where I can locate my own house on the map, allowing me the combined pleasures of voyeurism and narcissism by simultaneously being within and outside the represented space. There is a map of current zoning, dividing the neighborhood into big blocks of color-coded and categorized spaces of "R-3 Multi-Family," "C-1 Neighborhood Commercial," and so on; there is also a map of "Future Land Use" that is similarly color-coded and categorized.

These maps clearly embody the abstract "eye of power," which animates Lefebvre's representations of space, valorizing and fetishizing the visible and the geometric. Quite literally, they plot out spaces and places of identity, affect, and agency. Yet equally important to these maps is the narrative that accompanies them in the action plan. This discourse, along with the maps and their coding, functions as a *legend* that situates my neighborhood within the strategic social and spatial imaginary. All maps have legends and, as de Certeau points out, the word "legend" is derived from the Latin *legenda*, which not only means what is to be read, but also what *can* be read (de Certeau, 1984: 106). Thus, the legend of a map is a structure of inscribing meaning onto space. Moreover, in a broader sense, legends are also place-myths that rhetorically and narratively construct historical and temporal identities for specific locales. In this particular case, the action plan locates its strategy of neighborhood redevelopment within a fascinating legend or history of the neighborhood as an idealized middle-American community of interclass probity and decorum. According to this history, the

> "area in the 1890's began to take on the character it would hold on to for the next half-century. It was a multi-faceted character. Tolerance of belief and lifestyle were central to its nature. Carpenters and craftsman lived side by side with doctors and dentists. Corporate giants lived next to small shopkeepers. Ministers lived next door to evangelists. Professors and students shared accommodation...The people, like the houses, were not outside displays of pretension [sic]. The beauty of their homes was reserved for inside." (Carpenter/Drake Park Neighborhood Revitalization Task Force, 1995:2)

This peculiar legend functions as a mythic past against which one can read and evaluate the "ruins" of the present and chart a path of revitalization into the future. It is interesting to note this history's implicit valorization of bourgeois distinction between the private and public spheres, with the proper locus of "beauty" and aesthetic creativity within the solid utilitarian walls of the disciplined domestic abode and not in the streets outside. As cultural historians of the period have pointed out, a central feature of the Victorian ideology of domesticity was that the middle-class household was to be the primary locus of the moral and cultural education of children. Victorian mothers were considered the custodians of this education, and one can imagine that throughout the neighborhood in parlors in houses such as my own, mothers tutored their children's tastes and manners through piano and singing lessons. As Holly Kruse (1993) points out, the piano (and later the phonograph) was a key instrument in inculcating the values of "polite" and "civilized" American bourgeois culture. Moreover, the musical discipline of the piano provided an aural space of order, a "field of melody," which protected the middle-class household from the chaotic noise and moral turpitude of the emergent mass culture and the sounds of the immigrant quarters. Whatever the multifaceted character of this neighborhood in terms of occupations and religious denominations, it was, at least according to this account, a place with a remarkably tranquil and functional structure and order of differences. In a word, the spatial practices of the neighborhood supposedly embodied and exuded *harmony*.

The harmonious past of this place is long gone, however, displaced by a pathological present. According to the narrative of the action plan, the order of both domestic and public spheres was disrupted by a series of transformations in the spatial landscape of postwar American capitalist society that affected almost every urban center in the country: the rise of the mobile, privatized culture of the automobile and freeway system; the concomitant emergence of suburbs and the exodus of the predominantly white, professional middle classes to that space of the landed consumer; the erosion of the working-class occupational base in the inner city as industrial and manufacturing jobs left for cheaper labor and lower taxes; the increased segregation of the city along the lines of race, class, and ethnicity; and the steady decline in the quality and condition of schools, streets, residences, and city services. By 1979, this area was defined as the "city's most rapidly deteriorating" neighborhood. Although the neighborhood has made something of a recovery since that time, it is still classified in the curious language of the planners as "transitional negative" which means, according to the plan, "that it is likely to continue to decline without intervention." So, this is the legendary spatial story of the action plan: where there was order, there is now disorder; where there was once stability, there is chaos; where there was once harmony, there is dissonance.

And what once was will be again, for the action plan offers a series of goals and strategies for dealing with each "problem." Litter, sewers, sidewalks, streetlighting, traffic, commercial zoning, abandoned and deteriorating housing, vacant lots, owner-occupancy, landlord-tenant relations, community policing, graffiti and, last but not least, the noise of the streets are scrutinized, defined, and targeted for action in the narrative. As I read through this mapping of my neighborhood, one particular facet of the action plan, listed under "Community Enhancement Goals," stands out. The issue is "cultural and economic diversity"; the goal is to "support and promote the development of community identity"; the plan of action is to "organize a festival celebrating the cultural and ethnic diversity of the neighborhood." Right next to this particular emplotment of strategic rationality is a small drawing of a carnival tent. The tent has a little pennant sticking from its top, flickering in an imagined breeze, while three small balloons drift past the pennant, ascending gaily into the air. From a chaotic, pathological present, the action plan imagines a future where its crowning achievement is a festive party!

My quarrel with the spatial imaginary of the Drake action plan, and the strategic power it evinces, is not that the particular problems it identifies are not present. Nor is it that the specific plans of action are not worthy, particularly that of attending to the politics of community identity or "celebrating" cultural diversity. Rather, my quarrel with the plan is that its cartography is legible and not audible, that it is both silent and deaf. It offers a pale and pallid *vision* of a festival of cultural diversity that is disciplined and harmonious, without understanding the *sound* of the festival – that sonoric expression and excess that occurs everyday on the streets of this neighborhood. As the band Wire sings in "Map Ref. 41° N 93° W" (quoted above), "Beneath the rule, a country hides."

Thus, in spite of its desire for a celebration of difference, the space imagined by the plan in general, and the proposed festival in particular, is homogenous and constrained because it does not, or cannot, attend to what Lefebvre describes as the dramatization of space through sound and music: "[T]hanks to the potential energies of a variety of groups capable of divert-

ing homogenized space to their own purposes, a theatricalized or drama-
tized space is liable to arise. Space is liable to be eroticized and restored to
ambiguity, to the common birthplace of needs and desires, by means of
music, by means of differential systems and valorizations which overwhelm
the strict localization of needs and desires in spaces" (1991: 391).

In its desire for unambiguous order, in its yearning for a future that
echoes the past, the abstract space of the Action Plan effaces the reality of
this neighborhood's identity as a space of sound. This sonic reality, as Ian
Chambers has written, "is a reality that is multiformed, heterogeneous and
diasporic" (1993: 189). In the "atonal ensemble" of the festival of the street
one can hear "a creative disorder, an instructive confusion, an interpolating
space in which the imagination carries you in every direction, even towards
the previously unthought."

A festival of the street is underway right now, even as I write. A few
doors down, a boombox is blaring Toni Braxton's "You're Making Me High,"
a song about black female heterosexual desire. Yet it is a man who is dancing and singing along with the song, crooning the words as he lustily gyrates
his way from his front door to the sidewalk and back again. Who, I wonder,
is he singing to or about? In which direction is his imagination being carried? Is he imagining himself as Toni Braxton's lover and embodiment of
desire or is he imagining himself singing it to his own lover? Is the lover a
man or a woman, a specific or generalized other?

Directly across the street lives a family of Bosnian refugees. For reasons
that govern the flow of displaced people fleeing that civil war, and reasons
unknown to me, a fair number of Bosnians have settled in this neighborhood. On hot Friday nights such as this, the father will sometimes sit on the
front stoop, drinking and smoking. After a few hours, when darkness falls,
he will begin to sing Balkan folk songs. They strike me as sad songs, songs
of yearning for a place he once called home where his imagination carries
him. In contrast, his sons and daughters, young adults in their twenties, surround themselves with very different sounds. From their parked cars
emanate a hybrid of Balkan folk instruments, Middle Eastern vocal stylings,
and a furiously fast techno-jungle beat. It is a sound that is simultaneously
folk and electronic, undeniably local in its lyrical evocation of a place called
home (a place that is both the same yet different from their father's) yet
global in its instrumentation.

As I listen to this particular musical conjuring of a hybrid, diasporic place, I can hear the approaching WOMPH-WOMPH-WOMPH of a vehicle with a high-wattage stereo system . On this night, as on most nights, my street becomes a veritable valley of the jeep beats as a steady stream of low-riders, 4 X 4s, and customized vans hip-hop their way to the park at the end of the block, shaking the walls of the houses with their reverberations. It doesn't matter whether the particular recording is Dr. Dre, the Fugees, or A Tribe Called Quest, the effect on the aural landscape is the same. The drivers enact a territorial will to power that can not be ignored and is rarely challenged. In whatever ways the occupants of the vehicles are or feel themselves to be disempowered in everyday life, when they cruise here, they reign supreme over the sound of the streets.

Inside my house and in my home office, a different musical scene is being performed. I am listening to country music: Waylon Jennings's recording *Right for the Time*. All of the familiar country themes and tropes are present here: the remembrance of and nostalgia for rural roots; the loss of love, its pain, and its redemption; the romance of the road and its lonesome itinerant freedom; and the celebration of going on a drinking binge and the rueful remorse of the morning after. But what is perhaps most fascinating about my musical experience is noting the somewhat contradictory claims made for the efficacy and power of music in creating a sense of place. In the first song of the recording, "WBPT," Jennings (1996) closes by telling the listener:

> This little song means
> nothing to you
> Wouldn't matter at all
> if you wanted it to
> Just part of my life
> and part of the show
> Ain't that good –
> but I thought
> you'd want to know

In contrast to Jennings's classic country virtue of self-effacing humility about the ephemeral consequences of his music, however, are the liner notes on the CD. Here, the record's producer attempts to convince the listener of the manifold ways in which the music *does* matter. The mattering is in the mapping of the aural landscape:

> Ever the pioneer, Waylon's new record...takes the listener on a journey where space and time play the sidemen along with his band. Waylon gives us the opportunity to let all of our senses work when experiencing his new music. We can smell the dust in "Cactus, Texas," and taste the blood from "The Boxer." We feel the depths of despair in "Wastin' Time," and the pain from the hangover that will surely rock our world in "Hittin' the Bottle Again." We can see the borders of our imagination in "Lines." With this new album, Waylon allows us into his intimate world to experience the depth of what makes him such a force in our time. His sense of place, combined with his unique power, allow us the illusion of being able to reach out and touch Waylon.

In this passage, the writer quite clearly elaborates the power of music as a practice of the spatial imaginary. Of course, the writer embraces the romantic notion of the authorship, situating the power to create this aural landscape solely within the sublime creativity of Waylon Jennings as "pioneer." After all, as Jennings says, that is "part of the show": the marketing of "Waylon" as commodified star-text. Nonetheless, this doesn't erase the materiality of the "illusion of being able to reach out and touch Waylon" and his landscapes, nor that of Toni Braxton's geography of desire, nor the yearning for the Bosnian homeland, nor the reverberating territorializing power of the jeep beats. Perhaps this power of music as a spatial practice is best understood as "magical" rather than illusory.

"Magical" is how Michael Taussig describes the power of mimesis, of creating representations of others and other places, that allows one to "be lifted into other worlds" (1993: 16). Yet as Taussig points out, mimesis (the art of imitation) and alterity (the relation of self and other and the production of identity through difference) are inextricably bound together.

> 'The fundamental move of the mimetic faculty taking us bodily into alterity is very much the task of the storyteller, too. For the storyteller embodied that situation of stasis and movement in

which the far-away was brought to the here-and-now, archetyp-
ically that place where the returned traveler finally rejoined
those who stayed at home. It was from this encounter that the
story gained its existence and...it is here, in this moment of
apprehension, that the listening self is plunged forward into and
beyond itself" (1993: 40–41).

Taussig's description of the art of the storyteller can be applied to Waylon Jennings and his producer's account of his power; but it can also be
applied to all the other sounds of the street. Indeed, it is a perfect evocation
of the dynamics of what Chambers calls the "interpolating space" of the
noise of city, "in which the imagination carries you in every direction, even
towards the unthought" (1993: 189). We might call this ambiguity of the
unthought the sound of surprise.

THE SURPRISING SOUND OF NOISE

For twenty five centuries, Western knowledge has tried to look
upon the world. It has failed to understand the world is not for
the beholding. It is for the hearing. ..Our science has always
desired to monitor, abstract, and castrate meaning, forgetting
that life is full of noise and that death alone is silent: work noise,
noise of humanity, noise of beast. Noise bought, sold, or prohibited. Nothing essential happens in the absence of noise. Now
we must learn to judge a society more by its sounds, by its art,
and by its festivals, than by its statistics.
                                            —Jacques Attali, *Noise*, 1985, 3

So how might we map the space of "sounds of surprise," a space that is concrete and dramatically lived rather than abstract and geometrically petrified,
ambiguous rather than homogenous, audible rather than legible? The
themes that have emerged in our discussion so far may provide the groundwork. First, we must recognize that the architectonics of this space is produced by the cultural technology of popular music. That is, all of us on the
street are located in a technologically produced spatial field as individual listeners – individuals, yet linked together in common interdependence on the
organizational and electronic technologies of musical production that insin-
uate music in the spaces of our lives.

Moreover, although we are occupying the same physical landscape, we are located, too, within our own maps of aural emplacement and emplotment – those spatial stories and rhythms that position listeners in the social imaginary. In Foucault's (1986) terms, the aural landscape of the street is "heterotopic" – a bounded field of spatial practices in which a multiplicity of different *topoi* are performed and enacted. Of course, these spatial practices are as much about mobility and travel as they are stability and location, entailing movement towards other imaginary places while at the same time staking out a place in this specific space.

Finally, the simultaneity of travel and emplacement involve the processes of mimesis and alterity. The musical conjurings of place by Toni Braxton, Waylon Jennings, Bosni-pop, or Dr. Dre create a musical mode of identification and othering. Within the "magical" forcefield of sound, we become one with its place and, in so doing, mark a difference not only between the listening self and our "normal" selves, but also between ourselves and the others on the street.

Still, mapping the sounds of the street along these lines only takes us so far. Indeed, it might be argued that such a cartography is really not much more than a cartography of taste and consumer preference. Different people on the street like and buy different kinds of music, and when they listen to it they have different pleasures and travel to different imaginary places. What this kind of mapping evades, of course, are issues of power, issues that animate the designs and desires of the Drake Action Plan as well as our quarrel with its spatial strategy. What we need is not a populist cartography of taste and taste cultures, but a cartography of sound as a territory of power. Here we return to the issues of chaos and order, dissonance and harmony, and spaces of noise and places of music that, in turn, lead us to Attali.

Within the spatial imaginary of the Drake Action Plan, the festival is a celebration of difference that makes no difference as it fits neatly within the harmonious order of the city planner's rationalized future. For Attali, however, the festival embodies the ambivalent border between noise and music, dissonance and harmony, which is essential for the creation of difference and identity in society. As Lefebvre has argued, the concrete space of the everyday, the interpolating aural space of the sounds of the streets, "cannot live without generating, without producing, without creating *differences*. To deny them this is to kill them" (1991: 396).

Attali formulates the issues that produce a cartography of sound as power through an intriguingly idiosyncratic interpretation of Brueghel's *Carnival's Quarrel with Lent*. Heeding his own advice about putting one's "ear to sound matter as the herald of society" (1985: 5), Attali puts his ear to the sounds that he argues Brueghel makes audible "for the first time in Western art" (21). As such, *Carnival's Quarrel with Lent* can be both viewed and "listened to" as what Richard Leppert has called a "sonoric landscape" – a visual representation of sound in which "music connects to the *visible* human body, not only as the receiver of sound but as its producer" (1993: 18). According to Leppert, in sonoric landscapes a struggle between authorized and unauthorized sounds is represented. It is this "control over sonority" that Attali discerns in Brueghel's "cartography of noises":

> "Brueghel not only gives us a vision of the world, he also makes it audible... *Carnival's Quarrel with Lent* is a battle between two fundamental political strategies, two antagonistic cultural and ideological organizations: Festival, whose aim is to make everybody's misfortune tolerable through the derisory designation of a god to sacrifice; Austerity, whose aim is to make the alienation of everyday life bearable through the promise of eternity – the Scapegoat and Penitence. Noise and Silence....Brueghel saw the profound identity between noises and differences, between silence and anonymity. He announces the battle between two fundamental types of sociality: the Norm and the Festival" (1985: 21, 22, 23).

In Brueghel's landscape, Attali discerns relations of alterity that are central to a cartography of sound, aurality, and power and to a strategy of mapping spaces of noise and places of music. These relations are also present in our discussion of the politics of mapping a neighborhood and in the contrast between the abstract space of the action plan and the concrete space of the sounds of the streets.

According to Attali, relations of power are first located in the liminal and shifting boundary between "noise" and "music." Music is a channelization of noise into structured order through the endowment of noise with form. Music is thus constructed as a territory of harmony that provides a structure of interpretation and identity for those within its boundaries. More specifically, for Attali, music is *tamed* noise, a structural code that defines and maps positions of power and difference that are located in the aural landscape of sound. Noise, or sound that falls outside a dominant musical code, transgresses the dominant ordering of difference.

For those in positions of musicianship and listenership that are located within the dominant code of music, noise is "unlistenable" static and interference, a cacophonous anarchy of sound. Thus noise, as an element of the aural soundscape of society, can challenge positions of power and difference that are assumed to be "natural." On the other hand, if a dominant aural framing of power and difference is to be maintained, noise must either be silenced, contained, or domesticated and incorporated in the dominant culture. Accordingly, the history of music in general and of popular music in particular can be understood in terms of this dynamic tension between the popular noise of subordinate or marginal groups and the popular music of dominant culture.

Attali's distinction between noise and music not only foregrounds the social organization of sound as an epistemology of power, but also gives notice to the intensely phenomenological, bodily, and intersubjective effectivity of sound in the constitution of lived experience. For Attali, the epistemology of sound is manifested in music and noise as aural frameworks of perception and embodiment, knowledge and pleasure, and ideology and affect, through which we are emplaced and emploted in positions of personal and social identity. The social organization of sound into formations of music and noise highlights the dual nature of sound as both ineffably evanescent and material, imaginary and real, as sounds produce systems of identity and embodiment that are situated in the everyday world though sites of musical practice. Indeed, it is in the capacity of noise and music to operate across registers of space that Attali locates the power of sound to make a difference. And it is on the basis of this power that Attali invests so much importance in the notion of the festival and the carnival.

Networks, Festivals, Smooth and Striated Spaces

In his narrative of the use, meaning, and reproduction of music in Western society, Attali delineates four different networks. While the basis for these different networks is somewhat overdetermined, the most important factors are the political economy of each network as well as their logic as media and cultural technology. Paralleling Walter Ong's (1982) delineation of orality, literacy, print, and electronic media/culture, Attali provides a four-part typology focusing on music as sacrifice, as representation, as repetition, and, finally, as composition. In each case, music provides a different sense of order, a different aural, epistemological and sonic will to power. Hence, in the era of sacrifice, music creates order ritually by allowing people to ignore violence. Music acts in this network as the center of ritual, the focus of spiritual life rather than the means of commerce or trade.

In the network of representation, music creates order by allowing the belief in a world and social structure of harmony and order. Further, in anticipation of changing economic systems, music becomes a spectacle to be attended to in particular "places" (i.e., the concert hall). Moreover, music becomes a system of commerce and exchange in which people pay to listen and performers are paid to play.

In the third network – repetition – technologies of electronic reproduction of sound provide the means and locations for individuals to develop private relationships with music by listening on their own. However, even as we develop individual relationships to music, the music itself, Attali argues, has become a deanimated reproduction, a sound devoid of spirit and sociality. Because all sound then becomes a reflection of the recording and can be taken out of collective social spaces, music orders society through a privatization and individualization that is simultaneously shared.

Were it not for the suggestion of an oncoming network of composition, Attali's theorizing would end on a rather depressing note – with the familiar ring of those arguments put forward by the current crop of conservative media critics. Instead, in the network of composition, individuals take the elements of music as they exist in order to reproduce them in different arrangements according to their own desires. In the network of composition, music becomes less an expression of cultural hegemony and more a space for the critical reordering of sound.

Regardless of the network, however, what is key to understanding the space of music in Attali is understanding that music is always in a tenuous position. That is, while music itself is order, it is always already a contingent order, one that can become evident, and therefore rearranged, through the sound of noise. It is this metaphysical and literal space between noise and music that interests many of the contributors to this collection of essays. As critics besides Attali have noted, the carnival and the festival are locations for both social control and social protest (Stallybrass and White, 1986; Fiske 1989). The carnival exhibits not only the rituals of stability and music, but also spaces for the expression of the pleasures of transgression against established controls. Said another way, those who revel at the carnival bring the noise, creating a transgressive politics of sound. While music produces, and is produced through, familiar order, noise works against the order, creating a space for the imagination of multiple orders and disorders.

In their *Thousand Plateaus*, Deleuze and Guattari (1987) suggest a distinction between "smooth" and "striated" spaces. While striated spaces are those of division, clear differences, routine, objectivity, and rationality, smooth spaces are ones in which categories blur into one another, in which transformation and flight are highlighted over essence and stability. Deleuze and Guattari go on to note, however, that smooth and striated spaces exist simultaneously. We cannot live in a culture of pure striation nor pure smoothness. The point here is that it is in the transition of smooth and striated spaces, and the periods of smoothness before the return to striation, where politics, meaning, and identity change. Similarly, it is in those moments and sites of noise where the order of music changes.

When one brings the noise, then, one allows a different mapping of social space. One of the purposes of this collection is to explore the different locations of and routes for the creation of popular music and the spaces they open for transformation and flight.

In this first part of the book, "Noise, Performance, and the Politics of Sound," contributors explore "space" in terms of the cultural codes of sound and aurality. The chapters look at the disruption of certain musical codes through noise, and the ways in which the performance of noise creates not only new sounds, but new codes and spaces of identity and behavior.

Russell Potter, in "Not the Same: Race, Repetition, and Difference in Hip-Hop and Dance Music," examines the politics of the boundary between music and noise embodied in the strategies of rhythmic and vocal repetition in hip-hop, techno, and industrial genres of popular dance music. Taking critical aim at Attali as well as Adorno, Potter argues that structures of repetition created through use of sampling and other means of electronic reproduction must be understood as creative, dialogic practices of cultural resistance and not as proof of the selfsame beat of the commodification and industrialization of music.

In his chapter on the legendary Detroit band, the MC5, "Kick Out the Jams!: The MC5 and the Politics of Noise," Steve Waksman explores the phenomenological politics of one of rock's most compelling devices of structuring aural difference – guitar-based squalls of feedback. He explicitly brings to bear the noise/music distinction upon the complex and contradictory creation of gendered and racialized places of social identity, political affiliation (especially the White Panther Party), and embodiment through the performative use of feedback.

In "Can't We Just Talk About Music? Rock and Gender on the Internet," Norma Coates builds on work by Teresa deLauretis. Coates argues that rock is not only a technology of gender, but a *performance* of gender, a performance she traces by exploring three sites. The first two sites are Internet discussion groups – one representing men's "music," and the other representing women's "noise." The third site is an international conference on popular music studies.

In "If I Had a Dick: Queers, Punks, and Alternative Acts," Cynthia Fuchs examines the music and live shows of queer punk bands. Fuchs calls into question the binary opposition between incorporation and resistance, commodification and rebellion, by looking at how these binaries are "queered." Fuchs argues that the practices of queer punk narrate a social crisis of identity and authenticity that marks the liminal boundaries between noise and music. For Fuchs, "authenticity" is a performative act that must be negotiated within a system of power. At the border of incorporation and authenticity, Fuchs finds a transgressive place that is rich with political possibility.

The second part of *Mapping the Beat*, "History, Technology, and Policy," begins with "Drumming and Memory: Scholarship, Technology, and Music-Making." In this chapter, Andrew Goodwin discusses his own musical practices as a way of considering how listeners individualize pop through personal narratives that continue to elude the culture industry. Acknowledging that rock's "originals" were always less original than many thought, Goodwin argues that the rhythms and timbres of the past are very much alive for the current generation of music-makers and listeners – even while the sense of what constitutes both history and collective memory has changed significantly over the last few decades.

As it always has, rock proclaims the now, the new beginning, the absolute origin. But like all cultural forms, it is intertextual, always immersed in the past. Deena Weinstein notes in the provocative "The History of Rock's Pasts through Rock Covers" that the ways in which rock has referenced the past have changed significantly over time. She describes the history of these references by describing the different ways "past" has functioned for rock in different rock areas.

In "Repressive Representations: Patriarchy and Femininities in Rock Music of the Counterculture," Sheila Whiteley examines culturally dominant images of women in late 1960s rock from both British and American perspectives. She explores key figures and bands and the way their music situated women as fantasy figures and earth mothers. In building her argument, Whiteley looks at women's roles within the counterculture in regard to second-wave feminism, and situates women within the prevalent discourses of rock culture at the time.

David Sanjek, is interested in the market as it concerns popular music. In Popular Music and the Synergy of Corporate Culture," he examines two broad areas. First, he covers the corporate regime, with particular emphasis upon the recent proliferation of mergers and acquisitions; second, the legal-legislative regime, most notably the recent telecommunications bill, and how it impedes popular music as well as expands the opportunities for transitional conglomerates to dominate the marketplace.

The convergence of popular music studies, the market, and the state is an important and, at least in American popular music studies, neglected site. In her chapter, "Fields of Practice: Musical Production, Public Policy, and the Market," Holly Kruse suggests that popular music studies in the United States need to examine the degree to which market factors and state policy influence musical practices or help set scholarly agendas. In the absence of a significant tradition of integrated studies of policy issues and situated musical practices, Kruse turns to Pierre Bourdieu's work on "fields" of practice, and particularly to how Bourdieu conceptualizes cultural production, economics, politics and education – all of which exist within the field of power.

If the first part generally focuses on space in a metaphoric sense, or in the sense of codes and meanings, then the third part, "Location and Movement in the Spaces of Popular Music," leans more towards the study of space in a literal and material sense. While the chapters in this third of the book continue to focus on such issues as social, political, and ethnic identity in popular music, they also have more explicit ties to geographic or virtual spaces.

Part III begins with Ramona Leira-Schwichtenberg's "Crossing Over: Selena's Tejano Music and the Discourse of Borderlands," which examines the spatial metaphor of the "borderlands" as it is embodied in this particular form of popular music. Schwichtenberg argues that the notion of the "borderlands" is a synecdoche for the dynamic negotiation of place and identity among Mexican Americans. She then uses this trope to explore the liminal process of "crossing over," a process that continually renegotiates the borders and boundaries between the local and transnational, the community and the commodity. In the end, she argues that the aural politics of location in popular music can best be understood as the politics of the "in-between."

Robert Hanke, in "'Yo Quiero Mi MTV!': Making Music Television for Latin America," offers an intriguing look at this version of music television. The central issue for Hanke is not how MTV makes music television for Latin America, but rather how MTV constructs an *imaginary* "Latin America." Hanke argues that MTV Latino should be analyzed as an institutional site for the formation of new hybrid musical tastes and identities with yet unforeseen consequences for cultural politics.

Next, Tony Kirschner, in "Studying Rock: Towards a Materialist Ethnography" explores one way of engaging in a critical cartography of music and noise. Employing in part his own experiences as a band member, Kirschner develops a "materialist ethnography" of popular music as a cultural formation. Kirschner argues that such a methodology cuts across the tripartite conceptual orthodoxy of popular music studies (institution/text/audience) by focusing on "interconnectivity" in the specific locales of musical practice.

In "'Everybody Loves Our Town': Scenes, Spatiality, Migrancy" Mark Olson expands on issues addressed in previous chapters by examining the constitution of axes of communal identity, affiliation, and belonging in the spatial terrain of local sites of "scenic fandom." Rejecting the essentialism of identity politics, Olson argues for an analytical framework that can make sense of the diasporic and nomadic formations of community identity in postmodernity.

In the final chapter of *Mapping the Beat*, "Negativland, Out-law Judgments, and the Politics of Cyberspace," John Sloop and Andrew Herman take up the legal case and controversy that surrounded the release of the group Negativland's "The Letter 'U' and the Numeral '2'" in order to understand the potential politics of cyberspace. Exploring the structure of Negativland's site on the World Wide Web, the reactions of fans, and "alternative" systems of judgments made possible by the Web, Sloop and Herman explore the dynamics of smooth and striated space that the "noise" of hypertext and its transformation of judgment and identity represent.

NOTES

1. The classic statement of the Gramscian counterpoint is Hall's influential piece on "Encoding/Decoding" (1980). For a fascinating history of how this point/counterpoint has been played (and played out) in cultural studies over the past two decades, see Davies (1995) and Frow (1995).

2. This is not to conflate the important difference between work done on musical subcultures from a strictly Gramscian framework, such as Hebdige's, and the work of so-called cultural populists, such as Fiske, whose work is based on a very optimistic reading of figures such as de Certeau and Bakhtin. Hebdige wants to locate the workings of subcultural sonic and stylistic resistance within a flexible Marxist framework of overdetermination by the culture industry, whereas Fiske (especially in 1989) wants to disarticulate the workings of the industrial economy of production from the "cultural economy" of consumption, meaning, and pleasure. Yet, as Simon Frith ironically points out, work that emphasizes the politics of consumption is as rooted in the Adornian perspective on the culture industry as is work that focuses on the determining logic of cultural production. To wit: "The analytic move…has been to accept the Frankfurt reading of cultural production and to look for the redeeming features of commodity culture in the act of consumption. In British subcultural theory, this reworking took on the particular form of identifying certain groups with what we might call 'positive mass consumption'" (Frith, 1991: 103).

3. For instance, Andrew Goodwin's (whose essay appears as chapter 6) influential *Dancing in the Distraction Factory* (1992) examines music television and music video from within this analytic logic, while providing perhaps its most nuanced and compelling contemporary example.

4. This collection of essays follows important works on the musical conjuring of place and identity such as Cohen (1994, 1995), Frith (1996), Lipsitz (1994), and Shepherd (1993). It also follows works on music, sound, and spatiality including Hughes (1994), Jones (1996), Straw (1991), and Thornton (1995).

5. The voice and perspective of the first-person narrator in this section is Andrew Herman's.

REFERENCES

Adorno, T. 1990. "On Popular Music." In *On Record: Rock, Pop and the Written Word*, edited by Simon Frith and Andrew Goodwin, 301–314. New York: Pantheon.

Attali, J. 1985. *Noise: The Political Economy of Music*. Minneapolis: University of Minnesota Press.

Bennett, T., S. Frith, L. Grossberg, J. Shepherd, and G. Turner, eds. 1993. *Rock and Popular Music: Politics, Policies and Institutions*. London: Routledge.

Berland, J. 1992. "Angels Dancing: Cultural Technologies and the Production of Space." In *Cultural Studies*, edited by L. Grossberg, C. Nelson and P. Treichler, 38–55. New York: Routledge.

———. 1993. "Sound, Image, and Social Space: Music Video and Media Reconstruction." In *Sound and Vision: The Music Video Reader*, edited by S. Frith, A. Goodwin and L. Grossberg, 25–44. New York: Routledge.

Brackett, D. 1995. *Understanding Popular Music*. Cambridge, UK: Cambridge University Press.

Carpenter/Drake Park Neighborhood Revitalization Task Force. 1995. *Carpenter/Drake Neighborhood Revitalization Action Plan*. City of Des Moines Community Redevelopment Department.

Chambers, I. 1993. "Cities Without Maps." In *Mapping the Futures: Local Cultures, Global Change*, edited by J. Bird, B. Curtis, T. Putnam, G. Robertson, and L. Tickner, 188–98. New York: Routledge.

Cohen, S. 1991. *Rock Culture in Liverpool: Music in the Making*. Oxford, UK: Clarendon.

————. 1994. "Identity, Place and the 'Liverpool Sound.'" In *Ethnicity, Identity and Music: The Musical Construction of Place*, edited by M. Stokes, 117–134. Oxford, UK: Berg Publishers.

————. 1995. "Localizing Sound: Music, Place and Social Identity." In *Popular Music: Style and Identity*, edited by W. Straw, 61–7. Montreal: Centre for Research in Canadian Cultural Industries and Institutions.

Davies, I. 1995. *Cultural Studies and Beyond: Fragments of Empire*. New York: Routledge.

de Certeau, M. 1984. *The Practice of Everyday Life*. Berkeley: University of California Press.

de Lauretis, T. 1987. *Technologies of Gender: Essays on Theory, Film, and Fiction*. Bloomington: Indiana University Press.

Deleuze, G., and F. Guattari. 1987. *A Thousand Plateaus*. Minneapolis: University of Minnesota Press.

Fiske, J. 1989. *Understanding Popular Culture*. Boston: Unwin and Hyman.

————. 1993. *Power Plays, Power Works*. London: Verso.

Foucault, M. 1986. "Of Other Spaces." *Diacritics* 16(2): 22–7

Frith, S. 1991. "The Good, the Bad, and the Indifferent: Defending Popular Culture from the Populists." *Diacritics* 21(4): 102–15.

————. 1996. "Music and Identity." In *Questions of Cultural Identity*, edited by S. Hall and P. du Gay, 108–27. Thousand Oaks, CA: Sage.

Frow, J. 1995. *Cultural Studies and Cultural Value*. Oxford: Clarendon Press.

Goodwin, A. 1992. *Dancing in the Distraction Factory: Music Television and Popular Culture*. Minneapolis: University of Minnesota Press.

Gregory, D. 1995. *Geographical Imaginations*. Malden, MA: Blackwell Publishers.

Grossberg, L. 1992. *We Gotta Get Out of This Place: Popular Conservatism and Postmodern Culture*. New York: Routledge.

————. 1993a. "Cultural Studies and/in New Worlds." *Critical Studies in Mass Communications* 10 (1): 1–22.

————. 1994. "Is Anybody Listening? Does Anybody Care?" In *Microphone Fiends: Youth Music and Youth Culture*, edited by A. Ross and T. Rose. New York: Routledge.

————. 1996. "The Space of Culture, the Power of Space." In *The Postcolonial Question: Common Skies, Divided Horizons*, edited by I. Chambers and L. Curti, 169–88. New York: Routledge.

Hall, S. 1980. "Encoding/Decoding." In *Culture, Media and Language*, edited by S. Hall, D. Hobson, A. Lowe, and P. Willis, 128–38. London: Hutchinson.

Hebdige, D. 1979. *Subculture: The Meaning of Style*. London: Routledge.

Hughes, W. 1994. "In the Empire of the Beat: Discipline and Disco." In *Microphone Fiends: Youth Music and Youth Culture*, edited by A. Ross and T. Rose, 147–57. New York: Routledge.

Jennings, W. 1996. *Right for the Time*. Houston, TX: Justice Records.

Jones, S. 1992. *Rock Formation: Music, Technology and Mass Communication*. Newbury Park, CA: Sage.

————. 1996. "Rocking the House: Sound System Cultures and the Politics of Space." *Journal of Popular Music Studies* 7: 1–24.

Kruse, H. 1993. "Early Audio Technology and Domestic Space." *Stanford Humanities Review* 3(2): 1–16.

Lefebvre, Henri. 1991. *The Production of Space*. Malden, MA: Blackwell Publishers.

Leppert, Richard. 1993. *The Sight of Sound: Music, Representation and the History of the Body*. Berkeley: University of California Press.

Lewis, L. 1992. *The Adoring Audience: Fan Culture and Popular Media*. New York: Routledge.

Lipsitz, G. 1994. *Dangerous Crossroads: Popular Music, Postmodernism and the Politics of Place*. London: Verso.

Longhurst, B. 1995. *Popular Music and Society*. Malden, MA: Blackwell Publishers.

Negus, P. 1992. *Producing Pop: Culture and Conflict in the Popular Music Industry*. London: Edward Arnold.

Ong, W. 1982. *Orality and Literacy: The Technologizing of the Word*. New York: Methuen.

Shepherd, J. 1991. *Music as Social Text*. Malden, MA: Blackwell Publishers.

————. 1993. "Value and Power in Music." In *Relocating Cultural Studies: Developments in Theory and Research*, edited by V. Blundell, J. Shepherd, and I. Taylor, 171–206. New York: Routledge.

Shuker, R. 1995. *Understanding Popular Music.* New York: Routledge.

Stallybrass, P. and A. White. 1986. *The Politics and Poetics of Transgression.* Ithaca: Cornell University Press.

Straw, W. "Systems of Articulation, Logics of Change: Communities and Scenes in Popular Music." *Cultural Studies* 5(3): 368–88.

Taussig, M. 1993. *Mimesis and Alterity.* New York: Routledge.

Thornton, S. 1995. *Club Cultures: Music, Media and Subcultural Capital.* Hanover: Wesleyan University Press/University Press of New England.

Walser, R. 1993. *Running With the Devil: Power and Madness in Heavy Metal Music.* Hanover: Wesleyan University Press/University Press of New England.

Whiteley, S. 1992. *The Space Between the Notes: Rock Music and the Counter-Culture.* New York: Routledge.

Willis, P. 1978. *Profane Culture.* London: Routledge.

2

——— Not the Same ———

Race, Repetition, and Difference in Hip-Hop and Dance Music

Russell A. Potter

People, people we're all the same
No, we're not the same, coz we don't know the game…
                              –Chuck D, "Fight the Power"

I

In his recent study of the political figurations of blackface minstrelsy, Eric Lott quotes from Hans Nathan's (1962) theory of musical/racial *difference*: "Well into the 1850's much of the blackface repertory was of a mixed character…Nathan charts the convergence of cultural influences in the music as follows: 'Excessive repetition of single tones and of phrases of narrow compass derives from the Negro; on the other hand, the symmetry of phrase structure is a white concept'" (Nathan quoted in Lott, 1993: 177). Lott employs this dichotomy – rather uncritically – to distinguish supposedly *black* musical and lyrical forms (the repeated refrain of "I'm Gwine to Alabammy") from ostensibly *white* forms (the Irish hornpipes that provided the larger formal elements of tunes such as "Jump Jim Crow"). And yet within this distinction there is already a substantial and unexamined mistaking, one that Lott with his psychoanalytic frame of reference might have even

31

called a *méconaissance*: that excessive repetition, the "narrow compass" of the "same" is a characteristic of black musical forms. It is deceptively easy to recognize the inherent racism of statements such as "all blacks look alike," but evidently much more difficult to see the same logic (that is, the *logic of the same*) at work in characterizations, such as Nathan's, of black music as more "repetitive." The locus classicus of this logic is doubtless Adorno's infamous attack on jazz, which for him possessed at best a "monotonous attraction" born from a "perennial sameness" and was thus, if anything, a stultifying rather than liberatory influence – just another material echo of the industrial logic of assembly-line production (Adorno, 1983: 121–3). Lott is scornful of Adorno's oversimplifications, but his own analysis relies on the same underlying sense of what is "repetitious," a sense that is never fundamentally questioned.

Certainly jazz, like the blues before it, hinges on the repetition – with modulation and variation – of a central phrase or motif, often within structural patterns, such as the twelve-bar blues progression. Yet is such repetition in fact "the same" at all? Is the second time Robert Johnson sings, "Went down to the crossroads, tried to flag a ride," the same as the first time? Are the hundreds of recorded versions of "Staggerlee" from Mississippi John Hurt's in 1928 through Nick Cave's in 1996 repetitious? Are Miles Davis's sustained, multibar trumpet tones in *A Tribute to Jack Johnson* monotonous? What is excessive repetition? In contrast to these theorizations of a musical "selfsame," I would like to (re)iterate a theoretics of musical *difference* that, I would argue, is based on "repetition *with a difference*" (as Henry Louis Gates Jr. puts it), and that functions both within and against the logic of the selfsame of Euro-American musical modalities – and which has indeed become dominant as the "mix of black and white" in popular music has intensified (Gates, 1988: 51).

African American musical traditions have always operated from within a kind of Heraclitan ethos of difference. This ethos starts with the proposition that one cannot play or sing the same note (or word) twice – and that this is so whether the previous sound is as disparate as the latter bars of Coltrane's version of "My Favorite Things" are from the "original" melody, or as seemingly identical as a digitally lifted loop that reproduces the precise sound of an earlier performance, such as Big Daddy Kane's looping of the intro to Rufus Thomas's "I Think I Made a Boo Boo" in his rap "The Beef is On." This play of difference takes the ontological ground of musical form as its unit of (spare) change, by playing both ends of the street – veering as close to the same as it dares, or moving so far into difference that the figure of the previous music is rendered unrecognizable. It's a *practice* of difference that draws from (and folds back into) the theory of Signifyin(g) as developed by Gates.

The perception of "repetition" within the Signifyin(g) games of difference is accurate enough on one level – tropes are certainly being repeated. But this misses the point; what is at stake in repetition within African and diasporic traditions is not the same as what is at stake in European ones. Amiri Baraka has remarked on the inability of most white music critics to hear the blues as anything but a deviation from – even an attempt to avoid – "classical" principles of tempered scales and fixed tonal values (Baraka, 1963, 24–5). The same lack of awareness in the perception of repetition warps both Nathan's theory and Lott's extension of it, particularly since the music under analysis – the minstrel tunes of the 1840s – are, as Lott acknowledges, white attempts to mimic black music. It is as if one were to write a commentary on the classical ragas of India using only the recordings of George Harrison playing the sitar as a guide, a move no reputable musicologist would make.

There are really two issues underlying the perception of repetition: one being the sense of "return" time – the space between restatements of a trope or theme – and the other being a sense of what degree of variation is sufficient to judge something to be the same or different. On the first level, musicologists such as Richard Middleton have sought to separate music into "musemes" (the rough equivalent of phonemes in linguistics) and then distinguish between "musematic" repetitions (short tropes or riffs) and "discursive" repetitions (longer phrases set in a hierarchical or antiphonal relation to other phrases) (Middleton, 1986). Middleton regards some music, particularly the music of prenotational oral traditions, as being more musematic, while Western "classical" music is ostensibly more discursive. Yet there are clearly problems with this dichotomy, beginning with the judgment of what duration or periodicity is sufficient to qualify music as discursive – after all, all music has duration and unfolds over time, just as does language. Furthermore, there are certainly many musematic elements in classical music – among them traditional Baroque ornamentation of certain notes, the tags and motifs of operas and programmatic music, or for that matter vibrato itself, while black music contains unquestionably discursive elements such as the antiphonal call and response of the blues, or the rotation of suspension and resolution that shapes many jazz compositions.

On the second front, the question of *variance*, one has to examine the paradigmatic structures underlying the syntagmatic elements of musical movement or development. Just as no one would be satisfied with the grammar of a language that had no lexicon, no one ought to make an ostensibly "formal" analysis of a musical form without examining the differential possibilities of which it is composed. To complain that Chinese music is pentatonic, or that there is no music in E-flat for the guitar (which is customarily pitched in E), or that operas are full of melodramatic plots is to demonstrate a fundamental ignorance of the possibilities – and limits – of the forms or instruments in question. And, even assuming one is familiar with the possible range of musical utterances within a certain tradition, one must also be familiar with its history and repertoire. Just as few people would think much of an English professor who had never read a novel – even if he or she were a fluent and accomplished speaker – one would rightly denounce a jazz critic who knew nothing of Billie Holiday, or had never listened to Louis Armstrong's "Potato Head Blues."

It is this last presumption, as Baraka has pithily observed, that is the most common problem with white music critics' remarks about black music. Theodor Adorno was completely unfamiliar with the genesis and development of jazz, and couldn't tell the difference between Paul Whiteman and Duke Ellington – and yet his complaint that it was all "the same" has brought forth decades of serious head-wagging (and hand-wringing) by musical and cultural critics. Of course, historical knowledge is no guarantee; there are revival "Big Bands" today who can play Count Basie note for note, but what they play ain't jazz. Similarly, Lott's intimate acquaintance with nineteenth-century minstrelsy, impressive as it is, doesn't equip him to fully understand just what's at stake in *repetition*. He can see it as a parodic tool, as a means for translating class anxiety into race anxiety, as a signifier of mass identification – but ultimately, much like Adorno, he is suspicious of the minds that could consume it, of their "degraded and 'obedient' response" to its stimulus (Lott, 1993: 182).

Can there be a syntax of music that includes the vocabularies of repetition with all their cultural variability? Clearly, within almost any music of the world, whether classical in the sense of an inherited formal repertoire or wholly demotic and improvisational, there is much more internal repetition than would be tolerable in most verbal compositions. The "beat" itself has an inexorable periodicity that is nothing *but* repetition, however varied, and melodic units are scarcely less so. To the practiced listener, it is no more difficult to anticipate the chordal resolution of an unfamiliar Mozart sonata than it is to locate the "turnaroud" in a twelve-bar blues. The ostensibly formal question of "syntax," then, is no less imbricated in ideology than other, more visceral valuations. What is striking, indeed, is the degree to which the aesthetic laurels of classical music, like the nineteenth-century schoolbook's endorsement of lengthy periodic sentences with Latinate structures, are almost an anomaly within the global history of music. The aural continuity of music organized around tropological lines carried many things, from Child ballads to South Indian vocal music, across many centuries, and the arrival of technologies of reproduction (the phonograph and its descendants) has opened up a new age of aural transmission that has little need or use for written notation or formal schools. Chris Cutler, among others, has discussed this shift from the prenotational aurality of folk musics, through the retentive, notational structures of European classical music, and ultimately into a new, though also aural, postnotational tradition in which technological reproductions of music have deformed the "compositional" aesthetic (Cutler, 1993: 24–37).

But on a more microscopic level, if the understanding of tropes, musemes, or what have you is to be applied to the question of repetition, it's clear that the judgment of what is repetitious depends upon two things: (1) the listener's own position as to what length of phrasing constitutes a recognizable trope; and (2) the listener's familiarity with the particular tropes of a specific musical tradition or genre. For instance, the deepest tropological structure of all is the *beat* – a fact well known to both Homeric and Germanic bards, whose oral poetry structured itself around the variations possible given a certain absolutely regular set of permutations of length or stress in a given line. West African polyrhythms move in much the same way – that is, around beats with *even* divisions, grow beats with rigorously *odd* ones. This is the *syncope*, the *offbeat*, the difference whose unexpected expectedness marks all African American rhythms from Dixieland to swing to bop. Right behind this structure is that of the *tone*, which again moves both within and against the harmonic intervals by flattening and sharping itself at the crucial site of what European musics designate as the "seventh." In the place of Europe's tidy return to the tonic, African musics *sliiiide* home, passing intervening tones – tones of the voice, though also mimicked with other found technologies, like guitars played with sawed-off bottlenecks and slide trombones. Both in its rhythmic and tonal variations, black music goes far beyond the limits of what constituted "music" within the well-tempered classical tradition. It is not just the size of its tropological chops, but the fact that they defy the very definitional boundaries of what music is, that sets black music apart.

Repetition, in fact, is often perceived as a type of "noise" – not on account of its content (though as with hip-hop scratches, it may be "noise" in other senses as well), but on account of its interruption of the expectation of longer phrasal movement. The more one expects such movement, the more "noisy" a short cycle of tropes becomes. Hip-hop's "breakbeats" are in this sense just that; they "break" sampled beats away from their original aural context, and thus "break" down the sound into unexpected units, often using scratching to percussively flip-flop the initial sound, or leaving drops of sonic blood on the break, as with the clipped-off "hey" that Dr. Dre leaves in the loop when he samples James Brown's intro to "Funky President" in Michel'le's "Nicety." The effect is both to invoke the original sound and yet to puncture or punctuate it with the signs of its own status as a fragment; just as the surrealists made art by tacking urinals to a gallery walls, hip-hop DJ's tack up sonic ready-mades, "fresh" from their crates of dusty old vinyl. Drum machines, another trademark of early hip-hop recordings, made a similar intervention; when artists such as Afrika Bambataa or Davy DMX (named after his favorite drum machine) programmed a beat, they used its mechanical lack of variation *as* a variation, just as their Jamaican cousins capitalized on the "narrow compass" of cheap Casio keyboards to intensify the stark melodic hooks of dancehall styles.

To Adorno, reproducibility – predictability – could only be a sign of a loss; the idea that young people could hijack the means of reproduction and use them to produce something entirely different never occurred to him. He surely would have been revolted by hip-hop, especially in its techno-funk incarnation, which took its cue from Kraftwerk, whose musical aesthetic was the very antipodes of Adorno's. Electro-funk and its mongrel children, techno and industrial, seized upon the most irritating noises of the electronic age – Atari game beeps, telephone tones, 60-cycle hum – and pumped them into a maniacally sequenced, relentlessly recursive sound that became a banner for those who *opposed* the old industrial machine. This was a kind of motivated Signifyin(g), using repetition as a critique or parody of the repetitiveness of industrial society, that apparently fell entirely outside Adorno's imagination – something symptomatic of thinkers, such as the Frankfurt school, for whom the masses remain a phantasm, championed yet loathed at the same time.

There have been attempts in recent years to make culturally specific readings of repetition as it functions in black diasporic forms such as hip-hop. Tricia Rose, drawing on James Snead's suggestive consideration of the role of repetition in black culture, has forcefully articulated the cultural issues at stake in misreadings of repetition such as Adorno's (Rose, 1994: 67–9; Snead, 1981). Yet her reading of repetition makes no reference to Signifyin(g) as such, defending it simply on the grounds that it is a longstanding tradition within African and "African-derived" music. This has the unfortunate effect of seeming to concede that African traditions *are* indeed more repetitive, and that valuing repetition is simply a black cultural practice. She misses the continuous production of *difference* that is at stake in the Signifyin(g) game, both on the level of rhythm and lyrics, and thus its dialogic and antiphonal character. And, more importantly, by dismissing the idea of an "industrial correlative" (pace Adorno), she is unable to fully account for the deep imbrication of hip-hop within commodity capitalism, or for the uses that music and industry make of each other.

II

Our music is sampled
Totally fake
It's done by machines
'Coz they don't make mistakes

–KMFDM, "KMFDM Sucks"

Repetition per se, then, cannot be separated from the political motivations of those who produce or consume it. A couple of severe examples may clarify this. First, in December 1989, when he was holed up in the Vatican Embassy in Panama City, deposed Panamanian leader Manuel Noriega was subjected to the latest in army assault technology: he was bombarded with music. The program, though it included such "topical" titles as "No Place to Run," "Voodoo Chile," and "You're No Good," was chosen more for its volume and repetitiveness than for its content. Ear-splitting rock and R & B, the

Army assumed, would so irritate the opera-loving Noriega that he would decide to come out and surrender to U.S. forces. Of course, it's not only the Army who has discovered this particular use of amplified sound; when Jeeps loaded with bass-heavy speakers drive through the suburbs blaring hip-hop at top volume, there's another type of political action going on, one that many neighborhoods have sought to answer with "noise" ordinances.

Second, on his short-lived news program, Michael Moore pondered the bland repetetiveness of Muzak, the piped-in symphonic earwash that fills so many elevators and offices. He decided to see how the people who ran Muzak would feel about being forced to listen to it; he rented a flatbed truck and drove an immense stack of high-power amplifiers and speakers to the bucolic suburban lane where the chairman of the board of Muzak Inc. made his home. After a few minutes of being subjected to his own Muzak, the disgruntled chairman called the local police, who forcefully suggested to Moore that he turn off his speakers and move along. The humor of this incident is attributable not only to the way in which Moore mixed journalism with aural guerrilla action, but to the idea that Muzak, which is usually thought of as harmless "background" music, was so intolerable that even the head of the corporation that produced it regarded it as a nuisance when he himself was forced to listen.

Among the fans of many of current pop music genres, the awareness that their music constitutes noise to others has become a definitional aesthetic and driving force. For if "noise" means a good loud beat for the fans to dance to, it also signifies a delight at the irritation the same noises produce in those unsympathetic to the form. Heavy metal is often cited as one such genre, but hip-hop, techno, and industrial music have produced sounds in the past decade that far outpace conventional metal for sheer aural disturbance. Take for instance Public Enemy, whose recordings have featured, variously, air-raid sirens, phase-shifted and distorted banjo notes, the speeches of Louis Farrakhan, back-masked vocal chants, explosions, teakettle-like trumpet samples from T. S. Monk, James Brown shouts, and the inimitable scratching of DJ Terminator X. Or take a sample of industrial dance band KMFDM, whose live concerts have featured a drummer perched *atop* a drum machine, the machine dictating and punctuating the human rhythms, over which pre-programmed synth loops and jagged guitars mingled with lead singer En Esch's tortured German vocals. These are bands for whom aural assault – via repetition, distortion, and sheer volume – has been rendered into performance technique; whether it elates or offends, it *succeeds*.

Is such repetition *excessive*? Not by its own aesthetic, even though that aesthetic may include a tactical drive to interrupt the aesthetics of others. And yet there is another affective quality that has been associated with repetition even more firmly than irritation, and that is its *hypnotic* quality. "Tick-tock, tick-tock" goes the pocket watch, and the hypnotist intones, "You are getting sleepy …your eyelids are growing heavier and heavier…" The perception of a hypnotic quality was not necessarily a sign of peaceful intent; from the days of antirock crusaders such as the Reverend Jack Van Impe, who compared rock beats with Pavlovian behavior modification experiments and claimed they were part of a communist plot, the idea of repetition falsely lulling one into a receptive state has been a recurrent formulation of pop music paranoia. The latest avatar of this, I suppose, is New Age music such as that of Kitaro or Enya – music whose somnifacent qualities are undeniable, though no one so far as I know has suggested a warning label for them. But whether it is the beat of revolutionaries' boots or that of a calming metronome, repetition has been negatively associated by many music critics with mechanisms of social control, and with a receptive and vulnerable listening public.

Yet however vilified in these instances, repetition remains a central part of any music, and the opprobrium it receives is usually proportionate to the ignorance and/or hostility of the critic. As Gene Santoro has remarked, "One of the main things about pop that drives many jazz and classical performers and fans crazy is what they see as its narrow predictability. Of course, they manage to justify or overlook the predictability of forms they admire. Predictability, after all, is another name for syntax" (Santoro, 1992: 138). Santoro goes on to critique the romantic ideology of the "original" and the concomitant construction of the creative genius as "originator"; he sees pop music having more in common with pre-romantic tropologies of verbal and musical production in which "originality" as such was of only peripheral value. What counted for Chaucer or an Elizabethan sonneteer was not novelty at the level of tropes, but keen ability to wring new nuances out of the "syntax" of existing tropes.

While Santoro's comments invoke earlier European traditions, the same issues can be discerned in my opening questions about "repetition" versus "symmetry of phrase" – but what is being inadvertently voiced here suddenly appears not to be a difference between the *same* and the *different*, but between modalities of *difference*. The prehistory of this dissolving binary emerges from historical rather than aesthetic distinctions: between the residual orality of medieval and early modern Europe, where tropological syntax still held cultural power and the romantic/bourgeois ideology of originality, in which the trope becomes the cliché (a word that appropriately derives from the very *sound* of mechanical type).[1] Such was the repetition within which bourgeois subjects unhappily recognized their own eroding sense of difference – only to seek to recapture it, as Lott compellingly argues, by relocating it in an exoticized blackfaced other who is both a fantasy of class identification and a racialized syntagm of repulsion. When white audiences lined up to see the New Christy Minstrels in the 1850s – or lit out for Harlem nightclubs in the 1950s – what they were seeking, perhaps, was precisely this lost sense of difference, a sense that could only be recovered in a syntax that revivified the tropological mode of production.

For a trope is a part, even though it is never *partial;* like the shards of a hologram, tropes contain by inference the whole *materia musica* of their repertoire. A line of plainchant in a decaying manuscript, like fragments of alliterative Germanic verse, preserves the structure of the larger patterns, the intervals and the stresses with which they were woven. Adorno's mistake was to confuse the tropes of black musical traditions (albeit in their watered-down popularized form) for the *partial* parts of assembly-line production or mass society. Of course, in the hip-hop era, there is a secondary Signifyin(g), which in a sense takes mistakings such as Adorno's as its creative field. Hip-hop takes tropes from the continuum and deliberately renders their edges jagged, refusing to smooth them into a new composition, but pinioning them nonetheless upon a rhythmic scaffolding that invites fullness even as it speaks absence. Like the caesura in alliterative verse, the silent syncopes of hip-hop call up absent spirits as they mark its time.

In industrial and techno music, this logic goes one step further. Groups such as Frontline Assembly, Front 242, and KMFDM create a wall of noise, using explosive beats, broad-band synthesizer pulses, and fragmentary spoken-word samples; they mimic and (to some) satirize the empty plenitude and disconnected tones of postindustrial life. Other techno bands, however, such as Apotheosis and L.A. Style (whose big hit, ironically, was "James Brown Is Dead"), make careful use of a sonic caesura, stopping the high-paced pulse of the beat for a few seconds only to kick it up again, louder and faster than ever. Yet both styles are intensely tropological; techno-industrial bands have screaming guitars that could be taken for speed metal, if it weren't for the backbeats beneath them; techno deliberately makes riffs out of tightly packed clusters of sonic pulses, and deliberately chooses inane, disjointed verbal fragments to serve as its pivot point (calling it a chorus would be a bit much).

Techno or "rave" is perhaps the trouble child here, though – even some who celebrate the progressivity of everything from acid thrash to electro-funk have found that some techno music stretches their tolerance for repetition. Such repetition occurs not only with the beats, but in the verbal loops; "James Brown is Dead" spawned over a hundred clones with predictable titles ("Michael Jackson Is Shot Dead," "James Caan Is Dead," James Brown Is Alive," etc.). At its peak, techno-rave was a sort of postmodern echo chamber; partly on account of its mix-it-in-your-living-room ease of manufacture, partly because the recording industry was eager to clone whatever DJs could produce; it seemed there could be no sound or move that would not instantly reverberate through dozens of clones or near-clones. Yet in some odd way, this ultimately *technical* music claimed for itself a shamanistic collectivity, an "earthy" vibe that would appear to be a direct contradiction of its "manufactured" quality; at rural and urban raves and concerts, U.K. and U.S. youths drank nutritional yeast milkshakes and sought out natural highs (though synthetic ones such as "Ecstacy" were also near at hand); they danced with equal fervor under the stars and under the steel girders of abandoned warehouses.

The lesson of the development of forms such as hip-hop, electro-funk, and techno may well be that it is impossible to gauge the degree of a music's service to the bourgeois capitalist order by simply looking at the mechanical means of its (re)production. The troubadours – whose name derives from *trobar* (to find) – were finders and founders of a music that used material then at hand: lutes and chitterns, hurdy-gurdies and a'ouds – along with the voice itself. The kids in the South Bronx *found* their means in the vernacular technology of their own day; that this technology was constructed from metal and wires rather than wood and catgut was not the determining factor. Nor, for that matter, was the technology of reproduction, since at least in their earliest stages, hip-hop relied on the tactical aural recycling of previously existing sounds, a reclamation of the *consumed* (the vinyl record, whose value was supposed to be exchange-value) as a praxis of *production* (use-value). It is this kind of resistance – resistance that literally takes control of the means of production, that produces out of the consumed – which theorists from Adorno to Attali have missed, and that is most vital to charting the course of music at century's end. For it is not the case, as Attali claims, that when music became an "industry," it ceased to be collective, or that when sound could be mechanically reproduced, it was forever alienated from its makers and listeners (Attali, 1987: 88). Nevertheless, Attali's observations still merit a more detailed look, since they at least are cognizant of the necessary link between music and the political economy of society as a whole.

III

> Truly revolutionary music is not music which expresses the rev-
> olution in words, but which speaks of it as lack. Bringing an end
> to repetition, transforming the world into an art form and life
> into a shifting pleasure. Will a sacrifice be necessary? Hurry up
> with it, because – if we are still within earshot – the World, by
> repeating itself, is dissolving into Noise and Violence.
> –Jacques Attali, *Noise* (1987:141)

Jacques Attali's theories of music and its social and economic dimensions has been tremendously influential among musicologists and cultural critics alike. And yet, oddly, he makes many of the same presuppositions as Adorno: that repetition can only be a *loss* – a loss of the original, of the role of the artist (now reduced to being a mere "mold" for repeated forms), of the organic relations between musicians and their listeners. I think that Attali's larger conception of the historical modes of music – the sacrifice (music as ritual), representation (the "stately" music of the era of the court composers in Europe), and repetition (music in the age of mass production) is tremendously rich and suggestive, and resonates interestingly with Chris Cutler's triad of the "folk" mode, the written or "classical" mode, and the "recording" mode. Yet what Attali misses is that all three modes overlap to a tremendous degree, and while each perhaps has its quintessential historical moments, no one mode determines the social significance of music today. We still have our ritual music; what were the Grateful Dead, or what is Babatunde Olatun-ji, if not practitioners of ritual music? We still have our court composers, and although John Williams is no Haydn, he makes his living in a very similar way. And finally, repetition – clearly a term of repugnance for Attali much as it is for Adorno – is not necessarily the kiss of death to the two preceding modes (nor an obstacle for Attali's fourth and most elusive mode, that of "composition"). Attali idealizes the peripatetic troubadour and his nomadic lyricism; he seems to think that such people will rematerialize again with their lutes and tambors to save us from the world of mass-produced sound. It does not occur to Attali that the term "handmade" could apply just as accurately to the craft of a South Bronx DJ who wires up two turntables with a fader switch and cuts between them as it could to the itinerant bluesmen in the 1920s who smashed a wine bottle on a curb to make a guitar slide.

Attali's own "slide" – like Adorno's – is between the reproduction of a recording in its material form, the repetition of a beat or a tonality in a musical trope or figure, and the sensibility of the "same" – mindless music for a blandly complicit society. There are elements of both the "repetition as fascism of sound" element (Attali compares the beats of pop music to military music, and makes much of Hitler's remarks about the loudspeaker) and the "repetition as hypnosis" thesis, which Attali summarizes succinctly: "Repetition becomes pleasurable in the same way music becomes repetitive: by hypnotic effect. Today's youth is perhaps in the process of experiencing this fabulous and ultimate channelization of desires: *in a society in which power is so abstract that it can no longer be seized, in which the worst threat people feel is solitude and not alienation, conformity to the norm becomes the pleasure of belonging, and the acceptance of powerlessness takes root in the comfort of repetition*" (Attali, 1987: 125). The musical reference points of this passage are ambiguous; is it listening to too much Barry Manilow or too much Tupac Shakur that confers the "pleasure of belonging" – or *both*? I do not want to claim that complaints such as Attali's are misplaced or misinformed – only that they are incomplete, since they ignore the *tropological* mode of music altogether. Adorno is too busy mourning the death of the trouvères to perceive that their means of production could survive, even thrive, in the mirror house of mass-production, and too unfamiliar with the aural traditions of black American music to recognize, as Cutler does, its ability to continually defy and Signify on all attempts at cloning, all avatars of what funk guru George Clinton calls "the placebo syndrome." Attali's one example of the resistance of a black musical form – the "free jazz" movement – makes it sound like a last-gasp, isolated failure, rather than, as it was, one of a very long series of moves that aimed at and, in different ways, succeeded in taking black music to the next plateau while the "industry" was busy reproducing yesterday's sounds.

Attali's imperception of the underlying Significance of acts of repetition within black diasporic music forms is a product of his limited awareness that the black musical continuum does not correspond with his analysis of musical modes of production, almost all of which is concerned with develop-

ments in *European* musical history. For diasporic musics, which had already
come to terms many centuries ago with a loss of substance via a plenitude of
strategies, and which (as Cutler notes) were thus already practiced at side-
stepping the pressures of the bourgeois capitalistic order, there was a
tremendous stake in repetition and response, a vital antiphonal dynamic that
could be either reverent or bitterly satirical. Against the repetition of the
whip and chain, the repetition of slave labor (and, later, wage slavery), and
the repetition of the machine (John Henry *vs.* the steam hammer), the strategic repetitions of black music are both reply and critique. The music industry, as Attali observes, has from very early on staked itself on its ability to
reproduce and appropriate black musical forms, and yet this repetition
always comes belatedly. Attali's comments about repetition are surely accurate when it comes to the music industry as such, but he makes the mistake
of thinking that this industry has somehow succeeded in eliminating the
essence of the black aural tradition. But as Cutler notes, "Time and again, we
have seen that, no matter how abused and exploited it was, the force of the
communal spirit in Black music – its deep rejection of an oppressive culture
and its resilience as a folk form – kept its vital, liberating core undominated.
Black music continually throws up new, radical, and uncompromised forms,
forms which cannot and will not be contained, forms which reinforce and
reaffirm its generative life in the oppressed community" (Cutler, 1993: 53).
Attali's difficulty is that he is himself relying on what the recording industry
and the press have provided him. He has, to his credit, turned *on* his radio
(unlike Adorno) for more than a few minutes, and he knows something of
rock and R & B, but he really has no connection to street-level life, whether
it's that of a black kid in Detroit or a white kid in San Francisco. It is *he* who
has accepted the mediating hand of the technologies of repetition, he who
can see a recording only as an item of potential but unrealized use-value.
And why is this? I would suggest that it is because Attali, much like Adorno,
is an intellectual vanguardist who, whether he is wearing his culture-critic
clothes or not (and Attali was also a minister in the French government), is
always scanning the distant horizon for "organic" intellectuals, even as he
cannot hear the very sound beneath his feet.

In Paris in 1996, Attali might hear the rhythms of revolution a bit more
clearly, as rappers such as MC Solaar are rockin' the house with rapid-fire
rhymes *en français*. And, in these sounds, he might recognize something that

he himself anticipated under the name "composition," that next musical era, within which "differences are perpetually called into question," where "local knowledge" and the "availability of new tools and instruments" enables musicians to short-circuit the commodification of form. To be fair, Attali wrote *Noise* in 1977, when even the *Village Voice* hadn't quite caught up with the hip-hop revolution in its own backyard. But in his strange antipathy towards repetition, his inability to see the "trope" within the aesthetic of *trobar*, he reveals himself as a critic who, however much he regrets the old or hails the new, is still living within the ideology of what he himself thoughtfully details as the "representational" mode of music. For repetition, to the extent it is a "noise," is a noise *against* the lengthy hierarchical forms of the representational mode. Attali had thought only that composition might mean some new and welcomingly vernacular form of architecture, but never conceived that it might be, on the contrary, a matter of *Strategien gegen Architekturen* (Strategies against Architecture) — sonic graffiti, a brick at the window, underground passageways, and steam tunnels *beneath* the decrepit buildings of the age of the State.[2]

The moral of the story, if there is a moral, is that cultural critics, even those with the best of intentions, can't dip into the sonic archive of the moment and make pronouncements about its significance, unless they first take the time to understand what is at stake in the actual praxis and tropological vocabulary specific to these particular forms. One cannot, qua Leonard Bernstein, leap from Mozart to the Beatles, whether to praise or condemn them; one cannot invoke the "popular" if one lives a life schematically isolated from, or disdainful of, the codes through which the popular circulates. Cultural criticism, particularly of music, has suffered enough already from this sort of utopian window-shopping; if the *materials* of mass culture are worth analysis, the "materialist" thinkers must work against their own isolation from the masses themselves. Repetition, whatever its significance within mass forms, has almost never been used with any positive connotations by the critics of mass culture; the implicit elitism of their condescension lessens the value of their insights, even when, as with Attali, there is a tremendous synthetic project at hand. The work of the future must take a different turn, or else it must be admitted that cultural criticism is little more than the slumming cousin of cultural elitism.

NOTES

1. "Cliché," notes the OED, derives from the French *clicher*, "to click," a reference to the sound made when setting pre-cast blocks of type, which were employed for frequently used words and phrases.

2. *Strategien gegen Architekturen* was the title of Einstürzende Neubauten's groundbreaking first album (1983), in which these godfathers of the industrial genre made music by pounding on old metal scraps, springs, and (for one song) a rusty metal bridge.

REFERENCES

Adorno, T. 1983. "Perennial Fashion – Jazz." In *Prisms*, 119–32, translated by Samuel and Sherry Weber. Cambridge: The MIT Press.

Attali, J. 1987. *Noise: The Political Economy of Music*, translated by Brian Massumi. Minneapolis: University of Minnesota Press.

Baraka, A. [LeRoi Jones]. 1963. *Blues People*. New York: William Morrow.

Cutler, C. 1993. *File under Popular*. New York: Autonomedia.

Gates, Henry Louis Jr. 1988. *The Signifying Monkey: A Theory of African-American Literary Criticism*. New York: Oxford University Press.

Lott, E. 1993. *Love And Theft: Blackface Minstrelsy and the American Working Class*. New York: Oxford University Press.

Middleton, R. 1986. "In the Groove, or Blowing Your Mind? The Pleasures of Musical Repetition." In *Popular Culture and Social Relations*, edited by Tony Bennett, Colin Mercer, and Janet Woolacott, 47–59. Milton Keynes: Open University Press.

Nathan, H. 1962. *Dan Emmet and the Rise of Early Negro Minstrelsy*. Norman: University of Oklahoma Press.

Rose, Tricia. 1994. *Black Noise: Rap Music and Black Culture in Contemporary America*. Hanover, NH: Wesleyan University Press/University Press of New England.

Santoro, G. 1992. "Pop's Familiar Strains." *The Nation*, February 3, 1992, 138–40.

Snead, J. 1981. "On Repetition in Black Culture." *Black American Literature Forum* 15 (4): 146–54.

3

—— Kick Out the Jams! ——

The MC5 and the Politics of Noise

Steve Waksman

A RIOTOUS NOISE

In early 1968, that most momentous of years according to chroniclers of the 1960s, the MC5 released their second single, "Looking at You," a "mutinous" creation said by rock critic Chuck Eddy (1991) to have been recorded in downtown Detroit "sometime circa the [1967] riots or World Series" (24). Eddy's comment concerning the circumstances of the song's creation is probably a half-truth at best, but says much about the myth surrounding the MC5, in which the band were a group of "rock and roll guerrillas" who both fomented and embodied disorder with their rousing performances. Moreover, Eddy's association of the song with the riotous Detroit cityscape speaks to the sense of total unrest conveyed by "Looking at You," a sense present in so much of the band's music. The track explodes like a bull released from its pen, the bass and drums rolling atop one another while the guitars issue a screeching chaos that threatens to engulf singer Rob Tyner. John Sinclair (1969b), longtime manager of the band and producer of the single, offers a more hands-on account of its recording: "It was really a nonexistent production job, since I 'produced' it and didn't have any idea of what I was doing. I just knew that the music was killer and that we had to get it down, but I didn't know the first thing about mixing, and consequently the record was never really mixed, it was just released unmixed. I wanted to

47

make sure that all the high sound got in there because I had noticed that when records were played on the radio the high sounds dropped out, and I loaded them on to *Looking at You* to the point that the record was worthless for standard record-player playing" (10).

Thus was the feedback-laden sound put on tape, "unmixed" and, in Sinclair's description, thoroughly resistant to any standardization of musical product. "Looking at You" was designed not to be a hit, but to let the people of Detroit know "that the band really existed," to attract people to their live gigs at the Grande Ballroom, and to cultivate a following. In subsequent months, they accomplished their goal, becoming the main attraction in a burgeoning Detroit/Ann Arbor rock 'n' roll scene. During this time, the Five also became increasingly politicized; they became the musical arm of manager Sinclair's radical White Panther party and were the only rock band to perform at the Yippie-organized Festival of Life held during the week of confrontation at the 1968 Chicago Democratic convention, where their music was described by one astute observer as "an interplanetary, then galactic, flight of song, halfway between the space music of Sun Ra and 'The Flight of the Bumblebee,'...the sound screaming up to a climax of vibrations like one rocket blasting out of itself" (Mailer, 1968: 142). This sound was to become the basis of the MC5's politics, which were primarily a politics of affect. The stated goal was to turn the momentary synesthetic pleasures of musical experience into the basis for cultural revolution. These pleasures were the subject of many of the Five's best songs, such as "Looking at You," which recounted the singer's experience of being struck by desire in the midst of a rock and roll show:

> I stood up on the stand
> With my eyes shut tight
> Didn't want to see anybody
> Feeling happy having a good time yeah
> Feeling alright feeling alright
> Feeling alright feeling alright
>
> Danced out into the dancing crowd
> Felt like screaming out loud
> I saw you standing there
> I saw your long – saw your long hair.

Such lyrics no doubt bear witness to Dave Marsh's (1992) claim that the Five's politics had far more to do with "pleasure," in the sense of immediate gratification, than with transforming "modes of production" (8). Yet Marsh (1985), a noted rock journalist and Michigan native who attended many MC5 gigs, has also attested to the resounding sense of possibility that arose from his experiences with the band: "[S]o powerfully did the MC5's music unite its listeners that leaving those 1968 and 1969 shows, one literally felt that anything, even that implausible set of White Panther slogans, could come to pass. In that sense, the MC5, with their bacchanalian orgy of high energy sound, was a truer reflection of the positive spirit of the counter culture than the laid-back Apollonians of Haight-Ashbury ever could have been. And from the glimmerings of that confused babble, from the evidence of its hints of success, one could begin to construct an aesthetic and perhaps even a program that proposed how rock culture fit into society as something more significant than a diversion" (205).

Marsh writes as one who had been inside the MC5's grasp, who excited-ly went along with the band's rise to national attention only to be frustrat-ed, in the end, by their failure and dissolution. What he expresses in the above passage is not mere nostalgia (though there is much of that), but also a search for a usable past, for an aesthetic/political fusion that seemed as necessary in 1985, when he wrote his reflections, as it did in 1969 (and as it seems to me today).

With this chapter, I want to return to that brief period of possibility identified by Marsh, not simply to reclaim it but to explore it in its com-plexity. More specifically, I will examine the effects of the MC5's music within the context of the Detroit scene and the broader countercultural movement, with the ultimate goal of explaining how the use of maximum amplification affected the experience of watching and listening to rock and roll. This problem, essentially a phenomenological one, is directly related to the band's political stance. The energy that the Five generated was seem-ingly meant to break down the barriers between audience and performer and to radicalize the band's audience by awakening their deadened senses and compelling them to throw off the (mostly sexual) constraints imposed by the culture at large. Such a crude notion of sexual liberation was decidedly prefeminist if not antifeminist, as so much rock and roll has been and con-tinues to be, and was further built upon a pronounced fetishization of phallic potency that centered around an idealized notion of black masculinity common among white male radicals of the 1960s. To merely dismiss the MC5 as sexist and racist, though, is to unduly simplify the structures of desire articulated in their music and to gloss over the specific ways in which gender and race shaped their concept of liberation. Moreover, such a stance would overlook what I think are the legitimately positive elements of their aesthetic/political program, elements that have to do with their manipulation of electronic noise for the purposes of breaking aesthetic conventions and establishing the basis for an anti-authoritarian community of rock and roll devotees.

THE SCENE

One band does not make a music scene, but the fact remains that until the MC5's surge into local notoriety the Detroit/Ann Arbor area housed a scene-in-the-making more than a scene as such, at least with regard to rock and roll. Certainly there was music to be found, with Berry Gordy's Motown label issuing its stream of hits. Yet for white rock and roll bands, there was a severe shortage of places to play, as well as a shortage of radio stations that would play their music, and a shortage of media outlets that would cover their activities. Billy Lee and the Rivieras, a mid-1960s ensemble led by a white soul shouter named Mitch Ryder and identified by Dave Marsh (1985) as having laid the groundwork for the scene's later blossoming, spent much of their time playing "weddings, bar mitzvahs and lots of free hops" before settling in for a regular gig at "the Walled Lake Casino, thirty odd miles north of Detroit" (8). The MC5's career followed a similar path, performing in what guitarist Wayne Kramer called the "Downriver Rock and Roll scene" ("MC5 on the Cusp," 1969: 14) and what John Sinclair (1969b) called the "hickory rock circuit of fraternity parties, mixers at colleges, and the occasional teen-club job" (10). Making ends meet with this haphazard array of gigs was precarious, and the jobs seemed too much of the dead-end variety, a point of eminent frustration for a band with the ambitions of the Five.

Even in their earliest days, the members of the MC5 sought to be something more than just another garage band. Drawn to the hard soul sound of Stax records in Memphis, they were also beginning to experiment with their own version of "avant-rock" which sounded very close to some of the music coming out of England at the time, especially bands like the Yardbirds, the Who, and Them: three-chord rock with a strong blues/soul orientation, but also an aggressive use of electric instruments that set it apart from the music of most black musicians. The structure was simple but the sound was complex, verging towards a noisiness that, to untrained ears, did not sound much like music at all. Thus the original core members of the band, guitarists Wayne Kramer and Fred Smith and singer Rob Tyner, went through a number of musicians before settling on the rhythm section of Michael Davis on bass and Dennis Thompson on drums, losing a bassist and several drummers who could not relate to the band's sound. The band even structured one of its most "experimental" compositions, "Black to Comm," around drummer Bob Gasper's utter distaste for the piece, as Tyner recounted in a 1969 interview:

> [T]here's a thing that happens in *Black to Comm* that starts out with Fred playing the basic sound of the tune and the drums don't come in for a long time. Dennis waits and lets it build. That came from Bob Gasper's unwillingness to play the song, period. Sometimes the song'd go on for ten minutes with no drums. He'd sit there and sit there and get madder and madder and madder because he hated it so much and he couldn't relate to it at all. We're all flipping out, screaming into the mike, and finally he'd go crazy, and take out all of his frustrations by coming in very strong, maintaining the thing at a very high energy level. We always maneuovered [*sic*] him into that situation. So there's the Bob Gasper Memorial Wait at the beginning of *Black to Comm*. ("MC5 on the Cusp": 14)

Energy born out of anger and frustration: such is one crucial part of the Five's development and their myth, particularly that part of their myth that connects them to the later rise of punk rock. Anger is only part of their story, though, and the energy that motivated their music was neither so spontaneous nor so undirected as the above story might make it seem. However great a value the Five placed upon the spontaneous outburst, they were a band with at least some outline of a plan, and their plan crystallized upon meeting John Sinclair.

As the band tells it, they were drawn to Sinclair because of his preeminent place within the hip community of Detroit. At the time (1966) that community was quite small and, according to Sinclair (1972: 194), rather elitist in their attitudes toward rock and roll. Marijuana and jazz were the glue that held this enclave together; the goal was to live an alternative lifestyle in which everybody was free to do his or her "thing," and to live a life of art and poetry removed from the strictures of the workaday world. Into this classic bohemian setting the MC5 marched with the presumption that Sinclair and his fellow "beatniks" might be receptive to their music, and more importantly might serve as an important bridge in creating a following among the "kids" of Detroit ("MC5 on the Cusp": 15). What they found in Sinclair was not merely a conduit, though, but a collaborator and source of creative inspiration. Wayne Kramer described Sinclair as "a great big cat" with "all this energy, you know, and he just turns it on you....I had just left home, and here was this older cat who could explain all these things that I didn't understand about the world" (Fong-Torres, 1972: 32). What Sinclair explained to the band seems to have had much to do with the beauty and value of free jazz, itself a restless noisy outgrowth of African American culture that Sinclair perceived to parallel the Five's own brand of noise. With this initial bond established, Sinclair's association with the band grew, until he eventually signed on as manager and worked tirelessly to publicize the Five's exploits in the various underground channels growing in the Detroit/Ann Arbor area.

More than any single person, and probably at least as much as the band themselves, John Sinclair sought to cultivate a self-conscious recognition among Detroit's youth and counterculture that they were a part of a genuine rock and roll scene. In his columns for the underground newspaper *Fifth Estate*, Sinclair reported in issue after issue about the activities of the MC5 with a commitment that was at once self-serving and enlivening. At the center of the saga he constructed was the band's continual conflict with authority, which was part of a broader crackdown by police on the mounting youth culture of the Detroit/Ann Arbor region. One incident in particular, which occurred on May 31, 1968, reveals the dynamics at work in the relationship between the MC5, their audience, the police, and the club owners.

The situation begins with a small-scale drug bust: two cops come upon Sinclair and drummer Dennis Thompson as they smoke some marijuana outside the Grosse Point Hideout, where the band was to play that evening. When the police threaten to take everyone down to the station, Sinclair sends word to the rest of the band, who confront the officers while the band's equipment manager announces to the waiting crowd in the club that "the only way they'd get to hear the band would be to surround the cops outside and *make* them give us up." Sinclair (1972) continues the story:

> When the band, intact once again, returned inside to play the first set, the crowd went into a spontaneous scream scene to welcome them back to reality. And when Tyner kicked off the first tune with "KICK OUT THE JAMS, MOTHERFUCKER!" [the title of one of the band's songs] it was madness all the way, with wild applause and jubilation before and after every jam.

> The Hideout's manager was furious by this time, but he was caught in a simple capitalist contradiction: he couldn't move to censure the band because the paying customers were behind us all the way, and they were a lot more than "paying customers" by that time too – they were *ready*! When the chomp shut off the electricity during the closing energy – orgy "Black to Comm" to get the band off the stage, the crowd joined Fred Smith in chanting "Power! Power! Power!" until the juice came back on and the music soared to its natural climax. (p. 76)

I want to submit, along with Sinclair, that confrontations like this one had very much to do with the binding together of the Five's audience, and the broader rock audience of Detroit, into something approximating a self-conscious collectivity. As performing music and going to shows became contested activities, both the crowds and the band were compelled to take sides if they were to hold on to "their" culture in the face of police and club owners fearful of disorder. The actions of the police did much to cement the sense of solidarity between the MC5 and its audience, and also contributed significantly to the band's politicization.

Even more important for the purposes of my argument is the role that amplification plays in the above scenario. As much as the illegal substances and the unlawful cries of "MOTHERFUCKER," electricity itself becomes the source of contestation. More than a way to "turn on" a crowd, volume (or its lack) becomes a symbol of control, wonderfully signified in the crowd's multi-accentual chant of "Power! Power! Power!" The authoritarian impulse towards silence is countered by the restless noise of youth, which is in turn amplified by the band's sonic excess – all leading towards a restoration of "juice" (electric and otherwise) and a "natural climax" made possible by technology.

The role of technology in the above scenario has particular resonance within the context of Detroit, a city whose history has been linked with the achievements of industry and automation. Robert Duncan, longtime rock critic and former editor of the Detroit-based *Creem* magazine, observed some years ago that the style of rock centered in Detroit and practiced by the MC5 bore a clear relationship to the legacy of Fordism. Duncan drew attention to the music's (and the musicians') preoccupation with volume, and by extension with the technologies that made such volume possible, and suggested that this concern with playing *loudest* was what made Detroit rock "so suited to the cavernous, sound-devouring arena and so to the economy of scale that would be the linchpin of mass production rock 'n' roll, just as it had been the linchpin of Henry Ford's Detroit" (1984: 39). Of course, the MC5 never gained the sort of popularity that would have filled arenas, except perhaps in their native Detroit, but their use of extreme volume certainly set the stage for the later incorporation of "loudestness" described by Duncan with regard to heavy metal music and its attendant form of presentation, arena rock.

Where Duncan locates in the sound of Detroit rock the groundwork for a new "economy of scale" inextricably tied to the city's history as a center of mass production, others perceived resistance to that same cityscape not in the sound itself so much as in its reception. So did Lester Bangs declare in 1971 that "the only real hope" for truly vital rock and roll was Detroit, where "lots of people still care about getdown gutbucket rock 'n' roll passionately because it takes the intolerableness of Detroit life and channels it into a form of strength and survival with humor and much of the energy claimed" (1987: 69). In a similar vein, an earlier piece in *Creem* assessed the development of the city's scene in recent years:

> The alternative culture in the Detroit/Ann Arbor community is first and foremost a rock and roll culture. Whatever movement we have here grew out of rock and roll. It was rock and roll music which first drew us out of our intellectual covens and suburban shells. We got excited by and about the music and started relating to each other on the high plane of energy that has come to

be associated with our community; it is around the music that the community has grown and it is the music which holds the community together.

The reason is simple: there isn't anything else here....Life in Detroit is profoundly anti-intellectual. If you live in San Francisco or New York, the traditions are there, and even if you reject them wholly you've been shaped by them. Detroit is completely lacking in climate; our institutions are industrial and businesslike, not cultural or intellectual (Marsh, LaRene, and Kramer, 1970: 7).

Here the sterile industrialization described by Duncan is fused with the more hopeful observations of Bangs. Life in Detroit is pervaded by an over-arching boredom solved only by devotion to rock and roll; and that boredom is made even more unsettling by the specter of Fordism, which threatens to foreclose any alternatives to its totalizing presence.

Particularly for the white male youths who made up the core of the MC5's audience, Fordism represented both a legacy and a future without promise. John Sinclair powerfully expressed this sentiment in his response to the harsh criticisms put forth by Detroit Black Panther member William Leach (1969). Rejecting Leach's suggestion that white radicals go work in the factories to get to know the workers, Sinclair (1969a) countered that "our fucking parents have been working in those factories...for years and years so we won't have to do that anymore," and went on to assert: "We know all about the white working class, and the white lower, middle class and white middle class because that's where we come from. That's why we're the way we are, because we won't have anything to do with that bullshit. The way to change a system like this is to stop supporting it with your life, not to join the machine" (16). Sinclair gives voice here to the divided class identity that motivated the Five's music and gave force to the band's relationship with its audience. While this might have been a music born out of Fordism, and out of what might be termed a white male working-class sensibility, it was also founded upon a rejection of working-class life insofar as that life was perceived to be crippling in its lack of possibility.

Thus might the MC5's music, along with the music of other Detroit bands like the Stooges, be judged as an outgrowth of that moment in history when the significance of Fordism shifted from representing the American Dream to standing for the failure of that dream. As Detroit scholar Jerry Herron (1993) has argued:

> The history of Detroit…is also a history of humiliations; it is a history as humiliation. What I mean by this is summed up in the famous dictum attributed to Henry Ford…: "History is bunk." He may or may not have uttered the famous words; nevertheless, making bunk out of history was surely what "Fordism" was all about, and it's what the town that became synonymous with Ford's inventions came to be about: the creation of a material plenitude so vast that people would quit worrying about the past, and history would cease to matter. Detroit's humiliation of history seemed an exhilarating idea, so long as the good times lasted, but when they ran out, it left both the city and the people in it painfully undefended and up for grabs. (p. 9–10)

Whereas the counterculture has been interpreted by historians such as Gitlin (1993) and Leuchtenburg (1983) to have arisen out of the abundance of the postwar period, in Detroit we get a different story. Not simply the result of heightened expectations, Detroit's rock and roll counterculture also takes shape out of a fear that those expectations might never be met within the city's industrial economy, and thus from a sense of futility at even harboring expectations of advancement.

Following these observations, one can understand the intense, almost distressing energy of the music that came out of the Detroit scene at least in part as a product of this ambivalent network of expectations and desires, which gave the music a character not found in the more middle-class countercultural environs of San Francisco. I would further argue that the music of the MC5 and other Detroit bands like the Stooges did not simply reproduce the logic of repetition and standardization that undergirded Fordism, but rather stood as an attempt to turn that logic against itself. The production of a disorderly electronic noise in this context indicated a contradictory stance toward technology, a willful move to master the tools of standardization that at the same threatened to drown out the human presence with the force of the machine. Meanwhile, the repetition of the Five's music signified the boredom and sameness of everyday life, but also worked to counteract this boredom by producing a disorienting noise that brought listeners to an ecstatic pitch, as in the following account of one of the Five's shows written by Pam Brent (1969) for the first issue of *Creem*:

> The temperature soon becomes unbearable, and as the Five mount the stage, the place is literally an inferno. Rob Tyner invites us to remove any extraneous clothing, and in response, shirts, ties, scarves, etc. are removed The music begins. The wall of sound assaults every cell in these close quarters....Bold, exalting tones rip through the heat and set fire to the very air, as sweat drips down the backs and brows of all present.
>
> The roaring vibrations and now–language combine to put the audience in an indescribable and frenzied mood. The voice of the Five resounds all that is the youth of today. An aura of all our sought-after goals; love, peace, freedom, and f—king in the streets – they are echos, an incarnation of our will. We receive them with appropriate joy and rapture.

While Brent's description can only begin to do justice to the "heat" of the musical moment, she records a wave of synesthetic impressions very much like that articulated in the Five's lyrics: visual, aural, and tactile pleasures all blend together into a mood of "appropriate joy and rapture." Just as significant, though, is the political language of Brent's passage, the "sought-after goals" of youth that formed the basis of the MC5's political program. It is to a more detailed examination of those goals, and the means by which Sinclair and the Five sought to bring them about, that I now turn.

ROCK AND ROLL, DOPE, AND FUCKING IN THE STREETS

John Sinclair issued his "White Panther Statement," the official declaration of the formation of the White Panther party, in the November 14–27, 1968, issue of *Fifth Estate*. Drawing his inspiration from the combined influences of the Black Panthers and the Yippies, he outlined a movement of "visionary maniac white mother country dope fiend rock and roll freaks who were to parallel the move to Black Power in African-American politics with their own brand of cultural revolution." Stating the party's opposition to "the white honkie culture that has been handed to us on a silver plastic platter," he especially emphasized the centrality of rock and roll music to the group's platform. "Rock and roll music is the spearhead of our attack because it's so effective and so much fun," proclaimed Sinclair, who further cited the MC5 as the best example of the "organic high-energy guerrilla bands who are infiltrating the popular culture and destroying millions of minds in the process." To conclude the statement, he called attention to the absolute centrality of black politics and black music in the formation of the White Panther program:

> The actions of the Black Panthers in America have inspired us and given us strength, as has the music of black America, and we are moving to reflect that strength in our daily activity just as our music contains and extends the power and feeling of the black magic music that originally informed our bodies and told us that we could be free.

> I might mention Brother James Brown in this connection, as well as John Coltrane and Archie Shepp, Sun-Ra, LeRoi Jones, Malcolm X, Huey P. Newton, Bobby Seale, Eldridge Cleaver, these are magic names to us. These are men in America. And we're as crazy as they are, and as pure. We're bad. (p. 8)

This reverence for African American masculinity was essential to the White Panther program, and also to the music of the Five, which drew together a range of black musical influences – James Brown soul, John Coltrane free jazz, John Lee Hooker blues – out of the belief that these disparate styles were linked by a subversion of the "white honkie culture" and an affirmation of a new aesthetic/political order founded upon the celebration of bodily pleasure. That this return to the body was to be led by "pure" black men, and that it seemed primarily to be oriented towards a reconstruction of white males into sexually charged "rock and roll guerrillas," does not speak well for the Five's revolutionary vision. Indeed, it betrays the sort of "primitivization" of blackness, and of black masculinity in particular, that has characterized so many attempts by white European and American men to escape or transcend the constrictions of "their" culture. Marianna Torgovnick (1990) has discussed the ways in which "the idiom 'going primitive' is in fact congruent in many ways to the idiom 'getting physical.'" Fascination with the primitive "other" works to overcome "alienation from the body, restoring the body, and hence the self, to a relation of full and easy harmony with nature or the cosmos, as they have been variously conceived" (228). In this relationship, white men colonize the body of the "other" to resolve the split between mind and body that has been enforced by the "civilizing process" (Lowe, 1982: 85–108; Elias, 1978).

Indeed, one could say that for Sinclair and the MC5 it was only through the appropriation of black masculinity that white men could become any kind of men at all. Here the Five parallel that branch of 1960s radicalism that viewed the consumer-driven technocratic order to have had an emasculating effect upon American manhood. Todd Gitlin (1993) has discussed the strong masculinist impulse that underlay so much of the New Left and the counterculture, citing among other examples an outburst by Emmett Grogan, a member of San Francisco's anarchistic Diggers, at a 1967 SDS meeting. During a confrontational display in which he wrought havoc with the furniture and "slapped around" some of the women present, Grogan issued a challenge to the men of the movement: "Faggots! Fags! Take off your ties, they are chains around your necks. You haven't got the balls to go mad. You're gonna make a revolution? – you'll piss in your pants when the violence erupts. You, spade – you're a nigger, what are you doing here? Your people need you...." Grogan then followed his outburst with a poem by Gary Snyder that, according to Gitlin, included the line, "I hunt the white man down/in my heart" (228). The masculinist program of action performed by Grogan strongly parallels that of the MC5 with its denigration of a passive, tie-wearing masculinity, which comes to stand for white masculinity in general. Moreover, Gitlin goes on to explain how, as the movement turned towards a "revolutionary vision," the Black Panthers ascended to models of action for white men in the movement: "If revolution was imminent, the black under-class, rioting in the streets, were the plausible cadres. Who seemed to represent those specters better than Huey Newton, Bobby Seale, and Eldridge Cleaver, these intelligent brothers in black leather jackets, James Dean and Frantz Fanon rolled into one, the very image of indigenous revolutionary leadership risen from the underclass and certified in prison?" (349).

Whereas Gitlin provides substance for noting the connections between the MC5's fascination with black manhood and that of the political and countercultural movement at large, his allusion to the specter of the rioting black underclass should also force us back into a recognition of the specificity of this fascination within the context of Detroit. The Detroit riot of July 1967 was among the deadliest of the 1960s, with a death toll of over 40. While local authorities witnessed the event with fear, radicals like John Sinclair adopted a far different perspective. Writing in the *Fifth Estate* (1968) during the immediate aftermath of the "Rebellion," Sinclair responded to the action as a ritual of "purification" and went on to assert: "No, baby, it's not a 'race riot,' or anything as simple as that. People just got tired of being hassled by police and cheated by businessmen and got out their equalizers and went to town....Oh it was Robin Hood Day in merry olde Detroit, the first annual city-wide all-free fire sale, and the people without got their hands on the goodies" (5). Sinclair's imagination was clearly stoked by the spectacle of unrest, yet his rejection of the simple classification "race riot" was likely more than a rhetorical flourish; Gitlin (1993: 244–5) provides corroborating evidence that the unrest in Detroit was an integrated affair. Furthermore, Eric Ehrmann (1969), in profiling the MC5 for *Rolling Stone*, described a pact between the city's white and black militants "to stick up for each other," a pact that Sinclair himself was instrumental in engineering (16). Given the aforementioned dispute between Sinclair and Black Panther William Leach, one hesitates to conclude that there was a secure alliance between Detroit's countercultural enclave and the black community. If nothing else, though, what we can locate in Sinclair's words is a desire for a connection to exist between the two communities, a desire that became in the "White Panther Statement" a longing to participate in the "black revolution" itself, and to follow an aesthetic/political path that black men had already charted.

Given the political context of the time, Chuck Eddy's "half-truthful" association of the MC5's music with a riotous Detroit gains in symbolic truth-value what it might lack as a statement of fact. If the Five's music was not literally produced during the riots, it certainly gained much of its definition from the racial unrest that characterized Detroit during the mid- to late-1960s. Viewed from this perspective, the MC5's music can be taken as a response to the political imperative felt by Gitlin, Sinclair, and other white activists during the 1960s in the face of black political activity, an imperative articulated by Gitlin (1993) with the simple question: "What does Whitey do?" (245). Yet as far as this specificity with respect to time and geography might take us in understanding the context of the Five's politicization, it takes us only so far in understanding their music, which arose out of a broader mix of influences than any reference to the riots can explain. Furthermore, we should not lose sight of the extent to which the band's, and Sinclair's, attraction to black music predated the riots, and was rooted in patterns of racial and sexual desire that extend well beyond the 1960s.

Insight into these patterns can be gleaned from Eric Lott's study of minstrelsy, *Love and Theft* (1993). Seeking to move beyond the notion that black-

face minstrelsy arose solely out of twin white impulses to denigrate blackness and capitalize upon that denigration, Lott locates in the form evidence
of a "profound white investment in black culture" that cannot be explained
as mere racism (18). More specifically, Lott identifies in minstrelsy "a gendered pattern of exchange, a kind of commerce between men" motivated by
a "complex dynamic" in which white performers' tendency to dominate
black maleness "coexisted with or indeed depended on a self-conscious
attraction to the black men it was the job of these performers to mimic"
(1993: 49–50). Putting on blackface also involved putting on a particular
style of masculinity, one in which the qualities thought to belong to black
men – "cool, virility, humility, abandon, or *gaite de coeur*" – were transferred
onto the white male body (52). According to Lott, the sexual envy that
motivated this homosocial exchange betrayed a sort of homoerotic desire on
the part of white men; the desire to have what the black man had slid easily if uncomfortably into the desire to have the black man, with the ambivalence between economic and sexual possession residing in the word "have."

Although Lott's analysis is centered upon minstrelsy as an antebellum
form, he makes a convincing case that these modes of homosocial exchange
laid the foundation for the subsequent history of relations between white
bohemians and African American culture. The MC5 and the many legions
of other white musicians who drew from African American culture no longer
literalized the putting on of blackness through the application of blackface,
but did adopt other signifiers to mark the exchange (especially hair, in the
case of the Five). However, I would argue that it was primarily in their
"strapping on" of electric guitars, and in their use of technology more generally, that groups like the Five most clearly reproduced the logic of blackface.

Here we have to mediate between two sets of dichotomies, both of
which revolve around technology, that speak to a powerful contradiction in
the race/gender dynamic at work in this process of appropriation. First is the
opposition between black "nature" and white "technology," an opposition
that lays at the very heart of primitivist desires. Blackness gains its potency
from its closeness to nature in this paradigm of racial thought; it is the
embodiment of a primal essence that connotes a sort of purity. Technology,
by contrast, is an outgrowth of white rationality indicative of the alienation
of mind from body; it amplifies certain bodily effects and functions to com-
pensate for white bodily deficiency. So did Ron Wellburn (1972), an African
American poet, musician, and critic, label white rock music "a technology,

not a real music" and "an affectation, not a felt experience" in opposition to black jazz, which he judged to be marked by a natural expressivity (148–9). For Wellburn, the technological dependence of rock stood as a sign of its decadence, and of the "spiritual, creative, and sociological weaknesses of white America" (133); and he counseled black artists to avoid similar dependence lest they lose their vitality. That Wellburn writes from a black nationalist position demonstrates the power of these associations across racial lines, and gives evidence of the ways in which the "primitivization" of blackness was appropriated by black men during the 1960s as the basis for a critique of white masculinity (Wallace, 1979).

However, within another set of oppositions between female "nature" and male "technology," what is configured as a symbol of lack becomes itself a sign of mastery. Woman-as-nature connotes the passivity of an existence ruled by external forces, while men wield technology to display their transcendence of nature and their power to order the world according to their will. It is out of this second, gendered set of associations that Susan Hiwatt (1971), a feminist critic of rock music, pronounced the following: "It blew my mind the first time I heard about a woman playing an electric guitar. Partly because of the whole idea we have that women can't understand anything about electronics (and we're not even supposed to want to), and also because women are supposed to be composed, gentle, play soft songs. A guy once told my sister when she picked up his electric guitar that women were meant to play only folk guitar, like Joan Baez or Judy Collins, that electric guitars were unfeminine" (143). Technology in Hiwatt's account is clearly gendered in such a way as to reinforce associations of masculinity with knowledge as opposed to ignorance, force as opposed to gentility, and loudness as opposed to the "soft songs" that women are to play. Moreover, Hiwatt gives a rare moment of insight into the way in which men guard their privileged access to technology as a means of policing the boundary that separates maleness from femaleness.

In the MC5's approach to technology, these two paradigms – the racialized and gendered configurations of technology – are brought into an uneasy alliance. The electric guitar as an instrument of mastery amplifies the masculinity of the band's performers; even singer Rob Tyner gains force from the sheer volume surrounding and impacting his body, which also impacts the bodies of the audience. Yet this use of the electric guitar threatens to call attention to the artificiality of this performance of masculinity. To borrow a term from Marjorie Garber (1993: 374), the guitar "artifactualizes" the male body, insofar as it shows that masculinity can only be achieved by putting on certain appurtenances. This is where the recourse to racial discourse becomes so instrumental; for if white men take black masculinity as their model, they also aspire towards the "naturalness" that blackness signifies. The threat of artifice is therefore contained by putting on black manhood, which renaturalizes the virility of the male body.

Such a paradoxical mating of race, gender, and technology can be heard to great effect in the MC5's song "Rocket Reducer No. 62 (Rama Lama Fa Fa Fa)," the closing cut on side one of their first album, the "live" *Kick Out the Jams*. The very title of the song is indicative of the multiple levels of meaning at play in the Five's music: the rocket as technological signifier of potency coupled with the "nonsense" syllables so common to soul, rock and roll, and other musical forms derived from African American traditions. Similarly, the song itself couples a one-chord soul-blues vamp with the sort of maximum amplification that gave the Five's music its distinction. That this is a song about the power of the electric guitar becomes clear during the introduction, when Rob Tyner exclaims, "This song starts out with Brother Wayne Kramer, Brother Wayne Kramer," who proceeds to hammer out the main musical figure over a wave of feedback generated by fellow guitarist Fred "Sonic" Smith. As the entire band joins into the repetitive groove, Tyner sings insistently about his status as a "natural man." "I've got to keep it up 'cause I'm a natural man" is his constant refrain, leading to the reassertion of his masculinity in the chorus: "I'm the man for you baby/Yes I am for you baby." The climax of the song, though, comes at the end, when the two guitarists take off on an orgasmic solo flight, pursuing each other on their respective fretboards while the rest of the band lays silent. A full minute of rapid distorted runs is capped by a final bluesy bend, and when the rest of the band rejoins for a final crash of the chords, the "rocket" is "reduced" to a state of detumescence, signified by the ensuing silence as both the song and the album's side come to an end.

With this orgasmic outburst closing a rather explicit celebration of natural manhood, "Rocket Reducer" would seem to correspond to Susan McClary's (1991) analysis of the phallocentric narrative that has defined Western classical and popular musics during the past three centuries. Upon closer inspection, though, the song, and the Five's music in general, does not conform so easily to McClary's observations. For McClary, tonal music, that music which makes the most sense to Western ears, is organized according to a teleology in which the dominant musical mode states its control over "other" keys in a way that signifies both the assertion and the achievement of phallic mastery. She further explains that this narrative depends upon a song's departure from the tonic or dominant mode, so that the music performs "an adventure in which other key areas are visited...and in which the certainty of tonal identity is at least temporarily suspended. Otherwise there is no plot....To the extent that 'Other' keys stand in the way of unitary identity, they must finally be subdued for the sake of narrative closure. They serve as moments both of desire (because without the apparent longing to approach these other keys, there is only stagnation) and of dread (because they threaten identity)" (155–6). However phallocentric the Five's music might strike us, this "plot," with its emphasis upon the visitation and conquest of "other" musical areas, is absent in a great deal of their music, including "Rocket Reducer No. 62." Until the final guitar tirade, the song is most notable for its lack of narrative content, as the same chord and musical figure are struck again and again, establishing a tonic against which no other is defined. Moreover, when the guitars take off at the end of the song, it is not into a climactic tonal flourish but into atonality; the instruments abandon the relentlessly dominant mode of the song for a more "free" type of playing that obeys little sense of proper musical form.

The above analysis is not meant to deny the distinctly masculine bias of the MC5's music, but it is to show how they did not simply reproduce standard musical narratives of phallic achievement. Rather, the orgasmic imperative articulated in "Rocket Reducer No. 62," which I would argue was in many ways the driving force behind the Five's music in general, was divided in its motivation: while on the one hand it was offered as the supreme affirmation of the (white male) self, on the other hand this imperative pointed towards the obliteration of the boundaries between self and other. Thus, in his original liner notes for *Kick Out the Jams*, John Sinclair (1972) outlined a philosophy based upon the principle "Separation Is Doom," in which he stressed the Five's status as a *"whole thing:"*

> There is no way to get at the music without taking in the whole context of the music too – *there is no separation.* We say the MC5 is the solution to the problem of separation, because they are *so together.* The MC5 is totally committed to the revolution, as the

revolution is totally committed to driving people out of their separate shells and into each other's arms.

I'm talking about *unity*, brothers and sisters, because we have to *get it together*. We *are* the solution to the problem, if we will just *be* that. If we can *feel* it, LeRoi Jones said, "Feeling Predicts Intelligence." The MC5 will make you feel it, or leave the room. The MC5 will drive you crazy out of your head into your body. The MC5 *is* rock and roll. Rock and roll *is* the music of our bodies, of our whole lives – the "resensifier," Rob Tyner calls it. We have to *come together*, people, "build to a gathering," or else. Or else we are dead, and gone. (p. 110)

Consider alongside this statement of purpose the MC5 song "Come Together," alluded to above by Sinclair. Bearing no resemblance to the Beatles song of the same name (which was, in any case, released over a year later), "Come Together" was an explicit expression of the band's program of union through the musical enactment of orgasm. As with "Rocket Reducer No. 62," the song is characterized above all by an excess of volume and noise and by its unchanging harmonic structure: a single note struck for several beats, followed by two massive power chords, repeated throughout the course of the song without interruption. No guitar solos here; the band operates as a "whole thing" while Rob Tyner intermittently shouts vocals punctuated by the line "Together in the darkness," a line multiply inflected by the sexual/political command of the song's title. Any sense of variation comes from subtle shifts in the level of loudness; the thunderous density of the band's attack eases as Tyner announces that "it's getting closer...God it's so close now" with a voice that sounds pained with anticipation. The volume rises once again while the song rushes into its concluding gasp towards "togetherness," which ends with a progression of chords that ascends and then lunges back downward while becoming increasingly out of tune, the blur of the drums and the whirr of the feedback further contributing to the heightened disorder that immediately precedes the song's finish.

The prioritization of volume in this song – the way in which loudness was to provoke bodily excitement and changes in the level of noise provided the friction, if you will, that was to bring this excitement to its climax – lead us further into the MC5's aesthetic/political program. More specifically, it is here that we come to the Five's principles of "high-energy" music as a tool of cultural revolution. For the band, the "revolutionary" potential of their music lay in its presumed ability to drive people "into their bodies," to provoke what Rob Tyner called "purification and resensification on all levels." "Resensify you back to your meat, because that's the way you take it in. Your meat is your senses, because your senses are made out of meat. And if you don't keep in contact with your meat...that's why all these straight people are so fucked up, man, 'cause they let their meat loaf – and it just rots, it rots" (Walley, 1970: 283). Rock 'n' roll as an assault upon straight society might seem like the most naive sort of 1960s idealism, yet there is also in Tyner's statement what I think is a powerful recognition of civilization and its discontents. Here the primitivism that underlay the band's reverence for black manhood comes back into play: if "straight," civilized society required the dissociation of mind and body and the sublimation of physical pleasure, the Five would counter this system with a sonic assault on the senses that would, ideally, rid the body of its civilized trappings and return it to a purity of sensation that had long been lost.

Bodily pleasure, then, was not an end in itself for the MC5. Instead, the band's music was motivated by an impulse very similar to that described by Norman Mailer (1960) in his notorious and influential essay, "The White Negro." According to Mailer, the white negro, or "hipster," is a sort of psychopath seeking to resolve "those mutually contradictory inhibitions upon violence and love which civilization has exacted of us" (310). Refusing the negative associations of psychopathy, Mailer finds the hipster/psychopath especially adapted to the tensions of modern life, and defines the project of the hipster in terms that foreshadow the Five's own brand of sensual politics. The hipster seeks above all to "create a new nervous system" for himself, in Mailer's terms, and to overthrow "the inefficient and often antiquated nervous circuits of the past which strangle our potentiality for responding to new possibilities which might be exciting for our individual growth" (310). Similarly, the MC5 sought to escape the "reflexes and rhythms" of the past for a new mode of response. The desire to restore the body to a condition of purity, then, was not only a longing for primal return but also had a futuristic bent that envisioned the formation of "new possibilities." And again, the presence of blackness within this scenario is crucial; both Mailer and the Five located the model for these potentials of bodily experience in the "super-sensuality" of black men (Sinclair, 1972: 12).

Another comment by Mailer provides us entry into the language of the MC5: "The language of Hip is a language of energy, how it is found, how it is lost (1960: 314). Energy was the keyword within the Five's program – an energy born from sound, which was to effect the sort of reorganization of the senses discussed above. Indeed, as described by Rob Tyner, the effect upon the body was immediate and transformative: "Pure sound energizes. The more energy in the sound, the bigger the sound that gets to you, the more intense the experience is, and the more intense the experience is, the more intense reality is – your metabolic reality at that moment, you know, an intensive feeling of your metabolism – that's where you find your reality. And music is equated on that level too, because it does make metabolic changes. Like on the stage, I notice metabolic changes at every instant. So fast – your heart beat and your respiration and everything, because you're using your body 100 percent – that's what music is supposed to make you do" (Walley, 1970: 272). Tyner's words are echoed by John Sinclair (1969), who in a letter written after his break with the band offered his own articulation of their "high-energy" music: "[The MC5's stage show] was a beautiful demonstration of the principles of high-energy performance: as the performer puts out more the energy level of the audience is raised and they give back more energy to the performers, who are moved onto a higher energy level which is transmitted to the audience and sent back, etc., until everything is totally frenzied. This process makes changes in the people's bodies that are molecular and cellular and which transform them irrevocably just as LSD or any other strong high-energy agents do" (11). Sinclair brings us back to the collective basis of the Five's emphasis upon sound, energy, and the body. Energy in these passages acts as a metaphor for the ways in which sound acts upon the body, or more precisely, for the ways in which sound and body act upon each other, and the process through which the sensual experience of a single individual and a single body might be communicated to other individuals and other bodies. Thus was music not only to resensify but to spread that resensification, and to drive people "out of their separate shells, and into each other's arms."

Such a goal was utopian, to be sure, and what part of the band's audience shared this sense of thrusting towards communal ecstasy is all but impossible to measure. Nonetheless, I want to suggest that what the MC5 sought to do in statements like those above, and what they strove to achieve far more directly with their music, was to translate the powerful sensations they felt from their own experience of amplified music into a broad-based movement. In other words, their politics cannot be understood apart from their use of amplification, which opened for them levels of sensory experience that seemed fundamentally new.

As such, the Five's aesthetic/political program can be understood as an attempt to come to terms with the possibilities offered by new technologies in a way that paralleled the writings of 1960s media philosopher Marshall McLuhan. For McLuhan (1967), the present society was marked by a shift from the mechanical technologies that had dominated the age of industrial-ization towards a new electronic universe in which separation of all kinds was being overthrown. He described the message of the new technology as "Total Change," and declared that electric circuitry would end "psychic, social, economic and political parochialism" (16). Whereas Sinclair under-stood the Five's music as a "whole thing," McLuhan similarly believed that electronic media would abolish the boundaries that separated time and space, which in turn enforced the difference between self and other. Elec-tronic media would upset the relation between the center and the margins, converting the urbanized spaces of the imperializing West into nodes with-in a "global village." Perhaps more importantly, though, McLuhan claimed that electronic media would transform our sensorium, and would move us away from the objectifying emphasis upon vision and visuality that had been born with the Enlightenment towards a new prioritization of sound: "The ear favors no particular 'point of view.' We are enveloped by sound. It forms a seamless web around us. We say, 'Music shall fill the air.' We never say, 'Music shall fill a particular segment of the air.'...Where a visual space is an organized continuum of a uniformed connected kind, the ear world is a world of simultaneous relationships" (111). The reorganization of the ner-vous system, then, was already under way in McLuhan's conceptualization of electronic technology. Linearity and fragmentation were to give way to simultaneity and unification, all of which was to be embodied in the new "sound" relationships that people had with one another.

This sense of imminent possibility that McLuhan located within elec-tricity was in many ways also the crux of the MC5's music during the early phase of the band's career. One does not have to look hard to find traces of McLuhan's rhetoric, for instance, in Sinclair's writings on the band and on rock and roll in general. "Rock and roll kicked off the 21st century almost fifty years ahead of time," proclaimed Sinclair in the introduction to his

book, *Guitar Army* (1972). "It made the leap from the mechanical to the electronic age in the space of three minutes, 45 revolutions per minute" (9).
Meanwhile, McLuhan's idea that "the medium is the message" found its way
into Sinclair's (1970) discussion of the style with which the Five incorporated amplification into their music: "The power of the amplifiers was built into
the [MC5's] songs and arrangements of other people's songs they used, they
were not separable from it, and in that sense the MC5 made what can best
be described as a "post-Western" music, in the same sense that Archie
Shepp's or John Coltrane's or Cecil Taylor's or Sun Ra's music can only be
called post-Western. That is, these musics destroy separation on every level,
and separation is the basis of all Western musics up to and including most of
rock and roll expression" (54). McLuhan's categories not only justified the
prioritization of the medium in the Five's music, but also are used here by
Sinclair to situate the band within a global process of musical production. As
McLuhan (1967) suggested that "Electric circuitry is orientalizing the West"
(145), so Sinclair holds a similar faith in electricity's power to break free
from Western traditions. Underlying both versions of this faith is yet another idealization of the primitive as described by Marianna Torgovnick (1990),
one less concerned with "getting physical" that with "going home." She
writes: "Going primitive is trying to 'go home' to a place that feels comfortable and balanced....Whatever form the primitive's hominess takes, its
strangeness salves our estrangement from ourselves and our culture" (185).
So it is that the Orient, or blackness, symbolizes the extent to which electronic technology both breaks with the conventions of the West and
remains continuous with broader patterns of human existence. Electricity
takes us beyond ourselves only to restore us to our original state, a state from
which "others" (the East, blacks) never strayed so far: such is the trope
through which technology was imagined to be both radically different and
comfortably familiar in the writings of McLuhan and Sinclair, and in the
music of the MC5.

We should not forget, though, that it was not technology as a thing in itself,
but technology in its capacity to generate noise, that the MC5 found so full
of possibilities. In their use of amplified sound, the Five embody and perhaps
even foreshadow many of the ideas put forth by French social theorist
Jacques Attali in his groundbreaking musicological tract, *Noise: The Political
Economy of Music* (1985). Attali, in fact, locates in music a strong prophetic
tendency, and asserts that the forms and structures that organize music are

not determined by social forces but instead predict the future shape those forces will take. Sound, noise, and music are all fundamental to Attali's concept of the social order, and like McLuhan, but with greater intellectual rigor, he seeks a theoretical language that will overturn the hegemony of sight within the sensory hierarchy: "More than colors and forms, it is sounds and their arrangements that fashion societies. With noise is born disorder and its opposite: the world. With music is born power and its opposite: subversion. In noise can be read the codes of life, the relations among men. Clamor, Melody, Dissonance, Harmony; when it is fashioned by man with specific tools, when it invades man's time, when it becomes sound, noise is the source of purpose and power, of the dream – Music. It is at the heart of the progressive rationalization of aesthetics, and it is a refuge for residual irrationality; it is a means of power and a form of entertainment" (6).

So does Attali build an argument for the political centrality of music. Modern societies have been predicated upon the organization of noise into assimilable forms: the harmonious, rationalized tones of the Western musical canon convey a sense of the unity and order of all things, and at the same time urge us to forget the chaos of sounds that pervade our everyday life. With the move towards a consumer-driven musical economy, that chaos becomes normalized through processes of what Attali terms "repetition"; a greater diversity of sounds is present, but still operates to manage our desires into established channels. "Repetition produces information free of noise," writes Attali; it creates a "silence in sound, the innocuous chatter of recuperable cries" (1985: 106, 124). Where Attali locates the exercise of power in music, though, he also identifies possibilities for subversion through an emergent mode of musical production he names "Composition." He writes: "Composition...calls into question the distinction between worker and consumer, between doing and destroying, and fundamental division of roles in all societies in which usage is defined by a code; to compose is to take pleasure in the instruments, the tools of communication" (135). In Composition, music is no longer oriented towards demands outside itself. The musical worker uses his instrument to create his own musical code in which noise no longer signifies an unwanted dissonance but rather demarcates the autonomy of desire.

Attali's imagined utopia of musical practice resonates strongly with the MC5's own utopian goals. The Five were about nothing if not "taking pleasure in the instruments" of communication, and with those instruments they similarly strove to establish a realm of autonomous desire in which the "distinction between worker and consumer," or between audience and performer, was abolished. Of course, in the case of the Five, their utopia went unrealized, as perhaps only it could have – after an initial burst of public notoriety, their success fell rapidly, and by 1972 they were relegated to drifting around Europe, having lost the solid base of local support that had driven their early career. Nonetheless, in their short-lived prime the MC5 injected rock and roll with a level of hopefulness that continues to exert significant influence upon both the music's practitioners and its critics. Thus, 20 years after the band's demise, critic Chuck Eddy (1991) celebrated the Five's first album in the following terms: "Not merely the only live debut album that's ever mattered (damn few have ever even *not mattered!*), this is one of the livest *anythings* ever..., a toast to civilization and its discontents, pinkos-in-training defending armed love atop insurrectionarily inflamed National Guard jeeps on Murder City's East Side, dredging up hoodoo demons from the darkness....The MC5 were as American as apple pie, red-bleeding white-skinned blues-belters no matter how black they wanted to be" (34–5).

Where Eddy wants to recuperate the Five's whiteness in the face of their desire to "be" black, I would assert that the Five's whiteness cannot be understood apart from their fascination with black manhood, and that their utopianism could not have existed apart from this fascination. Indeed, it is interesting to note in this regard that for Attali, as for the Five, the music that most closely approximated his ideal of Composition was free jazz. In light of this convergence, and the recurrent privileging of "other" cultures in the revolutionary/utopian ideals that have pervaded this chapter (Gitlin, Mailer, McLuhan), one finally has to wonder whether white males of the late twentieth century can imagine a utopia that is not founded on the absorption of the other. Certainly during the 1960s at least, the use of primitivist rhetoric as a means of cultural critique was a fundamental part of the counterculture to which the MC5 contributed. Moreover, I want to suggest that it is specifically in music that we might gain clearest access to the complex range of desires that made up this countercultural moment. Race, gender, and technology were all mythicized through the MC5's music in ways that reproduced conventional hierarchies even as the band sought the abolition of those hierarchies.

By the same token, though, their music was marked by a restless exuberance that cannot be entirely explained by or reduced to standard academic categories, an exuberance contained within the band's rallying cry, "KICK

OUT THE JAMS, MOTHERFUCKER!" – a call to "break everything loose and free everybody from their very real and imaginary prisons" (Sinclair, 1972: 104). Flaunting Michigan's obscenity laws, the MC5 mobilized their audience and often called the police into action, much as they had in the earlier clash over the right to amplification.

> [Guitarist Wayne] Kramer kicked off the second set with "Ramblin' Rose," and when it came time for the magic moment Tyner strolled onstage and told the kids he needed some help. Everybody knows what comes next, he said, and we need your help in calling off the tune because we've been hearing all kinds of weird stuff about it. Everybody knows it's all right, don't you now (YEAH!!), so I'll just count three and then we can get this old tune started. But everybody's gotta do it together, or else it won't be any good.

> Tyner counted to three – the whole band counted – and then the place exploded: "KICK OUT THE JAMS MOTHERFUCKER!!" 400 deranged teen-age freeks screamed in unison, and the band *got down*. The pigs were infuriated, but they would've had to've arrested everybody in the place on the phony rap to get anyone. And after that it was freedom all the way. (Sinclair, 1972: 84)

More than a simple exhortation, "Kick out the jams" had the power to create a veritable collective euphoria, as both the band and the kids basked in breaking the rules of public decorum. Yet however much the phrase itself exerted a symbolic power over the events of the MC5's performances, it was ultimately the band's music that carried the proceedings. "KICK OUT THE JAMS, MOTHERFUCKER" as a shout would not have raised the audience to such a fever pitch if not for what followed: "Kick Out the Jams," the song, which was itself a sort of exhortation. Beginning with two crashing power chords that segue into feedback over the pulse of the drums, "Kick Out the Jams" was a musical statement full of both fury and joy. The four musicians – guitarists Fred Smith and Wayne Kramer, bassist Michael Davis, and drummer Dennis Thompson – locked into a fully amplified three-chord electric crush-groove while Rob Tyner sang in a voice, alternately soulful and manic, of the pleasures of experiencing just the sort of music the band was playing: "Well I fell pretty good and I guess that I could get crazy now baby…Yes I'm starting to sweat and now my shirt's all wet but I'm feeling" (in the background one of the band members laughs exuberantly). After Kramer's screaming spastic guitar solo, full of high-pitched notes repeated to the point of delirium, the song lunges towards its final chorus, a celebration of sound and self in which rock and roll is the key to liberation: "The wailing guitars and the crash of the drums/Make you want to keep a rockin' till the morning comes/Let me be who I am/And let me kick out the jams – Yes!/Kick out the jaaaaaaaams/I done kicked 'em out" (MC5 1969).

REFERENCES

Attali, J. 1985. *Noise: The Political Economy of Music*. Minneapolis: University of Minnesota Press.

Bangs, L. 1987. "James Taylor Marked for Death." In *Psychotic Reactions and Carburetor Dung*, edited by G. Marcus, 53–81. New York: Alfred A. Knopf.

Brent, P. 1969. "Crow's Nest." *Creem* 1 (1): n.p.

Duncan, R. 1984. *The Noise: Notes from a Rock 'n' Roll Era*. New York: Ticknor & Fields.

Eddy, C. 1991. *Stairway to Hell: The 500 Best Heavy Metal Albums in the Universe*. New York: Harmony Books.

Ehrmann, E. 1969. MC5. *Rolling Stone* 25 (January 4): 14–18.

Elias, N. 1978. *The Civilizing Process, Vol. 1: The History of Manners*. New York: Urizen Books.

Fong-Torres, B. 1972. Shattered Dreams in Motor City. *Rolling Stone* 110 (June 8): 30–2.

Garber, M. 1993. *Vested Interests: Cross-Dressing and Cultural Anxiety*. New York: HarperPerennial.

Gitlin, T. 1993. *The Sixties: Years of Hope, Days of Rage*. New York: Bantam Books.

Herron, J. 1993. *AfterCulture: Detroit and the Humiliation of History*. Detroit: Wayne State University Press.

Hiwatt, S. 1971. "Cock Rock." In *Twenty-Minute Fandangos and Forever Changes: A Rock Bazaar* , edited by J. Eisen, 141–7. New York: Random House.

Leach, W. 1969. The White Left – Serious or Not. *Fifth Estate* 3 (January 9–22): 7.

Leuchtenburg, W. 1983. *A Troubled Feast: American Society since 1945*. Boston: Little, Brown.

Lott, E. 1993. *Love and Theft: Blackface Minstrelsy and the American Working Class.* New York: Oxford University Press.

Lowe, D. 1982. *History of Bourgeois Perception.* Chicago: University of Chicago Press.

Mailer, N. 1960. "The White Negro." In *Advertisements for Myself,* 302–12. New York: Signet.

———. 1968. *Miami and the Siege of Chicago: An Informal History of the Republican and Democratic Conventions of 1968.* New York: World Publishing.

Marsh, D. 1985. *Fortunate Son: The Best of Dave Marsh.* New York: Random House.

———. 1992. Liner Notes For MC5, *Back in the USA* [compact disc]. New York: Atlantic Records, 1970.

Marsh, D., D. LaRene, and B. Kramer. 1970. [Untitled]. *Creem* 2 (11): 7–10.

McClary, S. 1991. *Feminine Endings: Music, Gender, and Sexuality.* Minneapolis: University of Minnesota Press.

MC5. 1969. *Kick out the jams* [compact disc]. New York: Elektra Records.

———. 1983. *Babes in Arms* [compact disc]. New York: ROIR/Danceteria Records.

"MC5 on the cusp." 1969. *Creem* 2 (4) (August 31): 13–18.

McLuhan, M. 1967. *The medium is the massage: An inventory of effects.* New York: Bantam Books.

Sinclair, J. 1968a. "Coat Puller." *Fifth Estate* 3 (August 1–14): 5.

———. 1968b. White Panther Statement. *Fifth Estate* (November 14–27): 8.

———. 1969a. Rock and Roll Dope. *Fifth Estate* 3 (January 23–February5): 16.

———. 1969b. "A Letter from Prison, Another Side of the MC5 Story, and (Incidentally) the End of an Era. *Creem* 2 (8) (November 28): 9–14, 27, 30–1.

———. 1970. "Motor City Music." *Jazz & Pop* 9 (December): 52–9.

———. 1972. *Guitar Army: Street Writings/Prison Writings.* New York: Douglas Book Corporation.

Torgovnick, M. 1990. *Gone Primitive: Savage Intellects, Modern Lives.* Chicago: University of Chicago Press.

Wallace, M. 1979. *Black Macho and the Myth of the Superwoman.* New York: Dial Press.

Walley, D. 1970. "MC5 Interview." In *The Age of Rock 2: Sights and Sounds of the American Cultural Revolution*, 271–86. New York: Vintage.

Wellburn, R. 1972. "The Black Aesthetic Imperative." In *The Black Aesthetic*, edited by A. Gayle, 132–49. New York: Anchor Books.

4

Can't We Just Talk ── About Music?

Rock and Gender on the Internet

Norma Coates

The lead story in the Music section of the April 30, 1996, edition of the *Village Voice* was about, of all things, an academic conference. In "Gender Theory Rocks: Feminism and Makeovers in Iowa," sociologist and writer Donna Gaines (1996) discussed her ambivalence about being an intellectual who likes rock through a consideration of the events leading up to and including a conference on popular music at a university in Iowa. Meanwhile, over on the Internet, fur was starting to fly on Rocklist, an electronic discussion group. The path that took Gaines to Iowa (along with others in this piece, including me) traveled through Rocklist. This is the story of that journey.

Rocklist is dedicated to the "academic discussion of popular music." This sets Rocklist apart from most music discussion groups ("fan lists") on the Internet that uncritically focus on particular artists or types of music. The formation of Rocklist was apparently motivated partially in response to the denigrated status of popular music studies in the academy. Rocklist is meant to bring together a community of scholars working within various branches of academia, as well as "noncredentialed" rock enthusiasts to further the serious discussion of popular music.

A male colleague told me about Rocklist in the fall of 1994; I have been an intermittently active contributor ever since. Although my scholarly inquiries often focused on trying to understand how I could love the Rolling Stones and still respect myself, I had given up trying to have intelligent discussions about rock long ago. I did this because of frustration with the hypercritical, "boys club" mentality of private and public (e.g., academic and journalistic) rock discourse. However, I continued to have an inexorable urge to think and write about rock. Rocklist, I hoped, would provide me with an opportunity to discuss my ideas, especially those about rock and gender formed by my experience of loving rock but not recognizing "myself" in it.

What I encountered instead was the same old scene. My messages and those from other women, particularly when we tried to discuss gender and rock, were ignored, argued with, or trivialized. A male respondent would generally proffer the "correct" take on an issue. To be fair to Rocklist, its discursive patterns and power dynamics are not exceptional. Moreover, the gendered nature of discourse on Rocklist is not unique to the discursive formation that situates rock in general. Grossberg (1992) calls the set of alliances that formed around (as well as the meanings attributed to and associated with) rock since its origins soon after World War II, the "rock formation." According to Grossberg, "the rock formation emerged out of and was articulated to the particular social, economic and political context of postwar America" (138): liberal pluralism. This context, in turn, constrained rock's political potential. Rock is not, according to Grossberg, a radical expression of alienation, but a reiteration if not a reification of the major ideological assumptions of liberal pluralism – assumptions with sexist, racist, and classist implications (144–5).

The historical specificity of rock's emergence in the 1950s "gendered" rock as male, and little has changed. Gender, according to Teresa de Lauretis, is a product of various social technologies, including forms of popular culture, institutionalized discourses, critical practices, and practices of daily life. Through these mechanisms, gender is at the same time constructed and always under construction (1987: 3). Rock, then, and the set of practices and alliances which form the rock formation can be characterized as a "technology of gender" that creates and reinforces particular gender representations to the exclusion of others. Such technologized representations of gender usually possess an aura of intractability.

However, de Lauretis's premise provides us with a possible way to represent alternative genders in rock by postulating the existence of that which is currently unrepresentable, excessive, and abject. The abject, according to Butler (1993) is always contained in that which is excluding or expelling it. The "return of the abject" radically destablizes that from which it was expelled, opening the site to reconfiguration and resignification (67). The gender of rock may appear stable, but it is "stabilized" through a constant process of reiteration and the performance of "masculinity," which act to keep that which is unrepresentable within it firmly outside.

In the case of rock, as in any popular form, there are any number of entities, tangible or ineffable, that could constitute the abject. In this chapter, I discuss "femininity" as the abject of "masculinity" in rock;[1] that is, femininity is at the same time all over rock yet evacuated from it. Further, femininity, the abject, is the glue that makes fluid and various masculinities appear to be a unitary "masculinity" when constructed in terms of an opposite.

This binary relationship is important for a number of reasons. Such a relationship sets up a number of other binaries, including subject/object, dominant/subordinate, and, most important to this discussion, representable or unrepresentable. Moreover, the performance of "masculinity" in rock, through any number of spaces and venues, including concert performances, written discourse, conversation, institutional setups and hierarchies, and distribution practices and policies, depends upon the containment of "excessive" femininity as well as the continued "expulsion" of the abject.[2]

These stabilizing binaries, relying as they do on a unitary male subject and a concomitant unitary masculinity, also depend upon a unified female object and subsequent unitary definition of femininity (and ultimately, feminism). This makes it as easy for critics and fans to exile women in rock to the bedrooms or to construct a ghettoized area within popular music called "pop."

When women have made themselves physically visible to the rock formation, they are seen through the lens of masculinity. One only need look at the "tom-boyization" of Patti Smith (cf. O'Brien, 1995; Reynolds and Press, 1995) to see this action. Or, as Kearney (1996) observes, rhetorical strategies are used within rock discourse to mark female rockers as other: "While much of the media hype surrounding today's female rock bands champions the success these artists have made in a conventionally male-dominated and misogynist industry, there are several journalists out there who...seem to ignore 'everything but the girl'"(3). Women, females, and femininity, therefore, remain invisible and unrepresentable.

In the body of this chapter, I examine an episode of the "return of the abject" to Rocklist. I problematize the day-to-day discourse of the rock formation, as enacted on Rocklist, to illuminate the extent to which performative masculinity has been so thoroughly reiterated within the rock formation as to have become normative and "second nature" or "commonsense." I will show how the performative masculinity in rock permeates discourse in this space, and how and why the revelation of the existence of a "counterpublic" troubled the coherence of that subsequent performance.

IT'S A MAN'S, MAN'S, MAN'S WORLD: DISRUPTING "MASCULINITY" ON ROCKLIST

Perhaps it was Donna Gaines's characterization of Rocklist in her *Village Voice* piece as humorless and pedantic, and even worse, as being like graduate school, that ruffled a few male feathers on Rocklist. More infuriating, I suspect, was Gaines's "outing" of a splinter group from Rocklist, a small number of women including Gaines and me. We called ourselves Clitlist (in opposition to what we occasionally called "Dicklist"). In this section, I explore why so many members of Rocklist found Clitlist to be a threat to Rocklist and even to rock.

This was the first post to Rocklist about Gaines's article: "Donna Gaines has a memoir of the Drake conference in this week's edition of the Village Voice. She also criticizes Rocklist and mentions a new alternat-list involving her and her cohorts. Instead of mis-summarizing her piece, I suggest all you meta-listers check it out" (Post to Rocklist, 1996). Although ostensibly innocuous, this post exemplifies the way in which Rocklist "performs" masculinity when faced with any trace of "femininity" in rock discourse. The post employs a series of binarisms common to Rocklist and to rock discourse in general, especially male/female and us/them (i.e., the "meta" versus "alternat" list split). The writer attributes hierarchized power dynamics to Clitlist in his implicit designation of Donna as the leader followed by the rest of her "cohorts." Using the term "criticizes" further reinforces an us/them binary. This move places Clitlist (and by extrapolation, its members) outside as well as subordinate to the discursive regime governing Rocklist – although we are very much within it some of the time.

As I've said, alternative gender performances are not visible in the current rock formation. To acknowledge them, or even see them, would undermine the sutured coherence of "masculinity" as represented in rock. Moreover, to acknowledge that there are alternative ways to perform gender in rock threatens to undermine the coherence of "rock" in general. The codes that signify rock, then, have become the "common sense" of rock discourse. A major tenet incorporated into this common sense is the notion that the primary spaces of rock are masculine, as this next response to Gaines's *Voice* article indicates: "Does anybody every remember Donna raising whatever concerns she raises in the article with us? When one is critical of a group from within it, one participates in a voluntary learning community. When one steps in and out of a group saying not much of substance for a long time and then talks negatively about us all in print….[expletive deleted]" (Post to Rocklist, 1996).

This post came from an active Rocklister who does not often participate in gender threads. His outrage over what he perceives as a violation of the Rocklist community is palpable. However, his comments underscore the common sense of masculinity in rock, and the invisibility of other gender performances. The writer speaks of Rocklist as a voluntary learning community, which to some extent it is. Like many if not most Internet fora, Rocklist is an affinity group. People become members after hearing about it from a friend or colleague, or by finding its web site while netsurfing. Membership is somewhat fluid, but there is a stable core of members who post with varying degrees of frequency – some say something at great length about almost every thread, others pop in and out. There also appear to be a great many "lurkers," those who read but don't participate in the exchanges. The relative stability of the list has indeed created a type of community.

However, Rocklist, as an affinity group centered around the discussion of rock music, not only replicates the gender dynamics of the rock formation in general but, as an Internet forum, also replicates the social dynamics currently operative in nascent cyberspace. Internet discourse has a male cast to it in this early phase of its existence. As Balsamo (1994) points out, "electronic discussion lists are governed by gendered codes of discursive interchange" (141). Balsamo also suggests that these lists are not only rendered inhospitable to female participants, but are "overtly subjected to gender, status, age, and race determination" (142).

Rocklist, then, may be a learning community in which the gender of the teachers and the content of the lessons have been established prior to the start of classes. The writer who complained about Gaines's article could not recognize that Gaines and others had indeed raised the concerns she discussed in *The Voice* piece with the Rocklist community – many times. The impression that this writer does not consider the occasional "gender wars" on Rocklist a contribution to its function as a learning community was as much a result of gender dynamics operating at the commonsense level as it was his own misremembering.

For example, in November 1995, the list discussed Courtney Love. Love was not analyzed in terms of her musicianship, but condemned as a bad mother because she lives the "sex, drugs, and rock and roll" lifestyle while parenting a small child. Rock generally constructs masculinity in rock as a site of unfettered and unencumbered sexuality. Parenting is not visible through this lens – the existence of rocker babies undermines the performance of male sexuality in rock. Babies of male rockers, for the most part, do not seem to exist. Therefore, there are no "bad fathers" in rock.[3] Yet wasn't Kurt Cobain's suicide the ultimate act of "bad parenting," given that he took one parent away from his daughter? When I posed that question to Rocklist, it was ignored, and the thread more or less ended. In this way, an opportunity for the community to learn another way of thinking about rock was refused.

The Courtney Love exchange was just one in a series of occasions when the list suddenly went silent when a female participant posted something that did not conform to the gendered wisdom of rock discourse. After months of mounting frustration, I seized an opportunity to directly raise the specter of femininity and rock on the list. When the list owner posted statistics indicating that the list was 75 percent male, I submitted a post asking, "Any thoughts as to why there aren't more females on the list?" Instead of serious answers, the replies started with "As James Brown said…[it's a man's man's world]" and degenerated to "too drunk to fuck." My question was not taken seriously, which I perceived as a "business as usual" trivialization of women and femininity on the list, and in rock discourse in general. I submitted this post in anger: "You know, I just want to point out that my original post was dead serious...Why is it that when questions about gender and rock (and women and this list) are posed, they are generally either: (a) answered by a male "expert"; (b) trivialized; or (c) just plain ignored?" (Post to Rocklist, 1995).

The replies to this were, in some cases, quite surprising, and in retrospect augured the reaction to Gaines's article a few months later. First, the reaction to my characterization of some of the men on the list as "experts" were vehement and defensive. For me, the term captured a certain dynamic of the list. Questions were frequently answered with long, informed posts, often studded with rock arcana. These posts would have the effect of offering the "final word" on a topic, although that may not have been the writer's intent. Nevertheless, to someone constructed as an outsider to the discourse, such posts foreclosed further discussion. I used the term "expert" to call out this dynamic and to indicate my reaction to it, not to castigate the list.

Those list members who responded to my question did not seem to understand that such posts are offputting. One member took it personally, writing that he's never presented himself as an expert; another forwarded this question: "Should the men here regard this as a request that we don't respond to questions about women, or from women?" At the time these reactions struck me as simply naive. In retrospect, I see these reactions as being entirely congruent with gender relations as constructed by and in the rock formation. For women to be heard, they must temporarily assume the expert position normally held by men in the formation. That is, they must talk like a man, or more accurately, as if they were men.

Moreover, the performance of masculinity on Rocklist and in other rock spaces requires that its subordinate be coherent as well. That is, there will be a "masculine" position and a "feminine" position. The "men on the list" will stand for one set of beliefs and the "women on the list" for another. The community, then, is split, with one side possessing more cultural capital than the other. The powerful side can invite the less powerful (e.g., "female experts") to contribute to the learning experience, but not vice versa.

This type of performance so permeates Rocklist that it is all but invisible to some. It is not invisible, however, to those who are marginalized by it as this next post makes very clear:

(writer) I'm not a frequent participant on Rocklist, mostly due to time constraints and devoting my time to formulating a response is, at times, not high on my priority list.

However, I felt compelled to interject my humble opinion/observation about this matter. I'm sure (?) ____'s questions was well intentioned, but it is exactly this kind of patronizing response that irritates the hell out of me. Obviously I'm making an assumption here, but I really don't think that's what Norma was suggesting *at all*. While I certainly don't have "the" answer as to why more women don't participate, etc., I believe there is value in exploring the topic. Unfortunately, I think ____'s "question" neatly avoids the topic...again. A perfect illustration of Norma's point that when questions regarding women and this list are raised: >they are generally either: (a) answered by a male "expert," (b) trivialized; or (c) just plain ignored?

And just so *I* don't avoid the topic, I can speak as to why I don't participate often:

1. Time
2. Recurring topics – little left to be said that hasn't already
3. Not all topics interest me
4. Fear of being "wrong"

(This last one probably is the most interesting – in a discussion where there really are no "rights" or "wrongs" I am amused that I feel the need to "check" myself before posting – to make certain I've dotted all the i's and cross all the t's. I feel a need to continually edit my response and by the time I get it sorted out, the moment is gone. Perhaps "men" are more confident at winging it.) (Post to Rocklist, 1995)

This writer eloquently expresses the process by which the male gendering of rock is made visible *and* reinforced on Rocklist and elsewhere. Her post captures the sense of outsiderness felt by those who are not explicitly visible to rock. Especially cogent is her description of the fear of being "wrong."

The very dynamic that this writer tried to both describe and speak against was active in this response to her post:

> A question was posed. Norma offers the passage you cite above. Now, pretend you're a man for a second. Most men here are probably fairly progressive types, and if they have been around the net any length of time at all they're aware of how woefully underrepresented women are here. If they're like me, they're bothered by this, because they don't see the medium reaching its potential as long as half the population is silenced. They're also embarrassed as hell by the behavior of men elsewhere on the net, because lots of times the reason [women] keep quiet is that they don't want to get slammed by the sorts of assholes who dominate certain usernet fora.
>
> So when a man like this sees Norma's post, he's likely a bit peeved…(Post to Rocklist, 1995).

Here the writer asks the women on the list to "pretend you're a man" – apparently the only way for women's "noise" to be heard among the men's "music."

At this point in the burgeoning debate, I wrote a long post that tried to explain what it felt like to be in my position, a perpetual outsider to rock. In retrospect, I see my response as one that is also coherent within the gender logic of rock; it is the outsider who has to explain herself. Nevertheless, I follow Probyn's (1992) suggestion that it is important to "speak oneself without reifying the self, of putting one's self to work discursively without taking oneself too seriously" (505). I tendered my personal experience as a woman who happens to be passionate about rock music in hopes of opening a dialogue about gender and rock without reverting in this case, to the clichés of sexism and male oppression. I hoped that sharing my experience was congruent with Rocklist's position as a space of learning.

Unfortunately, no one responded to my post. As one of the men on the list described the phenomenon, "On a list like this, I tend to read lack of response to ostensibly serious questions as a de facto acknowledgment that nobody there really knows the answer." Of course, this writer, like most others, had the luxury of being able to deem when a definitive statement or insight had been made. But, as Fraser (1992) points out, ignoring or not responding to women's interventions can be interpreted as a case of deliberation masking domination (123).

The thread finally died down when the following two messages crossed the e-mail transom:

> Please don't take this the wrong way, but this whole gender debate has been going on far too long (with this I am setting myself up for the obvious and highly intelligent retort, "Yes that's exactly the point it HAS been going on for far too long") and perhaps all of the parties involved could keep the discussion private. Maybe some of the silent Rocklist subscribers will agree that this whole nonsense is cluttering up their mailboxes. Nine out of ten intelligent men/people are not sexist, and some of you are merely trying to pick a fight. Perhaps we would do better to argue about rock and roll, instead. (Post to Rocklist, 1995)

> i agree. keep it private, or else change this thing to GENDER WARSLIST@KENTVM.KENT.EDU (Post to Rocklist, 1995)

These posts bring us back to the beginning of this section and to the charge that Gaines's airing of her "complaints" in a public forum had violated Rocklist's space as a learning community. Days of debate, which I have barely excerpted here, were reduced to "let's talk about rock instead." That is, most writers on Rocklist seemed to think that gender had nothing to do with rock.

Our posts on gender had indeed been brought up in the spirit of a learning community, but the community had refused to listen. More precisely, the community could not hear or see them. Not only had our arguments been made often, they also had been made more subtly by the slow retreat of Clitlist and other women from active, substantive participation on the list. Was this retreat an instance of regrouping for a form of identity politics or, a separatist move? Was it misguided, sanity-saving, or savvy? Moreover, how did it affect gender relations within the community of Rocklist? These are the questions I turn to in the next section.

GIRLS WANT TO BE WITH THE GIRLS: HIGH-TECH KITCHEN OR SUBALTERN COUNTERPUBLIC?

> We called ourselves grrrls, in honor of the riot ones…Even though Rocklist is 75 per cent male, it never occurred to me that my alienation might be gender-based until Norma and I began to exchange e-mail, mocking what we soon called Dicklist. Mary and Lori knew each other from [meeting of an academic organization]. Somewhere along the information stairway to heaven, we met Chris Cutler – she's an erstwhile heavy metal guitarist from Moline, Illinois, who writes about music for *Oil* magazine. Lori figured out how to link our names together and Clitlist was born.
>
> –Donna Gaines, "Gender Theory Rocks," 69

I don't remember exactly when I first started to chat with Gaines, but I remember that we bonded over our mutual frustration with Rocklist. I had also exchanged E-mail with Mary Kearney and Lori Tomlinson, other writers working on music and youth culture. Kearney and Tomlinson were among the founding members of Rocklist, but were becoming increasingly frustrated with it. Soon, we all decided to form Clitlist, a side discussion from Rocklist.

Clitlist enabled us to remain on Rocklist despite our frustration with it. In this sense, Clitlist served as an example of Fraser's (1992) concept of a subaltern counterpublic, a space outside of a hegemonic public sphere. Fraser contests some of the assumptions underlying the Habermasian liberal public sphere, particularly the notion that it is open to all, arguing instead that "where societal inequality persists, deliberative processes in public spheres will tend to operate to the advantage of dominant groups and to the disadvantage of subordinates" (122-3). The result is that subordinate groups cannot express themselves within the public sphere of the dominant. Subordinate groups, therefore, find it "advantageous to constitute alternative publics" or counterpublics, "parallel discursive arenas where members of subordinated groups invent and circulate counterdiscourses, so as to formulate oppositional interpretations of their identities, interests, and needs" (123).

As a counterpublic to the dominant public sphere of Rocklist, Clitlist had a much different discursive dynamic. For example, if we discussed rock, we related it more to our lives and the role that rock plays in them. We also spoke of mundane things, as Gaines (1996) reported in her *Voice* article:

> Everyday life was a central part of Clitlist: Should Chris go out with guy A or guy B? Should Norma paint her porch furniture black or blue? Should I go back with my boyfriend? And most importantly, what will we wear to Drake? Then there was the horror of Alanis Morissette. Mary offered me a bibliography on the girl groups of the early 1960s. Vegan Lori had nutritional tips for prevention of yeast beasts and urinary tract infections. And it continues. The elder Clitlister, I share dissertation and publication strategies. We ruminate on hair color, cats, and our relationship with Aunt Flo – the menstrual cycle. In contrast to the smugness of Dicklist, Clitlist offers a seamless landscape for shared experience: intellectual, emotional, sociological. (p. 69)

Clitlist provided its members with a way to connect with geographically dispersed cyberfriends as a respite from isolating lives as journalists, academics, and late-shift workers. Our bond was our common experience of being outsiders to a cultural form that supposedly celebrates outsiderness.

There are a number of things that we rarely talked about on Clitlist including, surprisingly, rock music. For example, I still cannot name the favorite band, or even favorite genre of other Clitlisters. We avoided the "baseball card" mentality, the power/knowledge equation that characterized much of the discourse on Rocklist. We spoke of riot grrrl bands, for example, on affective rather than competitive or hierarchical levels, focusing on what these bands meant to us and other people, and how their messages were deployed and mobilized, rather than which band was the "best one" or the most obscure one (a distinction frequently conflated in rock discourse and on Rocklist).

However, Clitlist's function as a counterpublic was opaque to many Rocklisters, as this next post indicates: "...if it has been "a man's man's world," and, similarly, males dominate the list, isn't it possible that something like "clitlist" is not a separatist caucus as much as it is recreating traditional, middle-class American gender roles? Think of the stereotype of a suburban bunch of men in the living room talking "politics" or "watching the game" while the women sit together in the kitchen "venting" (as Norma put it) and critiquing? In other words, is clitlist truly a caucus or is it more like a virtual coffee-clatch defended by theory?" (Post to Rocklist, 1996).

Was Clitlist a "coffee clatch," albeit one held in a burnished high-tech kitchen? According to Fraser (1992), one of the benefits of the emergence of counterpublics is that they help expand discursive space Further, counterpublics are not enclaves; "they also function as bases and training grounds for agitational activities directed toward wider publics" (124). Had it not been for the existence of another space in the form of Clitlist, the constant marginalization of our opinions and ideas on Rocklist would have caused us to leave it long before gender wars even had a chance to start. The discursive space of Rocklist would have been diminished by the defection of those who went on to form Clitlist. Instead, Clitlist enlarged that space, not in opposition to Rocklist, but in engagement with it.

Correspondingly, Clitlist did not plan and implement "attacks" on Rocklist. We did not have to do so because the performance of masculinity on Rocklist was coherent enough to ensure that any alternative performance looked cohesive as well. For example, reactions to Gaines's article seem to assume that it was the culmination of months of plotting and planning by Clitlist, which it was not. Like most published articles, Gaines's *Village Voice* piece transmogrified greatly from inception to publication. Clitlist's activities in this period and before were rendered coherent after the fact, by Gaines's journalistic need for a narrative and Rocklist's need to maintain a certain kind of discourse on the list. This is not to say that Clitlist members did not often take the same side in Rocklist debates. To a large extent, the positions that individual Clitlist members took on issues related to rock and gender were always already inscribed by virtue of Rocklist's position as part of the rock formation.

If Clitlist had "performed our gender," in this case, according to the masculinist ways of Rocklist, we would have had to slough off our construction as "females" to assume a male point of view, or we would have had to remain silent and invisible. Therefore, Clitlist was not exiled to Rocklist's kitchen, but we went voluntarily. We were compelled to go there in order to, paradoxically, make our voices heard above the din of "discourse as usual" on Rocklist.

The only time Clitlist ever met in real life was at the Conference on Popular Music in Iowa. Gaines's account of our performance there drew some of the most derisive comments from those who claimed to speak for the Rocklist community. It is to these reactions that I now turn.

I Enjoy Being a Girl: The Abject Appears

By now I'm in grrrlcult overdrive, so I decide to boycott all the boy panels...in between girl talks I spend my time doing calisthenics, retouching my makeup, teasing my hair and checking my answering machine every 20 minutes to see if my boyfriend called.

I came of age in the early 1960s, when the street gangs of New York's burbs and boroughs claimed turf by writing "D.T.K." (Down to Kill) on everything. But today we are rewriting D.T.K. for ourselves: Dress to Kill! In fine tones of black, blue, and gray, Mary and Norma wear tough little jackets, miniskirts, black opaque tights, and Doc Martens. Lori, known on the Net as "Goddess of Disco," goes for a softer look. I do Hannah Arendt meets Lou Reed in the '90s – long skirt, black top, combat boots, black leather blazer. Three out of four redheads on this panel.

As chair, I introduce our panel with a tape of songs by the obscure girl-group Reparata and the Delrons. Norma's paper opens with considerations of the political potential of gender, of rock as "an unquestioned performance of hegemonic tropes of masculinity," with women posing a threat to that hegemony. Earlier that day I did Norma's makeup in a palette of browns from M.A.C. Next on the panel, Lori examines the emancipatory power '70s disco offered women, creating autonomous space for us in music, clubs, and subculture. The night before, in an effort to present a unified front, Mary, the panel's only non-redhead tried in vain to locate some color in Iowa. Today, she goes for the jugular vein of the "women in rock" phenomenon, which she argues is both a feminist celebration of and conservative backlash against female-powered music.

–Donna Gaines, "Gender Theory Rocks," p.69

So far, I have been discussing rock as a technology of gender that both constructs and is always constructing "maleness" in its various spaces. I have tried to show that rock discourse is predicated on a system of binary structures which render that gender construction in rock coherent. I have also described an instance when an alternative gender performance has been attempted and failed within a discursive space of rock, the Internet discussion group Rocklist. In this section I describe a "real-life" performance, one that brought together some of the members of the virtual spaces I have been discussing. This real-life performance, and the reaction to it from the virtual community that was instrumental in spawning it, provides a telling case study about what happens when an abject tries to return to the "body" that has expelled it.

The abject, according to Butler (1993), designates "precisely those 'unlivable' and 'uninhabitable' zones of social life which are nevertheless densely populated by those who do not enjoy the status of the subject" (3). The subject, in Butler's view, is constituted by exclusion as well as inclusion of the abject. Swallowed up by and at the same time incorporated into that which is granted subjecthood, the abject is a "threatening specter" to the subject: "this disavowed abjection will threaten to expose the self-grounding presumptions of the sexed subject, grounded as that subject is in a repudiation whose consequences it cannot fully control" (3). Butler goes on to theorize how the abject, or "deconstituting possibility," can never be totally destroyed or erased by the naturalizing effect of the reiterated, sexed subject (10).

Since, as I have argued, rock is "sexed" in that it is gendered male by its technologizing processes, then an abject, in the form of the female or femininity, can put the naturalized effects and definition of rock, the *meaning* of rock, into what Butler terms a "potentially productive crisis." The ultimate effect of such a crisis could change the very meaning of rock. Gender instability in rock could have a domino effect with, at the least, unpredictable if not exhilarating results. Given the naturalized "maleness" of rock, and the systems of binaries, feints, and maneuvers erected to keep rock coherent and stable, how would such an abject "return"?

Gender in rock is naturalized, but it is also performative, in (at least) two definitions of the term. Butler asserts that performative acts are authoritative statements that both perform certain actions and execute binding powers. "Gendering" is such a performative act. In addition, one performs a conferred gender. This is not to imply that gender performativity is the same as a stage act; rather, performatives provisionally succeed because of the force of authority gained through repetition and citation of prior practices (225). Returning the abject, then, involves breaking the reiterative chain of a performative gender, substituting an alternative gender performance, or forcing an abjected gender into visibility through a theatrically informed performance.

For example, Butler in the context of queer politics, but applicable to other political stages, suggests a strategy of "occupation or reterritorialization of a term that has been used to abject a population" (231). Through this, an abject population can become a site or space of resistance; furthermore, the "possibility of an enabling social and political resignification" (231–2) of the abjected term is mobilized. In the case of the gendered nature of the rock formation, which expels "femininity" in order to reiterate and cite "masculinity," reclaiming "femininity" from its exile in abjection becomes a strategy of spatial reterritorialization. Theatricality, performing that which has been abjected, is key to this strategy: "This kind of citation will emerge as *theatrical* to the extent that it *mimes and renders hyperbolic* the discursive convention that it also *reverses*. The hyperbolic gesture is crucial to the exposure of the homophobic "law" that can no longer control the terms of its own abjecting strategies" (232). If we substitute "gynophobic" or some other term indicating "fear of women" for "homophobic" in Butler's theorem, we emerge with a strategy for returning the abject – "femininity," females, or women – to rock.

The Conference on Popular Music, Gaines's descriptions of the conference in the pages of the *Village Voice*, and the reactions of certain vocal Rocklist members to both occasions provide a study of this strategy at work. Until the conference, Clitlist's performance of an "alternative" gender lacked a degree of power because it was restricted by the space of the performance, which was oral and written rather than visual and "live." One may be able to perform "femininity" through writing, but the posts of Clitlist members to Rocklist, and to Clitlist for that matter, are not conscious examples of *l'écriture féminine*. Moreover, the written aspect of Rocklist does not foreground our "femininity." It is easy to abstract our sexed selves, or for others to dismiss us as "humorless, angry feminists." This marginalizing move is less easily made when the abject appears and physically performs some of the aspects of its gender that caused it to be abjected in the first place. However, as we will see, the force of the construction of masculinity in rock, as performed in its various spaces, remains strong and wily.

At the Conference on Popular Music, Clitlist finally met as a group. The conference was truly the first organized thing that Clitlist had done, in that we submitted a panel to the conference. We did not read each other's papers before the conference; nor did we plan anything besides trying to make sure we all hung out together. We did the typical things one does at an academic conference: met other scholars in the field, networked in order to learn about employment and publishing opportunities, went to a lot of panels, asked questions. But, as the above excerpts from Gaines's article indicate, Clitlist did indeed perform "femininity in rock" in a more literal sense of the term *performance*. We donned makeup and wore short skirts. We flirted with other academics. We partied and had fun. We managed to combine seriousness of purpose with gender politics, attempting to disrupt the smooth flow of normative masculinity in both rock and academic contexts.

In her discussion of our panel, Gaines juxtaposed the thesis of my paper with a description of my makeup, which, à la junior high school, she had applied in an adjacent bathroom not long before the event. Gaines's article also discussed our appearance, which we took a great deal of care with that day. Admittedly, we performed "femininity" that day in its rather normative state. At some level, one could say that we looked "sexy "for the sake of the (more than 50% male) audience. In reality, we were trying to subvert the normative performance of femininity in rock by performing it.

Our intent was not lost upon the conference attendees, particularly the audience for our panel, which included members of a rock band as well as a number of undergraduates, drawn out of their rooms on a rainy Saturday in order to see an academic discussion of women and music. The female lead singer of a band raised her hand and asked us to keep doing what we're doing; I received some applause when I responded to a question by proclaiming that Bonnie Raitt was a "goddess." We were also asked, by a female audience member, whether any of us were musicians. Had this question come from a male attendee, I might have interpreted it as an abjecting strategy. Rock guitars and drum sounds are coded as phallic, which is probably why girls have traditionally been channeled to "safer" instruments like the piano. However, the fact that this question came from a female attendee suggests that she was participating in our performance with us, bolstering our attempts to show that you could "do" an alternative gender in rock and still be "in" rock. Surprisingly, the voices heard in the lively discussion that followed our panel were female. Either the female members of the audience identified with the performative aspects of our presentations (both on the panel and through the other spaces of the conference), or the male rock fans/academics in the audience could not find a space for themselves in our performance of an alternative gender in rock. If this was indeed the case, which I believe that it was, then our performance succeeded. If only briefly, we had forced the unrepresentable into visibility.

Unfortunately, the triumph of Clitlist's alternative gender performance at the conference did not travel well on the road back to print media. The full impact of our performance did not carry over to Rocklist, as the excerpts I have been quoting throughout this chapter indicate. The reaction of some of the more vocal men on the list to our donning of makeup, wearing skirts, and generally acting "feminine" was particularly interesting. They equated our enactment of performative femininity, in which we dressed and acted "like girls," with some of the worst excesses of the Al Bundy–esque male. This is especially curious, in that, by wearing makeup, caring about our hair, and making a conscious effort to look "sexy," we more or less performed femininity as it is expected in rock. However, the twist was that we had *control* over the performance.

Our performance of "femininity" was unsettling to many of the male Rocklisters, I believe, because it subverted some of the neat binaries that enable masculinity in rock, and therefore rock itself, to cohere conscious performative femininity in rock exceeds and thus subverts the binary. It is important, then, to restore order and coherency by reinstating the binaries – that is, by resolving all contradictions. This is a circular operation, in that in order to restore performative masculinity to its "rightful" place, masculinity must be performed. In the case of the Rocklist/Clitlist contretemps, this was attempted by trying to marginalize Clitlist from that which was already abject. An analysis of this post illustrates my point:

> After reading Donna's piece I gave the article to a colleague, an accomplished female scholar here who describes herself in

staunchly feminist terms. Now, I know that "feminism" is a category, and a broad one at that, and that in some cases competing
theories and ideologies within the field crank up to such a level
of conflict you'd never know they shared a label. I know all that,
and as such I'm not trying to set my colleagues or anyone else up
as anything more than one well-informed perspective among
many. No, I'm just merely running a double-check on myself, just
making sure that it wasn't just ME.

Apparently, it isn't just me, because her reaction was that Donna's
piece was ANTI-feminist. I assured her that I didn't think either
Donna or the women she names in the article would see themselves that way, and so from this I conclude that something has
gotten way confused in this whole process. (Post to Rocklist,
1996)

Despite his long disclaimer, the writer assumes that there is one entity called
"feminism." Although he attempts to assert that there are differences of opinion within feminism, he apparently puts them on a continuum of a unitary
feminism, or worse, as catfights within that same unitary feminism. It strikes
me that feminism, for this writer, is still redolent with the smell of burning
bras and other clichés associated with the second-wave feminism of the
1970s. Feminism's goal, in this view, is gender-neutral equality. In this conception, equality feminism may mean that as a condition of that equality,
markers of "traditional," "oppressed" femininity, such as makeup, short skirts,
and other "girlie" things, fall away. That is, there is no space in his view of
feminism for *feminisms*, or for other ways of performing feminism.

Moreover, in this equation, feminism that is not equality feminism is
antifeminism. He asserts the correctness of his analysis by calling upon a
feminist to speak for him, thus absolving himself of charges of sexism. The
confusion that he speaks of, then, ultimately stems from the way in which
he perceives feminism, femininity, and gender politics in general, com-
pounded by the binary systems necessary to cohere gender as performed in
the spaces of the rock formation. Gender-neutral equality, the goal of feminism for this writer, does not jibe with hyperbolic femininity as performed
by Clitlist at the conference; nor does it jibe with gender separatism:

If I had devoted several column inches to describing how me and
___ and ___ had a blast sitting around at the conference in our
underwear, drinking beer, watching sports on TV, scratching our
balls and belching, I'd expect our female colleagues to be a little
put off. If it was further evident that we were sitting around
snickering about the grim self-importance of the clitocentric
feminist crowd and reveling in our rejection of pussylist hegemony, and if we then boycotted all the GIRL (or GRRRL, your
pick) panels (after all, what could a GIRL possibly say that would
be of any value to me), well, my guess is that we'd hear from colleagues like Norma and Mary.

And you know what? They'd be right.

But examine Donna's article and compare it to the above para-
graph. Substitute underwear for makeup and belching for Aunt
Flo and, well, you get the idea. And examine the characterizations of male scholars in the article. It's all pretty out in the open,
folks. (Post to Rocklist, 1996)

What the writer of this post, and some of the other male Rocklisters who
protested against the depiction of the list in Gaines's article, cannot or refuse
to see is that Clitlist served the same purpose for its members as Rocklist
does for some men. Rocklist discourse is not just about rock; it serves as a
stage for performing masculinity in various forms and guises. Rocklist shares
with rock the function of being a "safe" space for homosocial bonding without homophobic consequences.

When the initial protests against Gaines's article started to appear on
Rocklist, I sent an explanatory message to the list. In particular, I noted that
Clitlist was a critique of Rocklist, as well as a space both marked by our
shared experience of being outsiders to a cultural form that we love and
marked with the signs of "femininity" in a society that loves its binary gender demarcations. A particularly vocal male member, who wrote an extremely long post in reply, had this to say: "I disagree with Norma that Rocklist is
not criticized. While she quotes a particular section of the article and accurately notes that this is where Donna talks about Rocklist, if you read the
whole article it becomes clear that it's the dynamic of Rocklist which per-

vades the whole issue of gender and music for her and it is this community which represents the things she's attacking" (Post to Rocklist, 1996)

In hindsight, I now say that he's absolutely right, although he would not see Rocklist that way. The dynamic of Rocklist, which merely replicates the dynamic of the rock formation in general, does pervade the whole issue of gender and music for Donna, and for me, and Mary and Lori and Chris and countless other "women in rock." The Rocklist community does indeed represent what we're attacking. But only through a continued process of "attack," which I prefer to think of as forcing visibility, will women truly be able to be "in" rock.

NOTES

1. I place these terms in quotations to underscore both their constructedness and their contingency. Also included in these contingent deployments of the terms, as they refer to rock for the purposes of this article, are the adjectives white and heterosexual. Any of the three terms that I have conflated into the rubrics "masculine" and "feminine" – biological sex, race, and sexuality – could on their own count as an abject to the stable construction of "rock "

2. Of course, not all literal and figurative traces of the feminine have been expunged from rock. Groupies, female lead singers, screaming fans, and tight pants, big hair, and makeup are just some of the vestigial remnants of femininity in rock which have been used to prop up masculinity in rock. Those that remain, however, have been deployed or resignified in the service of the performance of masculinity in rock. However, traces of femininity which prop up hegemonic masculinity in rock are those which could threaten to expose it as a construction, or even a masquerade. Gender anxiety may indeed be behind the appropriation of normatively feminine visual signs, as Walser points out in his discussion of androgyny in heavy metal music (1993: 123–9). Such androgyny may also be conceptualized as a literal containment of excessive femininity through direct appropriation of its hegemonic signifiers.

    Other writers, such as Ehrenreich, Hess, and Jacobs (1986) and Douglas (1994), have read into phenomena such as Beatlemania and girl groups a form of female sexual empowerment, rather than a strict acceptance of their subordinate position under rocks hegemony of the masculine.

These important insights, however, move the subject away from rock and more toward reception. Ehrenreich and Douglas, and by extrapolation the female audiences they describe, are making oppositional readings to a cultural form with a dominant reading inscribed within it. They are not challenging the dominant meanings associated with rock, including its tight association with performative masculinity. In this way, these approaches reinforce and further replicate the binary construction of masculinity and femininity that stabilizes masculine hegemony in rock.

3. Kurt Cobain, however, was one rocker who was portrayed in photos with his daughter and wife, Courtney Love. Cobain, however, was an exception to the rule. In addition, Cobain and Love were, until Cobain's suicide, rock's royal couple of the moment, so the unwritten rules of rock discourse I am writing about were relaxed for them. In addition, Cobain was a rare male rocker in that he recognized and was outspoken about the hyperbolic construction of masculinity in rock.

References

Balsamo, A. 1994. "Feminism for the Incurably Informed." In *Flame Wars: The Discourse of Cyberculture*, edited by M. Dery, 125–56. Raleigh: Duke University Press.

Butler, J. 1993. *Bodies that Matter: On the Discursive Limits of "Sex."* New York: Routledge.

de Lauretis, T. 1987. *Technologies of Gender: Essay on Theory, Film, and Fiction.* Bloomington: Indiana University Press.

Douglas, S. 1994. *Where the Girls Are: Growing Up Female with the Mass Media.* New York: Times Books.

Ehrenreich, B., E. Hess, and G. Jacobs. 1986. *Remaking Love: The Feminization of Sex.* Garden City, NY: Anchor Press.

Fraser, N. 1992. "Rethinking the Public Sphere: A Contribution to the Critique of Actually Existing Democracy." In *Habermas and the Public Sphere*, edited by C. Calhoun, 109–42. Cambridge: MIT Press.

Gaines, D. 1996. "Gender Theory Rocks: Feminism and Makeovers in Iowa." *Village Voice*, April 30, 69–70.

Grossberg, L. 1992. *We Gotta Get Out of This Place: Popular Conservatism and Postmodern Culture.* New York: Routledge.

Kearney, M. 1996. "Exiled in Guyville? The Place of Female Rock Musicians in 'Women in Rock' Discourse." Unpublished paper.

O'Brien, L. 1995. *She Bop: The Definitive History of Women in Rock, Pop and Soul.* New York: Penguin Books.

Probyn, E. 1992. "Technologizing the Self: A Future Anterior for Cultural Studies." In *Cultural Studies*, edited by L. Grossberg, C. Nelson, and P. Treichler, 501–11. New York: Routledge.

Reynolds, S., and J. Press. 1995. *The Sex Revolts: Gender, Rebellion and Rock 'n' Roll.* Cambridge: Harvard University Press.

Walser, R. 1993. *Running With the Devil: Power, Gender and Madness in Heavy Metal Music.* Hanover, NH: Wesleyan University Press/University Press of New England.

5

———— If I Had a Dick ————

Queers, Punks, and Alternative Acts

Cynthia Fuchs

Once sex and gender are placed on equally fictive foot-
ing, the possibilities for multiple identities (and
alliances) are enormous.
> —Cathy Schwichtenberg,
> "Madonna's Postmodern Feminism"

I watch it like a movie
the details so consume me
what's real will surface when it's gone
(and then it's gone).
> —Bikini Kill, "For Only"

Would you like me if I talked with a lisp?
if I had a dick, put it away,
always had something to say.
> —Tribe 8, "What?"

During the winter of 1995, I attended a show at Washington D.C.'s
old 9:30 Club. The three bands appearing that night – Sexpod,
Tribe 8, and Pansy Division[1] – might all be called punk, though
their musical styles were quite different, ranging from three-chord rock to

DIY to perky pop-punk. They might also all be called queer. Their attitudes ranged from pissed off to charming to seductive to comic, and their topics from "dykes on bikes" to "cocksucker clubs." In other words, for all their differences, they shared an identifiable set of concerns with each other and with their audience (which remained fairly constant during the show's three -hours-plus running time, including song sets, breakdowns, and setups). While these concerns – with sex and sexuality, gender transgressions, unruly bodies, social offenses, and systemic oppressions, among other things – directly inform punk, postpunk, and queer sensibilities, they also illustrate the definitional messiness of punk, queer, queercore, and riot grrrl cultures, their predilections for mutation and motion, and their diverse modes of resistance to what might be understood as a dominant culture.[2]

I also want to suggest that for the brief time and space of the show at the 9:30 Club, band and audience members were aligned through a series of mutually appreciative acts, forging a loose community that was particular and performative, coalitional and conditional. I'm not saying that the experience constituted some kind of queerpunk mini-nation, that there was ever a moment when the crowd swayed as one body with their hands in the air, or that the room was continually awash in a tide of uniformly good will. But even while everyone looked, moved, and responded in individual ways, there were discernible moments of consensus. Spectators were clamorously enthusiastic, occasionally raucous: the mostly teens and twentysomethings danced, moshed (soft style, the kind dictated by a small space with wide hard columns), applauded, and sweated together. Like many punk shows, this one was premised on an ongoing exchange of energies and vexations: band and audience members tossed phrases – "Fuck you," "Suck me" – and plastic beer cups back and forth in a ritual that, for all its potent language and contentious gesticulating, was about community and shared identity. For this night, anyway, everyone here was "queer."

Of course, any claim for such "queerness" – and the quotation marks indicate both contingency and irony – is complicated by a variety of factors, not the least being the fact that some participants were heterosexual. But if this evening's queerness wasn't "literal" or even sustained once participants walked out the door, if it was "performative" in the most mundane sense, it was effective. It moved those of us who were there. This effect was as visceral as it was vocal, a volatile mix of sound (the amps were cranked) and movement, plus some wilder, in-between moments, approximating what Michel de Certeau calls "enunciative gaps." These "'obscene' citations of bodies," he writes, "these sounds waiting for a language, seem to certify, by a 'disorder' secretly referred to an unknown order, that there is something else, something other" (de Certeau, 1984: 163–4). Granted, this experience of "something else" may have been the function of a particularly hot moment. But what I want to stress here is the productive interplay of performance and authenticity, the ways that sexualized acts and exchanges can "speak," display a range of identities that are otherwise rendered invisible precisely because they're attached to such acts and exchanges.

Surely, demonstrations of community are not unusual at punk shows: images of moshing or pogoing throngs – occasionally mud-covered as if to underline their sameness – are familiar in contemporary mass media. But the nature of the identity shared by queercore and riot grrrl bands and their fans can be hard to pin down. On one hand, it seems clear that any common experiences at their shows are immediate and local, rather than universal or transcendent: folks slam up against each other, a few spill their drinks, and most go home with the people they came in with. Such collective experiences of identity are transient and typical, as Cathy Griggers observes, "The problem of identification is always a problem of signification within historically specific social situations" (Griggers, 1993: 179). And yet, on the other hand – because and in spite of their emphatic physicality – the shows take on exactly this "problem," by reframing identity not as something inherent in (pierced, tattooed, or painted) bodies, but as something more strategic and disturbing, something more perverse and imaginative.

The usefulness of punk aesthetics and politics for queer performers is in part premised on the genre's well-known rough-and-ready rebelliousness (not to mention its openness to a range of conventional and unconventional musical skills), a commitment to social protest that was simultaneously produced and consumed by a lack of polish and cash. It's frequently been asserted that since Nirvana's crossover success made punk bands commonplace – with platinum albums and labeled slots in Tower Records – whatever subversiveness was once assumed for it are now less obvious. As punk (and more generally, alternative music) has invaded, forever altered, and even become the Mainstream, the question of "authenticity" is both more and less important with regard to understanding fandom or possibilities for activism and social change.

In his famous study of subculture, Dick Hebdige observes that punk, from its inception, engaged with the perceived dominant culture, consuming and reinventing that culture, reconfiguring its restrictions as a means to exhibit frustration, innovation, and resistance. He writes that punk in its early forms narrated and communicated a sense of crisis by marking an edge of appropriable, understandable language, "challenging at a symbolic level the 'inevitability,' the 'naturalness' of class and gender stereotypes" (Hebdige, 1979: 89). While attempts to define punk typically set it against a fixed opposite (say, punk versus metal, or punk versus classic rock), its flexibility and resilience are typically matched by those of so-called dominant culture. Punk traditionally presumed a white, working- to middle- class, left-leaning, heterosexual male performer-and-fan base (not unlike most regular rock), but more recently (also like regular rock), it has shifted to include and appeal to a diversely raced, gendered, sexed, and classed set of artists and audiences (including girl and girl-fronted bands, mixed-race bands, and punk-hybrid bands, like punk-ska, punk-folk, punk-blues, punk-hiphop, etc.). The relationship between punk and mainstream, or punk and anything else, is, increasingly, by definition unstable.

The shift has produced neo-lite-punks (like Green Day, Offspring, Rancid, or Veruca Salt), whose derision by hardcore fans is understandable and politically important (as informed critiques of industry practices), but also potentially reductive and counterproductive, because it misses the ways that punk's incursions into commercial viability can complicate conventional oppositions. Hebdige proposes that punk's emphasis on "style" signals not straight-up capitulation, but simultaneous assimilation and resistance. "It is therefore difficult," he writes, "to maintain any absolute distinction between commercial exploitation on the one hand and creativity/originality on the other, even those these categories are emphatically opposed in the value systems of most subcultures" (Hebdige, 1979: 95). A similar rejection of "absolute distinction" also characterizes many queer and grrrl artists, audiences, and theorists, a diverse "community" whose markers of identity can be (deliberately) ambiguous as well as unmistakable, embracing a continuum of activism and incorporation, visibility and invisibility, private and public spheres, working against and through strictly oppositional structures.[3]

"Don't Need Your Dick To Fuck!"

As the above lyric from Bikini Kill's "Don't Need You" implies, the rejection of dominant cultural forms is a central theme for queercore and riot grrrl acts. If such protest is familiar from earlier incarnations of punk and rock more generally, its particular permutations in queercore and riot grrrl are less strictly oppositional, more disruptive. This practice allows for a range of alliances, in performances and audiences. Consider, for example, the striking display of collectivity when Tribe 8 singer Lynn Breedlove takes off her T-shirt: viewers typically respond in ways that suggest that they identify her as same and other, that they can imagine wanting and being her. Girls up front, near the stage, also take off their shirts – and often their bras, if they're wearing them – performing their solidarity with the dykes on stage, some-times moshing hard enough to push boys out of the pit.[4] And when Breedlove pushes her hand down into her jeans, simulating masturbation, the crowd also reacts enthusiastically, though usually not by mirroring her act.

The performance raises all kinds of questions about identity and authen-ticity. How, for instance, is Breedlove's authenticity entangled with that of her audience? Does she become a real dyke in and as her act, in taking off her shirt or in masturbating? Do her viewers also become authentic dykes if their responses conform to some idea of authentic dykeness? And how do these acts read differently for the women, straight or gay men who are watching her? The moment plays like drag at the same time that it's a punk-rock salvo, turning straight-porn conventions (the woman on display for a presumed male viewer) upside down, inviting girls to participate in sex fan-tasies, insisting on the fluidity of viewing and performing positions, and cre-ating a continuum of gender and sexual identities.

At the 9:30 club, for "Romeo and Julio" – a song about two gay boys "down by the schoolyard" – Breedlove pulled a dildo from out of her fly, put on a condom, and invited Pansy Division's bassist, Chris Freeman, to come on stage and suck her off, which he proceeded to do with comically exag-gerated zeal while men and women in the audience rooted them on. Then, during "Frat Pig," a song about gang rape ("In the name of male-bonding/In the name of fraternity") and revenge, Breedlove yelled, "Let's play a game called cas-trate!" and sawed off that faux dick with a hunting knife. Specta-tors cheered again as she held the pathetic item up on the tip of the knife, then grabbed for it when she tossed it into the pit. Tribe 8's set ended with a series of stereotypically masculine rock-star moves, with guitar players Lynn Flipper and Leslie Mah's and bassist Lynn Payne's legs thrust forward to the edge of the stage, available for fans' caresses.

Tribe 8's genderbending set turned out to be a provocative introduction for Pansy Division's. While the Pansies' on-stage style is more conspicuously and consistently playful than Tribe 8's, the boys' lyrics can be equally "lewd" (one reviewer has called them, admiringly, a "relentlessly filthy sex-positive fag band" [Baird, 1995]). At the 9:30 Club, they sang "Surrender Your Clothing" ("Zippers down, the prize revealed") and "Anthem" ("We wanna sock it to your hole"), sentiments clearly addressed to men, but also readable as paeans to queerness (or gloriously "deviant" sexual behaviors). Still, it's clear enough that the bands have very different takes on dicks and dick practices. How do audience members process this range of politics and performance, so they can applaud them within the space of a single evening?

Breedlove's donning of the dildo, for instance, can play differently for different crowds. I've seen the band perform for a mostly straight audience in Madison, Wisconsin, as well as for mostly lesbian audiences at other sites in D.C., and in each instance, she has pulled out the dildo and solicited an audience member to come on stage to "suck my dick!" While the possible meanings of this scene shift, depending on the gender and sexuality of the volunteer (and these may not always be immediately or ever clear), the easy read is that it constitutes a kind of continuum, of act and reaction, of attractive illusion and material reality. (At one show, she taunted the plainly straight boys moshing in front of her, asking how many of them had ever had dicks in their mouths? One of them made it to the stage for the "Romeo and Julio" routine, but backed off at the last minute).

Breedlove's literal apprehension of the (fake) penis brings various cultural assumptions to bear on the always complicated relationship between queer sexual acts and queer identity, or between performativity and authenticity. As Colleen Lamos argues, "the significance of the dildo is the manner in which it questions the nature of sexual difference" (Lamos, 1995: 110). Certainly this question is pervasive at a Tribe 8 show, as Breedlove all but embodies it. Her ironic self-display can, after all, be threatening to some boys, as when she warns them that their "cute girlfriends" might go home with her. Shirtless to expose her long torso, wearing sunglasses, blue or pink hair, baggy jeans, and her baseball cap backwards when she sings "Oversize Ego" ("I'm a real big deal!"), from the back she might pass for a guy. And then she turns around, displaying the A for Anarchy written on her belly, her breasts and nipple-ring, and her dildo. Perhaps needless to say, the dilemma of authenticity is repeatedly foregrounded by this body that won't conform to conventions.[5] You can"t help but look at the rubber dick that"s swinging from her crotch. As Lamos writes, "The dildo denaturalizes and renders perverse its subject so that the dildo's representation must continue to provoke uneasiness, especially the uneasiness of the loss of a secure gender identity" (Lamos, 1995: 118). Uneasiness, yes. At the end of some performances of "Frat Pig," I've seen Breedlove haul out a chainsaw, revving loudly, to chop the thing off.

Tribe 8's performances insist that authenticity is a perpetual act, not "artificial" as opposed to "true" or "real," but an act that carries with it consequences, meanings, and possibilities for transformation. For queers who are tired of trying to gain access to entrenched cultural hierarchies defined by (and defining) "original" and "copy," asserting an authentic (sometimes, though not always, formulated as "genetic") identity has been, in the recent past, politically significant and effective. At the same time however, drawing attention to the performances of everyday life has proven to be a useful tool for progressive social critique. As one measure of resistance to a commercializing and co-opting system, authenticity both establishes and diffuses the limits of popular representation. By the same token, punk's overt investment in affective cynicism, irony, and self-consciousness complicates any singular notion of authenticity, and insists on multiple identifications and fluid identities.

At least part of queercore's "subversiveness" is manifest in its self-ascribed authentic outrage, its rejection of orthodox conduits to success, financial and popular. "Contemporary gay punk," writes Matias Viegener (1994), insists not only on a generalized, transcultural "gender dysphoria," but as well rejects "'nice,' post-Stonewall gay culture, as it is manifested in disco, gay marriages, *The Advocate*, polo shirts, David Leavitt's fiction, and Calvin Klein advertisements" (117). Queer punk communities, he continues, "tend to be specific and local, centered in San Francisco, Toronto, and Los Angeles, among other cities, placed willfully beyond the 'mainstream'" (117). Such specificity grants queercore a sense of simultaneous risk and threat, vulnerability and aggression, as well as a "decentralization" that, Viegener argues, prevents any linear climbs to stardom or "typical" fan behaviors (118).

But insisting on the "beyond the mainstream" purity of this resistance can obscure what seems to me its potential to transform how "we" think about politics and products in contingent their relationship. That is, while Viegener's version of radical transience designates a specific authenticity in underground scenes, it also problematizes visibility outside immediate venues, and visibility is, after all, what being out is all about. And so, queer punks must negotiate among ironies, authenticities, and appearances that count.

"AGAINST ALL ODDS WE APPEAR"

In 1994, Pansy Division became particularly visible when they went on tour as the opening band for Green Day (the quotation above is from the Pansies). In doing so, they confronted a question that hasn't yet come up for most queercore bands: how is it possible to be visibly and actively political (as *being* queer would seem to demand) in a meta-media-universe? Is it possible to sell out when you're out, as a queer person and performer? What determines being out or selling out? Within the music business, answers to these questions are necessarily connected to the measures and readability of authenticity. Fans, record labels, promoters, and performers all have vested interests in claiming and defining authenticity. In a postmodern environment, Lawrence Grossberg has argued, there can be no such thing as authentic authenticity (if such a thing was ever possible, which is, at the least, debatable), only "authentic inauthenticity," a series of poses, mediations, and performances, alternately narrated by artists and judged by audiences who are, in turn, affiliated (or not) through taste, style, and affect (Grossberg, 1992).

Identification through such affiliation, as differentiated from, say, some notion of a shared inherent identity, makes people nervous. It doesn't seem committed, it could be faked, it might turn over tomorrow. But it also suggests another way to understand processes of identity and identification, one less invested in what appears to be real and more flexible with regard to lived experiences. Noting that it "became clear, particularly after punk, that this romanticism of authenticity was a false and idealized view," Angela McRobbie (1994) proposes that "subcultural life" combines commercial, aesthetic, and identificatory experiences; and these experiences, even if they aren't overtly "resistant," provide "young people in youth cultures with a way of achieving social subjectivity and therefore identity" (161).

Pansy Division is a case in point. They mix basic pop tunes and explicitly gay-sex lyrics, a combination that, depending on the venue, can be pretty regular or pretty outrageous. You could hardly call them intellectually complex or musically innovative, yet their expanding audience (in numbers and in demographic range) suggests that their charming and yet in-your-face performances of queerness are effectively creating affiliations, or what Robin Balliger aptly calls "sounds of resistance." Local and strategic, these "sounds," Balliger argues, constitute art that is not difficult or overtly "political," but rather appeal "to the senses, to physical pleasure." Balliger suggests that while it is typically dismissed by critics and theorists, this kind of pleasure is a means to conceive and build resistance (Balliger, 1995: 21).

Pansy Division seems especially able to faciliate such affiliations as resistance. At one point during their set at the 9:30 Club, for example, Pansy singer Jon Ginoli introduced the band's new drummer, Dustin Donaldson, as "heterosexual, but wearing a dress in solidarity" (a decidedly femme number he had borrowed from Leslie Mah). Donaldson stood up and bowed deeply, as viewers roundly applauded the courage of this outted "outsider." In this context, I think it's instructive to recall that a few months before this, I had been to another show at the same club, this one featuring Ice T's thrash-metal band, Body Count.[6] At this show I was surrounded by a spirited assembly of almost all white youths, who were more than happy to join in Ice T's call to "Fuck the police!" At one level this gleeful aggression seemed almost absurd: it's likely that most of these middle-class white fans had no experience with the cops resembling that described by Ice T in "Cop Killer." But they were more than willing to make an imaginative leap – whether to be cool or appropriative. They were part of a specific kind of collaboration that characterizes such moments (call them utopian, but they take place, however briefly), a collaboration that includes but isn't limited to an admiration for speedy guitar licks or a deep, chest-kicking bass.

I witnessed a similar unlikely crossover effect when I attended a Green Day show at the Patriot Center, a sports and concert arena in suburban Northern Virginia.[7] The audience was primed for Green Day, then enjoying the enormous success of their album, *Dookie*, and a quite hilarious punk performance at Woodstock II (during which frontperson Billie Joe Armstrong had exchanged insults and gobs of mud with his audience), which had been televised on MTV. The eager spectators – many wearing Green Day T-shirts, some just purchased at the arena – looked to be almost entirely white boys (teenagers and preteens), several of whom sat with parents (or I should say fathers, as I didn't see anyone who looked like a mother with her child or children). I doubt that most of them know that Green Day frontperson Billie Joe Armstrong had recently come out as "not fully straight" in a *Village Voice* piece about Pansy Division's "full steam ahead" gay punk activism (Herman, 1995: 57). (And besides, the glossy national magazines, like *Rolling Stone* and *Spin*, were leading with stories about his happy marriage and new baby.) And the majority certainly didn't recognize the warm-up band. But by the time Green Day came on, everyone in that space knew something about Pansy Division.

In fact, from the distance dictated by arena seating, the Pansies even looked like Green Day, three guys with shortish hair, dressed in jeans and T-shirts, and combining comic poise, nonthreatening aggression, and humorous self-deprecation on stage. Both bands depend on power chords, driving drums, and, between songs, well-rehearsed tirades by their respective frontmen. During both bands' sets, eager listeners reciprocated, throwing pieces of clothing onto the stage, along with cups half full of soda and (mostly empty) food containers. But for all their formal resemblances, the two bands part ways when it comes to subject matter. Though they both focus on young male experiences, where Armstrong sings about masturbation in "Long View" and angst-ridden insanity in "Basket Case" (both songs for which the spectators seemed to know all the words), Ginoli was describing gay club scenes ("Rock & Roll Queer Bar") and the ups and downs of gay romantic coupledom ("Hippy Dude"), with very little ambiguity regarding sexual acts ("We're butt-fuckers! Fuck you!").

It was, unsurprisingly, a very dissimilar show from the one I saw at the smaller club in D.C., where the audience was enchanted by the drummer's dress. The set list was similar – they sang "Fem in a Black Leather Jacket," "Bunnies" ("I got the carrot, you got the stick") and "Fuck Buddy" at both sites – but in Virginia, the crowd might have been from another planet, and Ginoli worked it differently (which is not to say he was less vigorous; rather, he was more cajoling, and even more energetic). I mean, he worked it like a hostile gathering, folks who probably wouldn't be converted to full-on support, but who might be convinced to be tolerant. Within a few minutes of stepping on stage, Ginoli asked them to identify themselves: "How many of you out there are homophobic?" Several dozen hands went up, and you could hear the groans and jeers as well. In front of me, four boys in baseball caps, knee-length shorts, and Chucks, yelled back to Ginoli, "Fuck you, homo!"

It seemed clear that such a response was routine for this tour. Most of the kids were there to mosh, however, so lyrics and pronouncements of identity ("homos" or "homophobes") were mostly beside the point. Shut up and dance. The Pansies launched into "Vanilla," their chords relentlessly bouncy ("People should do in bed whatever pops into their heads!") and then, "Anthem": "We can't relate to Judy Garland / It's a new generation of music calling." You could say that. "Basically," Freeman has said, "what we're doing is de-masculating men by telling them to bend over and take it. Come on, *enjoy* it, it's fun!" (Herman, 1995: 57). I've heard of a show where Freeman wore a nightgown and at the end of the night pulled it up to reveal that he was naked: the band is fun, no doubt about it. They sing about "getting tied up, and my boyfriend, Sean Connery" in "James Bondage," nonlethal STDs in "Crabby Day," and always, always, elusive "cute guys." And for all the potential and real tensions in the Patriot Center, that show actually seemed more compelling than the queer-identified one. By the time Green Day was ready to come on, much of the audience was fully "warmed up," writhing and flailing in the continually widening pit.

It wasn't as if there was a politically committed collective formed this night, or that the young (or older) phobes were reformed or enlightened. But the overwhelming effect of the spectacle on stage, the similarity of motion and emotion represented by the pit, was that change was possible, if not inevitable. Lynn Breedlove puts it this way in an interview: "There are different stages in revolution. The first stage is identity. That means you all have to get together very narrowly and limit yourself to just hanging out with people who are exactly like you. Once you're secure in who you are, and who your friends are, then you can start reaching out and building alliances. Once you have *alliances* you have power. Because there's numbers" (Juno, 1996: 66–7).

"I Can Sell My Body If I Wanna"

As Kathleen Hanna sings in "Jigsaw Youth," making and having options is key to this idea of "revolution." The differences among Tribe 8, Pansy Division, and Bikini Kill demonstrate the need for more than one "alternative." The rawness of Bikini Kill shows is a long way from the orchestrations of the Pansies or Tribe 8. Each time I've seen them, Bikini Kill has made do with lousy sound systems (one show, a benefit for a local organization to help young prostitutes, was in a room with gymnasium-style acoustics). Each time they've played with three to four other grrrl bands. While Bikini Kill is by now very well-known as one of the initial acts in the movement afterwards called "riot grrrl," they have also resolutely refused to record for a major label, to claim a singularly "representative" position. Their album, *Reject All American* (1996) has been praised by music critics (for *Rolling Stone*, *AP*, and other publications), but the crucial energy of the band remains focused through and at their live shows.

The first time I saw them, they appeared as the last band, after Slant 6 and Team Dresch. The second time I saw them, they also served as anchor, for a four-band lineup including Team Dresch. While Team Dresch's lyrics focused on women's relations, their act was consistently rough and overtly politicized. Their first album, *Personal Best*, features cover art recalling the poster for Robert Townsend's movie: two girl runners posed on a track, looking at each other, ready to "break all the rules," as the accompanying text has it. But there are other rules at stake in punk, imperatives to disorder, or at least a convincing show of same. The Team Dresch–Slant 6–Bikini Kill show, at a small D.C. club called the Black Cat, opened with a demonstration of self-defense for women.[8] Without microphones or props, members of all the bands acted out various parts, including would-be victims and aggressors, male and female (including a scenario where a lesbian imposes on a straight woman). As Team Dresch then started their set, the mostly white and female audience was more than ready to appreciate their every pro-girl gesture and inflection.

As the night went on, the audience became more gender-mixed, men arriving late, in time to hear Bikini Kill, the biggest name up that night. By the time frontperson Kathleen Hanna took the stage, the crowd was restless and excited. She instructed the men in the audience to step to the back so women could see the stage (only a few men complied). "Girl power now!" she screamed, leading into "Rebel Girl" ("You are the queen of my world"). When Hanna erupted into "White Boy" – "I'm so sorry if I've alienated some of you! Your whole fucking culture alienates me!" – it was clear that no one in the audience was going to be identifying as a "white boy." "It's hard to talk with your dick in my mouth," sang Hanna, and all heads in the audience nodded, as if swept up by a single rhythm, moved by a single cause and a lively chorus: "White boy, don't laugh, don't cry. Just die!" Some of the guys moved off to the sides of the room, as if to fade into the crowd or walls. But most of them hung with their girl companions, their flannel shirts and baggy pants providing precious little camouflage. And yet this apparent capacity to make white-boy-ness invisible, or at least negotiable, becomes more complicated when you consider that I also saw several girls at the front, in the very small pit, being shoved by boys. Hanna stopped the show, and refused to continue until the rest of the audience stopped these guys from misbehaving.[9]

There seem to be at least two ways to read this scene, and both have to do – perhaps ironically – with knowing your options, with understanding what constitutes a "crisis" (as Hebdige uses the term), and with negotiating between authentic and performative transgressions: the white boys in the audience are in deep denial, or they are quite self-aware and able to make a serious leap, of faith, of imagination, of empathy. (Actually, there are a number of other ways to read the scene that fall in between these poles, and each of the young men in the audience must have his own perspective on his experience of the evening.) What I'd like to suggest, though, derives from Eve Kosofsky Sedgwick's (1995) proposition that "masculinity and femininity are threshold effects." She defines these effects as "places where quantitative increments along one dimension can suddenly appear as qualitative differences somewhere else on the map entirely" (16). I find this spatial metaphor useful, in the sense that it might address the various spaces (though the differences among them are worth noting, as they indicate and shape audience responses, the bigger venues allowing more room for less unified-looking reactions), because of the surprise she describes – "suddenly," as if gendered and sexual identities might "show up," uninvited and unanticipated, complicating and challenging expectations.

This effect seemed, perhaps, most obvious during Pansy Division's appearance at the arena, but there was a way in which the Bikini Kill show pressed its audience to make choices about their identifications, which were immediate and temporary, but choices with consequences nevertheless. This wasn't an atmospheric shift that changed the world forever. Granted, some made lousy choices: they pushed girls even as Hanna was singing (or rather, yelling, which is closer to describing her performance style), "It's about wanting you dead" (in "Outta Me"). But everyone (or nearly everyone) in the room acted as if they were aware of the stakes inherent in his or her behavior. Hanna is nothing if not an aggressive and "confessional" performer, incorporating her own experiences into her work, and also laying responsibility onto her audience, making them into a "community" that can act to stop violence or abuse.[10]

While an ostensible singleness of purpose is surely integral to punk's aesthetics and politics, confusion has also long been an important factor, mounting a particular challenge to linearity, binarism, and coherence. The increasing availability and accessibility of a popular, "commodity" queerness (lesbian chic in *New York* magazine [Kasindorf, 1993], for instance, a "gay" episode of MTV's *Dating Game* ripoff series, *Singled Out* [1995], Ellen's coming out [1997], or a wholly sympathetic, even heroic, gay boy in Amy Heckerling's *Clueless* [1995]) seem less a loss of authentic marginality than an invasion and expansion of the mainstream. Punk emulates a kind of acting out and giving in, simulating resistance to exacerbate linguistic and generic instabilities, acting out and acting up to kick listeners into gear. Transforming the mainstream – injecting it with good music, no less – queer punk translates experience into performance and vice versa, collapsing expression onto identity, fiction onto productive politics. As Kathleen Hanna sings, "There's more than one way of going somewhere."

NOTES

1. Sexpod's members are Karyn Kuhl on guitar and lead vocals, Alice Genese on bass and vocals, Billy Loose on drums; Tribe 8 is Lynn Breedlove on vocals (and chainsaw), Lynn Flipper on guitar, Leslie Mah on guitar, Lynn Payne/Tantrum on bass, and Slade Bellum on drums; and Pansy Division is currently composed of Jon Ginoli on guitar and vocals, Chris Freeman on bass and vocals, and Dustin Donaldson on drums. Donaldson, who replaced Patrick Hawley and has been with the band for a little over a year, is the only straight member of the group.

2. For the sake of drawing some broad generic lines, I'm using the labels punk, queercore, and riot grrrl, even though they are notoriously inaccurate and many bands reject them on principle (that such labeling is designed to enable more effective marketing rather than describe music or performance styles). And yet, as Tom Frank points out, the "expres-

sion of dissent" that characterizes such "alternative" cultures retains a persuasive power for its local, immediate constituencies. He writes, "through its noise comes the scream of torment that is this country's only mark of health: the sweet shriek of outrage that is the only sign that sanity survives amid the stripmalls and hazy clouds of Hollywood desire" (Frank, 1995: 118). Pretty to think so, and sometimes effective.

3. John Champagne, in his formulation of an "ethics of marginality," describes a difference between "liberal criticism" and an "ethical criticism." The first "extends to the Other a greater subjectivity" (working within an established, hierarchical social and political system); the second "deploys the Other towards a resistance to subjectivity" as subjectivity constitutes a restrictive dichotomy of subject and object, in order to challenge this established system (Champagne, 1995: xxxiii).

4. A friend of mine overheard one young man at the Madison, Wisconsin show complaining to his male friend that "some chick" had pushed him so hard and aggressively he was reluctant to return to the pit unless his friend accompanied him, as a kind of reinforcement: they decided to hang back in the crowd.

5. And the band, which identifies itself as "pro-SM," has been challenged by other feminists. The most famous instance of this occurred at the 1994 Michigan Womyn's Music Festival, when their performance was interrupted by women carrying banners that read, "Tribe 8 promotes violence against women and children" and "If you're a sexual abuse survivor, you may not want to attend this concert" (Thomas, 1995: 22). And Evelyn McDonnell (1995) reports that one speaker at an antiviolence workshop at the festival called the band "pornographers."

6. While the 9:30 Club is a self-designated site for "alternative" music (that famously bland and amorphous category) and tends to attract a caucasian, middle-class, straight clientele, such demographic generalizations make presumptions (sometimes warranted, sometimes not) about performative possibilities.

7. I've written elsewhere about this show, with more specific focus on Green Day (Fuchs, 1996).

8. This educational "self-defense" performance is part of an ongoing collaborative project, with other women's bands, which has produced two recent CDs, *Free To Fight* (Portland, OR: Candy Ass, 1995), and *Home*

Alive: The Art of Self-Defense (New York: Sony Music, 1996). The latter comes with a "People Advisory Sticker," which reads: "Contents of this record represent the views of people who have been affected by violence. This is a topic that inspires various responses. Some people may be offended by the language and views on this record. Home Alive believes that awareness, communication and responsibility, rather than silence, censorship or denial of these complex issues, will lead to change. We all have a lot to learn. Warning: This world contains people and events that can be harmful to your health."

9. I've seen Tribe 8 and other women's bands deal with this behavior as well: L7 stopped singing and playing at one performance, to demand that a singled-out young man stop sticking his elbow in a woman's face. He complied; they played on.

10. See also Hanna's project with a group called the Fakes, *Real Fiction* (Portland, OR: Chainsaw Records, 1995), which the liner notes describe as a "rock opera" (not unlike the Who's *Tommy*), about a girl's abuse by her father. She also discusses this notion of audience as "community" in an interview with Andrea Juno (Juno, 1996: 90).

REFERENCES

Baird, D. 1995. "The King is dead... Long live the Queen." *Monk* [on-line zine, at http://www.neo.com/Monk/SanFrancisco/].

Balliger, R. 1995. "Sounds of Resistance." In *Sounding Off! Music as Subversion/Resistance/Revolution*, edited by R. Sakolsky and F. Wei-Han Ho. New York: Autonomedia.

Butler, J. 1989. "Imitation and Gender Insubordination." In *Inside/Out: Lesbian Theories, Gay Theories*, edited by D. Fuss. New York: Routledge.

———. 1993. *Bodies that Matter: On the Discursive Limits of "Sex."* New York: Routledge.

Champagne, J. 1995. *The Ethics of Marginality: A New Approach to Gay Studies.* Minneapolis: University of Minnesota Press.

de Certeau, M. 1984. *The Practice of Everyday Life.* Berkeley: University of California Press.

Frank, T. 1995. "Alternative to What?" In *Sounding Off! Music as Subervsion/Resistance/Revolution*, edited by R. Sakolsky and F. Wei-Han Ho. Brooklyn, NY: Autonomedia.

Fuchs, C. 1996. "'Beat me outta me': Alternative Masculinities." In *Boys: Masculinities in Contemporary Culture*, edited by P. Smith, 171–97. New York: Westview Press.

Fuss, D. 1989. *Essentially Speaking: Feminism, Nature, and Difference.* New York: Routledge.

Griggers, C. 1993. "Lesbian Bodies in the Age of (Post)Mechanical Reproduction." In *Fear of a Queer Planet: Queer Politics and Social Theory*, edited by M. Warner, 178–92. Minneapolis: University of Minnesota Press.

Grossberg, L. 1992. *We Gotta Get Out of This Place: Popular Conservatism and Postmodern Culture.* New York: Routledge.

———. 1993. "The Framing of Rock: Rock and the New Conservatism." In *Rock and Popular Music: Politics, Policies, Institutions*, edited by T. Bennett, S. Frith, L. Grossberg, J. Shepherd, and G. Turner. London: Routledge.

Hebdige, D. 1979. *Subculture: The Meaning of Style.* London: Routledge.

Herman, J. P. 1995. "Orgasm Addicts." *Village Voice*, January 10, 57–8.

Juno, A. 1996. *Angry Women in Rock, Volume 1.* New York: Juno Books.

Kasindorf, J. R. 1993. "Lesbian Chic." *New York*, May 10, 30–7.

Lamos, C. 1995. "Taking on the Phallus." In *Lesbian Erotics*, edited by Karla Jay, 101–24. New York: New York University Press.

McDonnell, E. 1995. "Riot Grrrls Invade the 'Lesbian Woodstock.' *Addicted to Noise* [on-line magazine at http://www.addict.com/].

McRobbie, A. 1994. *Postmodernism and Popular Culture.* London: Routledge.

Schwichtenberg, C. 1993. "Madonna's Postmodern Feminism: Bringing the Margins to the Center." In *The Madonna Connection: Representational Politics, Subcultural Identities, and Cultural Theory*, edited by C. Schwichtenberg, 129–45. Boulder, CO: Westview Press.

Sedgwick, E. K. 1995. "Gosh. Boy George, You Must Be Awfully Secure in Your Masculinity!" In *Constructing Masculinity*, edited by M. Berger, B. Wallis, and S. Watson, 11–20. New York: Routledge.

Thomas, T. 1995. "Music for the Tribe: Interview with Tribe 8." *Girlfriends*, July–August, 20–22, 46.

Viegener, M. 1994. "'The Only Haircut That Makes Sense Anymore': Queer Subculture and Gay Resistance." In *Queer Looks: Perspectives on Lesbian and Gay Film and Video*, edited by M. Gever, J. Greyson, and P. Parmar. New York: Routledge.

CD's Listed in this Article

1. Bikini Kill. 1993. *Bikini Kill: The CD Version of the First Two Records* [compact disc]. Olympia, WA: Kill Rock Stars.

2. ———. 1994. *Pussywhipped* [compact disc]. Olympia, WA: Kill Rock Stars.

3. ———. 1996. *Reject All American* [compact disc]. Olympia, WA: Kill Rock Stars.

4. Pansy Division. 1993a. *Deflowered* [compact disc]. Berkeley, CA: Lookout Records.

5. ———. 1993b. *Undressed* [compact disc]. Berkeley, CA: Lookout Records.

6. ———. 1995. *Pile Up* [compact disc]. Berkeley, CA: Lookout Records.

7. ———. 1996. *Wish I'd Taken Pictures* [compact disc]. Berkeley, CA: Lookout Records.

8. The Fakes. 1995a. *Real Fiction* [compact disc]. Portland, OR: Chainsaw.

9. ———. 1995b. *Home Alive* [compact disc]. Portland, OR: Chainsaw.

10. ———. 1995c. *Free to Fight* [compact disc]. Portland, OR: Chainsaw.

11. Tribe 8. 1995a. *By The Time We Get To Colorado* [compact disc]. San Francisco: Outpunk.

12. ———. 1995b. *Fist City* [compact disc]. San Francisco: Alternative Tentacles.

13. ———. 1996. *Snarkism* [compact disc]. San Francisco: Alternative Tentacles.

Part II

HISTORY, TECHNOLOGY, AND POLICY

6

—— Drumming and Memory ——

Scholarship, Technology, and Music-Making

Andrew Goodwin

To begin with, two small questions, both from my teenage years, where I can see myself now, if memory serves me correctly, on the one occasion thinking about the Who (I was in the bus station next to our house), and on the other (I was walking along an alley just off Facto- ry Road) thinking about electronic music. How could it be, I wondered, that the Who would ever get old, and what would *we* be like if we listened to them in the future? And what, I also wondered, would the music of the future sound like? Would synthesizers replace guitars, so that tomorrow's music would sound futuristic? Would entire songs be made that had nothing but synthesizers in them? Another future that seemed hard to imagine.

Of course, today's music *does* sound futuristic, although it is not of the future, guitars have not been replaced, a synthesizer's unique timbre can still conjure up science fiction visions, and the Who play on, reuniting again to premiere *Quadrophenia* for the Prince's Trust in London's Hyde Park, available live on pay-per-view in the United States, courtesy of HBO. What might scholars teach us about these developments? If we are to have anything to offer beyond journalistic histories and endless discussions of the various postmodernisms, then I believe that we will look again at the concepts of time and memory.

121

Certainly there is much that could be done here if practitioners – journalists, DJs, musicians – and scholars could enter into dialogue, as only a few really have. One of the problems is that the practitioners too often sound like Stanley Fish (1995) in his book *Professional Correctness*, overeager to celebrate an unbridgeable divide between what media studies calls "theory and practice." This point was made for me recently at an academic conference where the audience heard from a distinguished panel of journalists and academics, who, as is usual, talked past each other about their work. What invariably happens is that the academics, eager (like me) to find ways of addressing a nonacademic audience, make all kinds of concessions to the difficulties and limitations of journalism, engage in autocritique concerning the politics of academic writing, and discuss our yearning to work as or with media producers, and so forth. We are then treated to career histories from the practitioners, who berate the professors for using bloodless "jargon," without revealing the slightest interest in figuring out why academics use technical language, or what forms of knowledge might be produced on campus that cannot emerge in a 200-word record review. Because they operate just a little closer to the marketplace than the professors, the critics evidently believe that they are also closer to "the street."

If there is to be any point in such dialogues, then the communication must take place on a two-way street. That is, we should acknowledge that we are talking about different kinds of work. There is a division of labor here: journalists (like musicians and DJs) know more facts, and facts are not stupid, they are valuable. Musicians, DJs and journalists often listen to more music than do professors, and from them we can learn a great deal. Many journalists are better writers than professional academics. There are too many academic books on pop that fail because the author lacks three basic qualities: knowledge of facts, understanding of music, ability to write. However, there are far fewer bad books on pop by academics than there are *useless* books by rock critics, most of which lack ideas, argument, critical thinking, analysis, theory, social context, political sophistication, or indeed any quality that would give the reader some hint as to why the book was written in the first place, save the lure of what the Sex Pistols have taken to calling "filthy lucre." And this is not to mention bad radio programs of a purely promotional nature and interviews with musicians that teach us nothing. It is time for the professors to stop apologizing for being academic, since finally we often do the job of rock criticism better than anyone else.

II

Musicians and professors certainly share at least one vital capacity, although this essential quality often goes unremarked: memory. I have often thought that at least half of the credit for what is assumed to be our intelligence as professors resides in fact in the ability to remember things that we have read, or heard about, or, frankly, said before. Rock and pop musicians rely on a similar trick. Music that has been heard before, or played before, can be reproduced at will. Even those musicians who read music often play it from memory, without notation; and in any case, as Robert Walser (1992) and others have pointed out, traditional musical notation contains insufficient information for the performance of pop and rock. Perhaps the relative ease with which rock musicians and producers have come to terms with auto-mated music machines, sampling computers, and so forth reflects in part a simple recognition that electronic machinery is sometimes better suited to this task than the human body.[1]

Nowhere is the link between music and memory more evident than in the case of drumming. Indeed it was Pete Townshend who once comment-ed that drummers are distinguished by their powers of recall – evidence that even musicians are sometimes better at theorizing than journalists! Drum-mers practice independence. We train our limbs to forget to listen to one another. And we must also be in two places at once – inside the groove of the piece, and yet at the same time observing it from outside, charting where in the song we are. The whole band depends on the drummer's ability to sit-uate the players within the pulse of the song, while simultaneously keeping track of its structure. As Townshend noted, the other players usually have some means of knowing where the song is – words, chords, progressions. These elements all give out stronger clues concerning structure than the repetitive beat that the drummer lays down for everyone else.

In this respect Geoffrey Curran's (1996) account of the differences between jazz and rock drumming is quite interesting. Starting with the observation that "the world of drumming revolves around classifications of 'styles,'" Curran sees the differences between jazz and rock drumming as entirely conventional, having more to do with the social construction of "thought communities" than the music itself. From the manner of playing to the choice of drum set (bigger drums for rock, smaller kits for jazz) and even hairstyle and appearance, Curran critiques a divide between jazz and rock that almost always involves a hierarchy, with jazz drummers at the top: "If there were not general agreement among drummers that jazz players are "better" than rock players, the boundaries between rock and jazz drummers would still exist, but they would likely separate two different but equal groups" (Curran, 1996: 48). The word "better" is in quotes here because this is sociology. That jazz drummers do in fact have more developed technique, can often play rock (where the obverse is not so), and bring the drums more to the foreground than is usually the case in rock, where the drummer focuses more on keeping time, is what drummers mean by "better," as Curran points out. The article concludes with a call for the breaking down of barriers between the two styles and for an end to rigid classifications of how drumming works in jazz and in rock.

Curran's account excludes too many examples of crossovers between rock and jazz; British progressive rock, rather than Frank Zappa (whom Curran cites), would provide several examples of drummers who play carefully composed art-rock music (not jazz) using jazz drumming styles – Bill Bruford, Carl Palmer, Phil Collins, and Pip Pyle come to mind. But Curran is essentially correct in his description of premechanized drumming, even if he is silent on the virtues of introducing new modes of drumming into preexisting genres, which are taken for granted. Curran's one comment on drum machines is as follows: "In this age of drum machines which sound a lot like (and to some ears, better than) drummers, it is not surprising that drummers rest their identities and find comfort in their bounded world of categories" (Curran, 1996: 56). However, the relationship between drumming and the new technologies is a little more complex than this, and in fact addresses Curran's goal of bridging different styles.

Drum machines have certainly changed the function of the drummer in live performance. These days it might be the keyboard player who sets the tempo, from a click track to which the drummer might be playing. If you had seen the set list for the Rolling Stones Voodoo Lounge tour, for example, you would know that every song was timed out, *to the second*, and from a count that was often set by a keyboard player. But even in this case Townsend's dictum still applies – once the tune kicks off, Charlie Watts, that professor emeritus of time-keeping who these days gets his kicks from playing jazz, still has less to go on than his bandmates do.

His room to maneuver is, however, significantly curtailed, as is Mick Jagger's ability to change the set or improvise his patter between songs, since the gaps between the songs are also timed out on the set list. In fact, Mick Jagger has less space for spontaneity than we professors enjoy on an average day in the lecture theater. He is now trapped in the Rolling Stones machinery, even as the band engages in what is widely, and wrongly, perceived as the most authentic and spontaneous moment in the cycle of pop production. In this respect, we see further evidence for the argument that pop is becoming more and more like cinema, and less and less like theater.

Yet with regard to drumming, I am struck by one key similarity between the old flesh-and-blood "spontaneity" and the new machinery. As a drummer, one trains the body to memorize patterns and moves until the memory can be recalled and reproduced at will. Hitting a good groove as a player is an almost Zen-like practice involving both awareness and effortlessness; thus, there is also a distancing and a forgetting that goes on in the training of a drummer, too. For "independence" is impossible without the ability to "forget" that your right hand is playing four-to-the-bar, while your left foot is playing threes. Syncopation, the very essence of rock "grooviness," relies upon the drummer's ability to play off the beat (ahead, behind, in between), without forgetting "where," mathematically speaking, the music is. Similarly, while the drummer must know key figures and tropes (if not the rudiments, then at least the basic pattern of, say, a reggae beat – this is what Volosinov [1986] might have called the "inner speech" of the drummer), it is also necessary to know how to use them without simply repeating clichés. The great strength of the drum machine in this respect is that it may encourage the programmer to avoid the tried and tested conventions that the body unthinkingly repeats. The famous drum break that interrupts New Order's "Blue Monday" is a good example of a fill that few drummers would have considered trying to play, not only because it would be technically quite demanding, but because it is just very slightly removed from what one's hands and feet would normally do with a rock drum set.

The inner speech of the drummer is, then, a problem, from Curran's point of view, since this language system, once internalized, prevents drummers from using their imaginations to the full. There is some irony here. For if one wants to reproduce a groove, "real" playing will often be looped and perhaps sampled, because a few bars of keenly syncopated playing are quite hard to write into a machine. Sometimes, for instance, where a drum machine has been used, a drummer will be brought in to add cymbals and hi-hat on a kit, to give the drum track a real feel. On the other hand, if one wants not a simple groove, but something shocking and different, it is often the computer or the drum machine than can provide it, unhindered as it is by the "thought communities" of flesh-and-blood musicians. (Provided, that is, that the programmer is either not a drummer at all, or someone who has specialized in programming.) I am thinking here, for instance, of the work of drum programmer Keith Le Blanc, and of the percussion parts executed by him (and others) in the recordings of producer Adrian Sherwood.

In a sense, then, the human body is simply a precursor to the drum machine – a device that remembers rhythms. In this respect, the cold mechanical features of the machine merely *embody* the phenomenon that musicians, critics and fans claim to dread – a *mechanical* reproduction. One thinks of the story of Brian Eno, who is purported to have quit Roxy Music after he found himself on stage wondering about whether or not he had taken his laundry off the washing line.[2] That other British art-rock quitter, Peter Gabriel, wrote a song about this, which celebrates walking out of the machinery.[3]

I want to suggest, then, that it is a paradox of contemporary music production that self-consciously programming a machine may well free the musician from overly memorized routines.[4] It seems to me that in recent years British pop, and dance music, and hip-hop the world over, have been more innovative than American rock and pop for precisely this reason. On the US scene it is to the mechanized musics of rap and techno that one looks for sonic and structural innovations. And there is no small paradox in noting that sampling and computer-based technologies have generated music that is unarguably more original than that produced by the traditional human centered rock "band".[5]

However, programming drum machines, which has now been largely superceded in any case by the use of computer software (which triggers the drums via MIDI), has now established its own routines and norms, from which pop is in urgent need of release. Recording drums was not so long ago the craft of reproducing the sound of a drum kit. As one trains the limbs to hit specific parts of the kit with hands and feet, that kit takes on a particular dimension. Certain predictable patterns emerge. I still cannot play a drum part into a computer via a keyboard without my right hand reaching for the hi-hat and my left for the snare drum, as I would seated at a drum set. An early skill that can be learned on the simplest of drum machines is to program in a manner that reproduces kit drumming, so as to create the illusion that acoustic drums were used. Then of course the next move is to invent new patterns – hand claps on the first beat of the bar, a cowbell playing the kick drum (bass drum) part, snare rim-shots in place of the hi-hat, and so on. This technique was developed in the 1980s and has taken on a new dimension with jungle, or hard step, or drum and bass, where the rhythmic patterns are rendered at a tempo that few pop drummers would attempt. Dance music drum programming routinely announces its machinelike qualities, with grooves that make no attempt to reproduce the patterns that would be deployed by a real-time drummer.

If there is something reminiscent of punk in this strategy, then I think we can see the link – in what is called "Brit-pop" – between the dance music of acts like Goldie, Portishead, and Everything But the Girl, and the guitar pop of bands like Oasis, the Bluetones, Lush, and Echobelly. Both refuse the particular version of funkiness that was introduced, towards the end of the 1980s, by computers and sampled grooves. There was a period in the early 1990s when it seemed that every song from a new act used the drum track from James Brown's "Funky Drummer." While this was a welcome nod towards pop's African American roots, it also made it less accessible to many musicians. That groove is very difficult to play and needs a considerable degree of competence to play *around*. Sampling it (or something like it) is an option. But in this respect the democratic features of sampling technologies have perhaps been overstated. For once it was established that the *creative* use of sampling involved *changing* the original sample (a tactic that had its roots in legal strategy every bit as much as aesthetics) then the stakes were upped, in time-honored tradition, and once again the means of musical production were found at some distance from workaday or amateur musicians. There are several reasons for this.

In the first place, changing samples often involves mixing them with other samples or "original" drumming or drum machine patterns, which makes the whole process more complex than simply copping a riff from your favorite record. Second, samplers and computer software developed so fast that the ability to program on the latest machinery became a specialized skill. That is why studios and producers will often employ engineers and programmers who specialize in particular kinds of equipment. Third, in aesthetic terms the 1980s ushered in an era where it was considered de rigeur to create synthetic and sampled textures that were original – not merely copied from a sample, or called up from a preprogrammed, preset sound.

This requires time and more specialized knowledge. In this respect, fears that the new technologies would replace musicianship were misplaced. The very opposite was the case, and the problem: Only musicians, engineers and producers had the time and the competence to keep up with technological developments. Furthermore, the highly produced and layered nature of the new rock and pop meant that sophisticated outboard effects and processing devices were needed – devices that usually went beyond the budget of a bedroom or basement studio. The simple grooves and textures of jungle, trip-hop, and of Brit-pop (like lo-fi in the United States) have in common a desire to make music production more accessible once again. A radical example of this is the shift in the music of Blur from the "baggy" 1991 sound of their hit "There's No Other Way" to the more straightahead punk patterns of "Jubilee" (1994).[6]

Law played its part here, too. In defence of its intellectual property, the music industry began policing the use of samples, making the semiotic guerrilla tactics of hip-hop less attractive.[7] Of course, the new technologies had, to some degree, negated the need to sample. With the use of "virtual tracks" and MIDI, computer software enabled musicians and producers to program parts and then select among hundreds of different options in terms of texture and timbre. This made it easier to fake samples. I know from experience that it is sometimes easier now to copy, rather than sample. On seeking a pastiche of Propaganda's piece "Jewel,"[8] I discovered during one recording session that it was in fact quicker and easier to copy the drum pattern, enter it via software, and then select the right sounds, than it would have been to sample the groove. This occurs because of two factors: the new flexibility in software when it comes to rhythm; and the range of timbres available in many of today's drum boxes.

III

The song "Professor of Pop" by the band I play with, Theory Sluts, was recorded for pleasure, and not as an exercise in participant-observation. However, it was impossible not to notice things during the recording process, many of which indicated how much times have changed – not only since the days of playing kit drums in real bands, but even from the early days of mechanization and recording with drum machines. There was much to be learned here about the effects of the new technologies on music-making dynamics and the process of decision making. Indeed, one might say that increasingly a music-making project *is* a decision-making exercise, first and foremost. "Professor of Pop" was recorded, like a great deal of modern pop, by a small group of people who stood around a computer terminal for much of the time. A microphone was used for some vocals, and "real" guitar was played; but most of the time, three of us simply sat there in a room and made decisions about song structure, rhythm, and timbre. As Brian Eno (1992) has observed: "Artists are people who specialize in judgment rather than skill." The implication of this comment (which is, in my view, only a half-truth — where would Eno be without the skill he has developed in understanding how different synthesizers operate?[9]) is that music practice comes to resemble criticism — the ability to discriminate between the "right" sound and the wrong one; the capacity to select the most effective structure for a song; a knowledge of the current field of practice that enables one to know which sounds and structure will sound current and which would sound old or tired. This is of course the very skill that producers must possess. An acute understanding of timbre is important — and this matters in drumming, too. The gated snare drum sounds deployed on Peter Gabriel's second solo album were so widely recognizable that they became known as "the Phil Collins" drum sound (after the drummer who played on that album and then appropriated this sound) and dominated production (in ever more monstrous proportions) throughout the first half of the 1980s.

Like music itself, timbre is a powerful memory-trigger.[10] Pull the wrong trigger, and you can shoot yourself in the foot. When the band Counting Crows set off to record their hugely successful debut album *August and Everything After* with producer T-Bone Burnett, a million dollars was spent in southern California, in an effort to reproduce the simplicity of the band's demo tapes.[11] The key production tactic was apparently Burnett's understanding that an overproduced recording using the latest effects and processors too obviously would be one that was tied to a particular moment in time. To create a "classic," timeless piece of music, such memory-triggers had to go.

Of course critics and producers usually ply their trade alone, where musicians work in groups. "Professor of Pop" was recorded on an eight-track ADAT machine, with many of the parts existing as "virtual tracks" on the computer.[12] It has been suggested that technologies such as multitracking inhibit interaction between musicians. Yet the existence of virtual tracks dilutes and perhaps even reverses this trend.

The flexibility of virtual tracks is such that it becomes quite simple and time efficient to change parts in relation to newly recorded multitracked (or virtual-tracked) parts. After drums and a bass-line were laid down via the computer, vocals and two guitar tracks were recorded onto ADAT. It was then possible to alter the keyboard parts to accommodate the voice and guitar, literally with the click of a mouse. Of course the great difficulty with this system lies in its capacity to delay decisions about timbre. Producers have often bemoaned the fact that 64-track mixers and so forth allow the moment of truth to be avoided for too long concerning which performances should be kept. Virtual tracks also allow for an infinite combination of sound textures to be deployed at mix-down – even with some material on ADAT, almost everything beyond the actual structure of the song could be decided upon at the mixing stage.

As pop becomes more and more a producer's and programmer's medium, so it increasingly is a sphere of composition, as opposed to performance. This has implications for the debate about whether or not theories of "serious" music (symphonic, classical, and so forth) have anything to say to students of pop. For it is an axiom of the critics of traditional musicology that pop is unlike symphonic music in that performance supersedes composition (see Baugh, 1993). It is a sign of progress that pop scholars have been able to mark out territory for research that transcends the approach to more conventional musics; nonetheless, I suspect that we will find a merging of the two areas in the future, and perhaps a new appreciation of what the two have in common. James O. Young has argued that pop theorists too often exaggerate the differences between serious music and pop, arguing that "a good classical performance can be expressive, stress the beauty of individual notes, bear a loose relation to a score, inspire the body to movement, be very loud, and employ unsophisticated means of expression." (Young, 1993: 98)

Despite both the new flexibility of technologies like virtual tracks, and the extent to which they override the moment of performance, accidents will happen; and accidents are of course at the heart of the rock aesthetic. One can think of dozens, perhaps hundreds of examples. A favorite example that triggers happy memories for me, because I recall hearing this song in my head (repeating it from the radio) during a Biology class at school and anticipating the moment of purchase, is that wonderful introduction to the T. Rex song "Jeepster," which is in fact the sound of Marc Bolan jumping up and down, as accidentally amplified via the microphone stand.[13]

Computer technologies could edit those sounds out these days, and we are hardly likely ever again to hear a major band like Led Zeppelin begin a song ("Celebration Day") in a very peculiar and exciting place simply because someone inadvertently wiped the introduction from the master tape. But what of the accidents that will happen using the new technologies? Are these to be different kinds of accidents? Strange problems can arise can using the new systems. By clicking on the wrong sound, we happened upon the odd brasslike texture that interrupts our song "Professor of Pop" on two occasions. None of us had thought of using such a sound – the mouse found it for us. At an early stage, we made a mistake that could never have occured in a regular band. By miscalculating the number of bars, we cut-and-pasted a structure for the song and left out a 16-bar instrumental sequence. This would have been easily remedied, except that we did not discover this until after the voices had gone onto ADAT. Thus the 16-bar section could only have been reinstated had we re-recorded the vocals. Since there was no time for this, we decided to like the new structure. It is almost inconceivable that a band playing in real time would make such a mistake – for the drummer would have memorized the song structure and noticed the gap. Had the drums been programmed on a machine in what is now the "old-fashioned" way, this error is also hard to imagine – the drum programmer would lay down a structure and have a very clear idea of the different sections in his or her head. Perhaps, then, as with the word processor and its effects on writing, computer recording and composition is going to generate its own results, including perhaps its own sloppiness, its own mistakes, and its own miscalculations.

IV

The new technologies certainly open up ever more sophisticated possibilities for recalling the past, for dialing into a collective pop memory. I have tried to show how this is the case not only for sampling music computers, but also via virtual tracks and the increasing number of options available to music-makers.

But to speak of a collective pop memory is to beg the question: whose memory?[14] Counting Crows delighted millions and repulsed many of us because their sound was so redolent of soft rock from the late 1960s, perhaps early 1970s. This, for T-Bone Burnett, sounds 'timeless.' Just as readings of the analog synthesizer changed from "cold" to "warm" in the space of a few years (and in part because of the advent of digital keyboards), so the "cold" mechanical drumming of today's jungle sound is affective – we might conclude not because of its inherent features, but because of its function within a system of difference.

None of this means that we have entered a postmodern moment that is his-toryless and postmemory. I want to end by suggesting that the postmodernisms in some of their features are symptoms of a generation of intellectuals who expected the young to forget the past, only to find that a mediascape scored both for and by baby boomers, which is unsurprisingly awash with music from the sixties, eventually generated two responses. On the one hand, there is an antirock shift to postrock[15] (Flying Saucer Attack, My Bloody Valentine, Stere-olab) and prerock forms (Tony Bennett, easy listening, space-age bachelor pad music, John Barry soundtracks). On the other, there is so much "new" music res-onant with memories – of punk (Green Day, Rancid, Elastica, Offspring), pro-gressive rock (the Orb, Porcupine Tree), the Beatles (Nirvana, Oasis, Guided by Voices), the Who (Paul Weller, Cast), James Brown (the Artist Formerly Known as Prince, Public Enemy), and the Grateful Dead (Blues Traveler).

We do not know very much about how today's listeners hear this music, but it is clear that a major element in consuming pop these days is what Adorno called "part-interchangeablity," and what others term "pastiche." In an exploration of time and memory in music Alfred Schutz comes to this conclusion: "The composer, by the specific means of his art, has arranged it in such a way that the consciousness of the beholder is led to refer what he actually hears to what he anticipates will follow and also to what he has just been hearing and what he has heard ever since this piece of music began. The hearer, therefore, listens to the ongoing flux of music, so to speak, not only in the direction from the first to the last bar but simultaneously in a reverse direction back to the first one" (Schutz, 1964: 170). Pop, of course, operates differently than a symphony. Nonetheless, Schutz offers a useful comment on how music is listened to, and the parallel with pop, obviously enough, is that its repetition allows us to "listen back" towards three discrete moments: to previous instances when we heard this same recording; to the particular memories that it might trigger; and to the musical forms from which it draws its material (familiar lyrics, chord progressions, guitar tim-bres, drum patterns, etc.). The music industry is too fond of gimmicks for us to deny the pertinence of Adorno's notion of "pseudo-individualization,"[16] but it is clear also that we individualize pop through more personal narra-tives that continue to elude the culture industry, as a result of music's peculiar ability to trigger memories. Schutz has something to say about this: "It can be said that the social relationship between performer and listener is founded upon the common experience of living simultaneously in several dimensions of time" (Schutz, 1964: 175). That is to say, the intimacy of music, its ability to get under our skin, is founded at least in part on the illusion of *shared time* spent with the performer and/or composer.

Of course, popular music introduces a new element into this process. Ever since teenagers have had their "own" music, pop has accompanied us from adolescence to adulthood (now, with baby boomers stretching into their fifties, with little sign of the connection breaking down because of age) and some artists have been associated with the ability to develop and "grow up" with us (the Beatles, Bob Dylan, Stevie Wonder, Bruce Springsteen, Pete Townshend, Madonna, Paul Weller). So pop's use of time is especially intense, and the shared journey is one that flows with the star-text, as well as with the music.

If memory is collective, and if the collective memory of pop began sometime around 1954, then youth today has more to remember than ever before. However, its use of memory, like its deployment of sampling technologies, cannot be adequately understood from the point of view of a modernist rock criticism that fetishizes "originals." Rock's originals were always much less original than we thought, as Deena Weinstein points out in the next chapter and as Kevin Holm-Hudson (1996), among others, has argued. And the rock "pastiche" of, say, Oasis (when I saw the band in San Francisco, they played the Who nonstop before taking the stage, which almost answered my teenage question) is neither lacking in originality, nor is it "blank" or parodic in nature. That the rhythms and timbres of the past are alive for this generation suggests a sense of history and an interest in a collective pop memory, albeit one that is different than that of the baby boomers, whose insistence on decrying today's music for failing to rebel in the "correct" manner remains both funny and sad.

NOTES

1. For a fascinating series of interviews and profiles dealing with this issue, see Armbruster (1984) For a more critical discussion, see Theberge (forthcoming).

2. This story came to me courtesy of Lucy O'Brien. For a detailed discussion of Eno and his career, see Tamm (1989).

3. The song is "Solsbury Hill," from Gabriel's first solo album.

4. This argument, which I am about to undermine, is elaborated further in my essay (Goodwin, 1991).

5. I am not arguing that one kind of music is "better" than the other, or that originality is necessarily desirable. My point is simply that Orbital is more imaginative than Pearl Jam.

6. Available on Blur's albums *Leisure* and *Parklife,* respectively.

7. See Negativland (1995) and Cutler.

8. From their album *A Secret Wish*.

9. See Jim Aikin's interview with Eno, in Armbruster (1984), and also Tamm (1989).

10. Grimshaw (1996).

11. I am grateful to Steve Bowman for this information.

12. "Virtual tracks" are not commited to the multitrack tape, existing only as computerized information that is fed, usually via MIDI, directly to a sound source, and thereafter to whatever mastering system records the final mix. For further discussion, see Goodwin (1991).

13. "The footstomps you hear at the beginning of that weren't overdubbed or anything, that was just an enthusiastic Marc Bolan jumping up and down on the floor while he was laying his guitar live, and shaking the mike stands" (Visconti, 1982). "Jeepster" is available on the album *Electric Warrior*.

14. For an informative discussion of this issue, and in my view a model approach that could be applied to pop, see Schudson (1992).

15. On "postrock," see Reynolds (1990).

16. See Adorno (1990).

17 See Theodor Adorno (with George Simpson), "On Popular Music", reprinted in Simon Frith & Andrew Goodwin (eds.), *On Record: Rock, Pop, and the Written Word*. New York: Pantheon.

References

Adorno, T. (with G. Simpson). 1990. "On Popular Music." In *On Record: Rock, Pop, and the Written Word*, edited by S. Frith and A. Goodwin. New York: Pantheon.

Armbruster, G. (ed.). 1984. *The Art of Electronic Music*. New York: Quill/A Keyboard Book.

Baugh, B. 1993. "Prolegomena to Any Aesthetics of Rock Music." *Journal of Aesthetics and Art Criticism* 51 (1) (Winter 1993): 90–107.

Curran, G. 1992. "Dancing in the Distraction Factory." In *Dancing in the Distraction Factory*, edited by A. Goodwin, 40–58. Minneapolis: University of Minnesota Press.

Cutler, C. 1995. "Plunderphonics." In *Sounding Off: Music as Subversion/Resistance/Revolution*, edited by R. Sakolsky and F. Wei-Han Ho, 57–72. New York: Autonomedia.

Eno, B. 1992. "Interview with Brian Eno." *Mix*.

Fish, S. 1995. *Professional Correctness: Literary Studies and Political Change*. New York: Oxford.

Goodwin, A. 1991. "Rationalization and Democratization in the New Technologies of Pop Production." In *Popular Music and Communication* (2nd ed.), edited by J. Lull, 146–60. Newbury Park: Sage.

Grimshaw, M. 1996. "Remix Technologies: Sound and Music," paper presented at the Drake Conference on Popular Music. March 29–30, Des Moines: Drake University

Holm-Hudson, K. 1996. "Sampling and John Oswald's Plunderphonics: Quotation and Context," paper presented at the Drake Conference on Popular Music. March 29–30, Des Moines: Drake University.

Negativland. 1995. *Fair Use: The Story of the Letter 'U' and the Numeral '2'*. Concord: Seeland.

Reynolds, S. 1990. *Blissed Out: The Raptures of Rock*. London: Serpent's Tail.

Schudson, M. 1992. *Watergate in American Memory: How We Remember, Forget, and Reconstruct the Past*. New York: Basic Books.

Schutz, A. 1964. "Making Music Together: A Study in Social Relationships." *Collected Papers. Volume II: Studies in Social Theory*, 102–09. The Hague: Martinus-Nijhoff.

Tamm, E. 1989. *Brian Eno: His Music and Vertical Color of Sound*. Boston: Faber and Faber.

Theberge, P. (In press). *Any Sound You Can Imagine*. Middletown: Wesleyan University Press.

Tobler, J. and S. Grundy (eds.). 1982. *The Record Producers*. London: BBC.

Volosinov, V. [1929] 1986. *Marxism and the Philosophy of Language*. Cambridge: Harvard University Press.

Walser, R. 1993. *Running with the Devil: Power, Gender and Madness in Heavy Metal Music*. Hanover: Wesleyan University Press.

Young, J. O. 1993. "Between Rock and a Harp Place." *Journal of Aesthetics and Art Criticism* 51 (1) (Winter 1993): 69–91.

7

— The History of Rock's Pasts — through Rock Covers

Deena Weinstein

s rock slouches in 4/4 time to the millennium, it is up to its ringing ears in history. There are tribute albums, several "history of rock" TV miniseries repackaged as video collections, a plethora of bands such as the Rolling Stones reprising their own larger-than life history on gargantuan stages, major record labels growing fat on CD reissues, and dozens of tribute bands. If that isn't enough of the past in the present, there's the Rock and Roll Hall of Fame. Rock is dead. Long live rock?

Rock proclaims, as it always has, the now, the new beginning, the absolute origin. But like all cultural forms, it is intertextual, always already immersed in a past. My argument in this chapter, then, is that rock has always referenced a past, despite its "nowness," but that the way it has referenced the past has changed significantly over time. I want to describe both the historiography and the history of these references – that is, the differing ways in which the "past" has been constructed by and functioned for rock in different rock eras.

I will explore this history – through one of the major forms of rock's intertextuality, the cover song, which is intrinsically a relation to the past.

Cover songs, in the fullest sense of the term, are peculiar to rock music, both for technological and ideological reasons. A cover song iterates (with more or fewer differences) a prior recorded performance of a song by a particular artist, rather than simply the song itself as an entity separate from any performer or performance. When the song itself (as opposed to the performance) is taken as the reference for iteration, each performer does a version or a rendition of the song, and none of these versions is a necessary reference. Forms of popular music other than rock, then, generally do not have covers as I have defined them; rather, they have versions.

Technologically, the electronic reproduction of the performance in recordings makes it practical to take a particular recorded performance as one's reference for iteration, rather than an abstracted "song" per se. But covering a song also presupposes an ideological element. That is, the practice assumes that the "original" recorded performance is privileged, and that in some way the song belongs to that performance and by extension to the original performer.

The following discussion will show that the rock cover has changed its signification over time. I'll briefly define three epistemic breaks that have distinctive relationships to the past – individually, they mark a modern, a modernist, and a postmodern moment in rock's history.

THE PAST AS ETERNAL NOW: FIFTIES COVERS

"Sh-Boom," Crew Cuts, 1954
        (Original: Chords, 1954)

"Shake, Rattle and Roll," Bill Haley, 1954
        (Original: Joe Turner, 1954)

"Ain't That a Shame," Pat Boone, 1955
        (Original: Fats Domino, 1955)

"Hound Dog," Elvis Presley, 1956
        (Original: Willie Mae Thornton, 1953)

Rock 'n' roll emerged from an amalgam of rhythm & blues ("race music" rechristened for commerce), country and western music, and pop music, some time during the first half of the 1950s. This reflected the appearance of a definable youth market on the economic side, and the emergence of a distinctive youth culture on the ideological side. Rock 'n' roll might be said to be coconstituted by a relation to its immediate past – by covers. "Sh-Boom," for example, originally done by the Chords, was a hit on the R & B chart in 1954. By July of that year, it also made the Top 10 on the pop charts when the Crew Cuts' cover of that song was issued. The Crew Cuts'"whiter" version made the pop Top 10 one week after its release.

Not all covers in the 1950s were covers in the full sense of involving reference to a particular performance, but they were appropriations of current recorded music within genres, across genres, and into genres-in-formation. Cover songs during the decade were done for commercial purposes – the original was seldom something the intended audience had heard. That is, although 1950s covers constituted a relation to the (immediate) past, that relation was not generally grasped by most audiences as it was not part of their listening experience. In the 1950s so many of the originals had been released only a few months prior to covers that even if some in the audience did know the original, they did not attach any particular past to it. Mid-1950s rock 'n' roll was constituted by timeless moments of now; the past was an eternal present.

Most 1950s covers modified the original in order to reach a wider and whiter audience. One type of modification was merely to cover the original using artists on a major label that had greater marketing clout than the independent label on which the original had appeared.[1] When the sound of the cover was as close as possible to the original it was called, at the time, a "copy."

Successful cover records combined both commercial and aesthetic mediations. Often a few words were changed to make the lyrics less racy. Georgia Gibbs's cover of Etta James's "Wallflower" is a case in point. "Wallflower" was an "answer" record to "Work With Me, Annie" by Hank Ballard and the Midnighters.[2] Ballard's song used the word "work" as a double entendre for sex, imploring Annie to "work with me" and to "give me all my meat." James's reply, "Wallflower," using a similar tune and arrangement, challenged Henry's dancing ability (a code for sexual potency). Gibbs's cover, released by Mercury Records, retitled the song "Dance with Me, Henry," burying the sexual double entendre more deeply.

In general, the covers of 1954 and 1955 transformed the R & B arrangements in the direction of pop. Singers' voices were chosen for polish, rather than rawness, and their enunciation of the lyrics was clear, not gritty, as in many of the originals. Moreover, in contrast to the R & B arrangements, pop clearly segregated the vocal and instrumental parts of the song, subordinating the instrumentals. This Tin Pan Alley style allowed the Crew Cuts, the McGuire Sisters, and Pat Boone, among others, to have hit records covering more raw, mainly black, and generally indie-label, artists.

The mediation between the R & B and pop styles of the early rock 'n' roll covers served to make many white artists popular, while providing paltry songwriting royalties to mainly black musicians. In this way marginalized music crossed over to a white youth audience that was not yet prepared for its full counterhegemonic impact. By 1956, the ears of the white youth audience had been trained away from their parents' pop, and the ministrations of white pop musicians were no longer needed. In that year, Little Richard's "Tutti-Frutti" was a bigger hit than Pat Boone's criminally bland cover.[3]

Elvis built his early career on covers and succeeded in avoiding sounding like either black R & B or (before his Hollywood-Las Vegas careers) white Tin Pan Alley. His first record for Sun was a double-sided cover, Arthur "Big Boy" Cruddup's "That's All Right" backed by Bill Monroe's "Blue Moon of Kentucky."

By 1958 "rock 'n' roll" was transformed (aided by Dick Clark, major record labels, and ASCAP) into the domesticated-for-mass-consumption "rock and roll." With this change, rock became self-conscious of its own history. Songs from the first era became "oldies," grouped in radio formats and snipped into collages in novelty records.

THE PAST AS AUTHENTIC SOURCE: SIXTIES COVERS

"Roll Over Beethoven," Beatles, 1964
        (Original: Chuck Berry, 1956)

"I'm a King Bee," Rolling Stones, 1964
        (Original: Slim Harpo, 1957)

"House of the Risin' Sun," Animals, 1964
          (Original: Bob Dylan, 1962/Anon.)

"Mr Tambourine Man," Byrds, 1965
          (Original: Bob Dylan, 1965)

"All Along the Watchtower," Jimi Hendrix, 1968
          (Original: Bob Dylan, 1968)

The British Invasion hit the American shores in early 1964.[4] It was a modern "retro" movement, reviving the cultural menace that rock 'n' roll had been at its inception, and reclaiming rock, once again, for the young. Led by the Beatles and the Rolling Stones, the invaders used weapons that were stamped, almost illegibly, "made in the USA," to conquer the American youth market. Cover songs were a staple of the invaders' early arsenal, but unlike the covers of the 1950s, these were covers with a past.

The 1950s cover usurps the original, asserts itself as freestanding, and functions as its own absolute beginning. The 1950s cover constitutes a relation to the past by negating that past. But in the 1960s British bands constituted for themselves a new relation to their origins, which were the components of the initial rock amalgam and its crystallization in early rock 'n' roll. Rather than seeking to usurp or efface these origins, British bands celebrated them and in doing so used them to validate their own authenticity as musicians.

The music of the early Beatles and Rolling Stones is saturated with intertextuality beyond the cover songs themselves. Belz (1969: 128) and other critics contend that "early Beatles records contained an encyclopedia of Chuck Berry guitar licks, Buddy Holly harmonies, and Little Richard falsettos." The early British invasion nodded to American black music at the same time that Americans were involved in the Civil Rights movement and Motown was supplying homegrown blackened pop.

The Beatles chose songs that had been successful in the United States. Many covers found their way into their April 1964 album (Beatles' Second Album), including Chuck Berry's "Roll Over Beethoven," Little Richard's

"Long Tall Sally," and the Marvellettes's Motown hit, "Please Mr. Postman." In contrast, the Rolling Stones tended toward covers of songs found on the R & B charts, such as "Time is on My Side" by Irma Thomas, Slim Harpo's "I'm a King Bee," and Jimmy Reed's "Honest I Do."

As the episteme of 1960s rock crystallized, it included new emphases on the original sources of rock 'n' roll and new sources of authenticity. The Delta blues and its Chicago and Detroit offspring became the sources of white blues rock. Bands such as John Mayall's Blues Breakers, the Yardbirds, and Cream covered blues songs. (They also helped to resurrect the careers of older, underappreciated bluesmen.) The blues-rock audience was, at least initially, unfamiliar with the originals, but no doubt heard the covers as referencing "real blues." Examples of blues-rock covers include Cream's Howlin' Wolf covers ("Spoonful" and "Sitting on Top of the World"), the Yardbirds' cover of Bo Diddley's "I'm a Man," and Led Zeppelin's cover of Muddy Waters'"I Can't Quit You Baby."

In the last part of the 1960s, cover songs were done less frequently. They tended to be relegated to B-sides and encore material at live shows, distancing the band from material that it didn't write, while at the same time maintaining some connection with authentic origins. The modern romantic notion of authenticity – creating out of one's own resources – became dominant over the idea that authenticity constituted a relationship, through creative repetition, to an authentic source.[5]

Notable examples of covers at the time, however, included the many covers of Bob Dylan's songs, such as Jimi Hendrix's "All Along the Watchtower." Moreover, about this time, as rock performance became increasingly skewed toward a style of the arena-rock spectacle, a style that indexed the general reactionary political and cultural moment, authenticity increasingly became a pose. This was most clearly expressed in the singer-songwriter style, made popular by Joni Mitchell, Jackson Browne, James Taylor, Carole King, Neil Young, Paul Simon, and John Denver. "And the appeal of each of them," Janet Maslin (1980) contends, "at least initially, had far less to do with either singing or song writing, than with the sheer allure of personality."

FRAGMENTARY PASTS: SEVENTIES COVERS

The Romantic Continuation: Heavy Metal

"Green Manalishi (With the Two-Pronged Crown)", Judas Priest, 1978
(Original: Fleetwood Mac, 1970)

"Beethoven's Ninth," Rainbow, 1980
(Original: Beethoven, 1823)

Slayer, "In-A-Gadda-Da-Vida," 1986
(Original: Iron Butterfly, 1968)

Megadeth, "Anarchy in the U.K.," 1988
(Original: Sex Pistols, 1977)

Heavy metal, initiated by the ur-metal band Black Sabbath, continued the blues-rock tradition of the 1960s. Black Sabbath did not do covers, in part, the band said, because no extant songs embodied their vision of existence (an inversion of the "love" of the counterculture). As the style of heavy music became a genre with a subcultural audience, some bands did covers, but, as in the 1950s, the audience had not often heard the originals. For example, Judas Priest, definers of the classic metal that came to dominate the late-1970s and early-1980s heavy-metal sound, redid early Fleetwood Mac's blues-rock "Green Manalishi (With The Two-Pronged Crown)." The song became a well-loved anthemic staple of Priest's repertoire; hardly any fans knew the original, or even that there was one.[6]

Metal did not acknowledge a premetal past. The classical music motifs and the few metal covers of modern classical music (Rainbow's rendition of the fourth movement of Beethoven's Symphony no. 9; Manowar's remakes of the "William Tell Overture" and "Flight of the Bumblebee"; and Accept's "Metal Heart," a remake of Beethoven's "Für Elyse") were not meant to provide an authenticity rooted in a valorization of the past, but to validate and proclaim a musical virtuosity valued by the subculture.

The Past as Object of Parody: Punk Covers

"Eve of Destruction," Dickies, 1978
        (Original: Barry McGuire, 1965)

"Viva Las Vegas," Dead Kennedys, 1981
        (Original: Elvis Presley, 1964)

"Eight Miles High," Hüsker Dü, 1983
        (Original: Byrds, 1966)

A new episteme emerged with the eruption of punk rock in the mid-1970s. As a fundamentalism in revolt, punk drew much of its vitality from its engagement with the musical past. Punk adopted intentions ranging from playful irony laced with tribute, to scathing, high-energy parody. Following the example of the Ramones, covers became a common punk practice. But punk covers were of a different order then previous rock covers. They tended to be stereophonic, depending for their full impact on the audience being acquainted with the originals and thus reminding listeners of the past. Punk covers deconstructed their originals, removing and/or exaggerating the pretty, the pompous, and the pop. The audience's knowledge of the original allowed it to hear punk's fast and raw style more clearly. The Ramones' revision of the Contours'"Do You Wanna Dance?" the Dead Kennedys' remake of the bloated late-Elvis trademark, "Viva Las Vegas," and the Dickies' sarcastic delivery of Barry McGuire's "Eve of Destruction" all subverted the originals by transposing them to an irreverent musical attitude.[7]

Through parody, the punk cover attacked the conventions of authenticity in rock as pompous, pretentious, and (laughably) lame. The punk cover took the new position of distancing criticism, opening up an intentional gap in attitude between original and cover that had not been present before. Covers in the 1950s often attempted to escape their status and be taken as self standing (perfect simulation where the simulation substitutes for the reference), whereas 1960s covers paid homage to their referents. Punk covers negated the originals without attempting to obliterate them; consequently, they keep the originals in play by constituting themselves over and against them.

THE PAST AS ARCHIVE FOR APPROPRIATION: EIGHTIES AND NINETIES COVERS

"Mrs. Robinson," Lemonheads, 1993
  (Original: Simon and Garfunkel, 1968)

"Girl You'll Be a Woman Soon," Urge Overkill, 1995
  (Original: Neil Diamond, 1968)

"Lay, Lady, Lay," Ministry, 1996
  (Original: Bob Dylan, 1969)

"Unplugged" albums by Eric Clapton, Nirvana, Rolling Stones, etc.

Tribute albums to Kiss, Tom Petty, Jimi Hendrix, Joy Division,
  Thin Lizzy, John Lennon, Black Sabbath, etc.

The postmodernist, postpunk moment of rock music negates punk's negation of the 1960s, not in order to restore authenticity, but to explore the gap opened up by punk between original and cover. The past now becomes not something to transcend, to honor, or to criticize and parody, but something to appropriate. Facilitated by audio technologies that allow sampling, the postmodern past is transformed in any way that one wishes.

In the postmodern moment, covers are no longer relegated to the periphery but share the center with original work. The raw material of rock is no longer life, but culture. If God is dead and all things are allowed, the god that was knocked off by punk was the myth of the individual, along with its master name, Authenticity. Musicians can now plunder the past with abandon. The immediate postpunk "new wave" did covers, but extended reinterpretations far beyond parody. Devo's cover of one of the most central and praised rock songs of all time, "(I Can't Get No) Satisfaction," fully removed the romantic individual from the first-person pronoun.

Postmodern covers are generally stereophonic: the audience is aware of the original and hears the cover in terms of it. Well-known originals are often chosen, but more importantly the audience for rock now is far more knowledgeable about rock's past. The looming presence of the past for the current rock audience and potential creators is a complex phenomena. Rock is no longer confined to adolescents or even youth. Youth became a free-floating signifier in the postmodern moment and many who were young during the 1960s or later see no reason to give up youthful lifestyles and attitudes, including rock music, which is one of the prime signifiers of youth (Weinstein, 1994a).[8] These chronological adults, some pushing into late middle age, want access to the music of their youth.

CD reissues and box sets of extinct rock acts and artists have made record companies fat with profits. New albums by the older bands (including once defunct but now profitably reformed bands, such as the Eagles and the Sex Pistols), and groups sounding like them, have cross-generational appeal. (Indeed, the notion of generations has been blurred in postmodern culture.) Television, Hollywood soundtracks, and retro radio formats ("oldies," "classic rock," "retro flashbacks") make rock's past available to everyone. The most lucrative tours in recent years have been those of Pink Floyd, the Rolling Stones, and the Grateful Dead – all 1960s bands.

Record companies are releasing compilations of the original artists whose songs were the basis for hits by other bands.[9] Most listeners will hear these originals as covers of the far more familiar rock hits. Covers have become so fashionable in the 1990s that the Association of Independent Music Publishers has an award category for "Best Pop Cover Song."

Covers are done in every conceivable way now, ranging from radical modification to slavish imitation. The reasons for doing covers in the postmodern moment are as varied as the ways in which they are done: the commercial advantage of familiarity, homage, introducing obscure artists to a wider audience, gaining credibility, criticizing the past, appropriating a song from one genre into another, demonstrating one's roots, finding the original song to express the cover artists' views or feelings as well as if not better than anything they could write, and lack of creativity.

The so-called hip bands of the 1980s (lumped into a category called "indie rock") played with rock's past via covers. The Rolling Stones' *Exile On Main Street*, released in 1972, was remade by Pussy Galore.[10] Sonic Youth's side project, Ciccone Youth, did a noisy remake of several Madonna (Ciccone) hits in 1988. Hüsker Dü released a souped-up version of the Byrd's

"Eight Miles High" in 1983. R.E.M.'s many covers, including those of "Superman" by the obscure psychedelic band the Clique, and Wire's "Strange," as well as the covers on their 1987 album, *Dead Letter Office*, were never hits as originals, but were influential in underground rock culture. The Residents did a whole album of Elvis covers, *The King and Eye*, which combines the punk practice of deconstructing bloated rock with the postmodern penchant for tribute albums.[11]

Mainstream listeners have heard a fair number of cover songs become hits, including remakes of Neil Diamond's "Red Red Wine" by UB40 and "Girl You'll Be a Woman Soon" by Urge Overkill. Artists such as Guns N' Roses, the Ramones, Slayer, and Pat Boone have put out entire albums of covers.

A torrent of cover songs has flooded the market in the 1990s in the form of tribute albums, in which an artist's songs are covered by a variety of current artists. Tribute albums have become so ubiquitous that record stores stock them in a separate section. Some are put out by indie labels to gain exposure for new, unknown groups. Other compilations have well-known bands doing the covers. (And some even have the tributee producing or playing on the album.) Releases have honored a wide variety of artists, including Kiss, Tom Petty, Kraftwerk, Lynyrd Skynyrd, Richard Thompson, Black Sabbath, Arthur Alexander, Roky Erikson, Van Morrison, and the Carpenters, to name only a handful.[12]

As heavy metal fragmented in the 1980s, both the punk-influenced thrash bands and the more pop and popular hard-rock groups were not averse to doing covers. Metallica redid songs by obscure bands that had influenced them. Megadeth's reworking of the Sex Pistols'"Anarchy in the U.K." has been the highlight of their live show since they recorded it in 1988.[13] Thrash bands have even covered classic heavy-metal songs. For example, Sacred Reich and Faith No More each redid Black Sabbath's "War Pigs," Exodus did AC/DC's "Overdose," and Metal Church revisited Deep Purple's "Highway Star." The pop metal covers that became well known include Great White's cover of Ian Hunter's "Once Bitten Twice Shy," White Lion's reinterpretation of Golden Earring's "Radar Love," and W.A.S.P.'s version of the Who's "The Real Me." (Death metal, more than just commercially underground, is probably the only style that avoids covers.)

Rap and hip-hop practiced their own strategy of aural collage via sampling, exploiting the archive by recombining the past while at the same time affirming authenticity by adopting their own attitude toward the material. Associated with hip-hop, dance mixes are covers of songs specifically made for play at urban clubs. The key to these covers is the use of a drum machine to manufacture a made-for-dancing disco-style beat to any song. Mainstream exposure of this style began with the remixes of Suzanne Vega's "Tom's Diner" and Bruce Springsteen's "Dancing in the Dark." The original Springsteen performance, from the megaplatinum *Born in the USA* album, was well known, helping to promote the cover (Tankel, 1990).

It is no small irony that a feature of the 1990s rock scene, tribute bands (Dasein, 1994), which cover other bands' sounds and images in live shows, honor just those bands, such as Rush, the Rolling Stones, Pink Floyd, and the Doors, that privileged authenticity and the romantic self. Tribute bands do not put out albums; they are only heard live. Without merchandise to sell and without the possibility of large tours, such bands, despite their musical expertise (often exceeding that of the bands to which they pay tribute) are not especially lucrative. Other sorts of tribute bands (let us call them "indexical" bands) skirt the tribute band's limitations. They do not cover the songs but imitate the original band's arrangements and performance style. Kingdom Come indexed Led Zeppelin and Phish indexes the Grateful Dead. This form of intertextuality allows the bands to make albums and have arena tours.[14]

Does the pan-appropriation of the past from a simultaneous archive that makes everything contemporaneous spell cynicism and the passing over of creativity as a value? The situation seems far more complex than that – allowing for, as it does, the emergence of new genres, recurrence to external sources, and, most importantly, authentic appropriation. Perhaps the notion of an authentic relation to the past, in which one draws upon the resources of that past to find oneself in the present, is the living alternative to cynicism in the postmodern moment of rock. Or perhaps, as Simmel noted in "The Metropolis and Mental Life,"(Simmel, 1950) the overwhelming din of the past will finally obliterate people's ability to hear themselves.

NOTES

1. With the Fontaine Sisters, Pat Boone, and other artists, Dot became a major label by doing covers of upcoming R & B songs.

2. "Answer songs" were a common practice in early 1950s R & B that came close to being covers. In answer songs, the words are changed and the new lyrics respond to the original lyrics.

3. Little Richard's "Tutti-Frutti" "was considerably cleaned up and censored before being released in the famous version which went on to become a hit. That immortal tag line from the song 'Awop-Bop-a-Loo-Mop Alop-Bam-Boom' actually began as 'Awop-Bop-a-Loo-Mop-a-Good-Goddam.' Another line expunged was 'Tutti-Frutti good booty – if it don't fit don't force it.' The song was written originally by Richard but a second writer was called in to help provide the cleaner lyrics" (Martin and Segrave, 1988: 73).

4. In April 1964 the top five songs were by the Beatles. Number two was a cover of "Twist and Shout."

5. For a discussion of authentic repetition, see Heidegger (1962).

6. Judas Priest also redid Joan Baez's "Before the Dawn," fully covering over its folky roots.

7. The Dickies did many, including the Moody Blues' "Nights in White Satin."

8. See also Weinstein (1994b) and Weinstein (1995).

9. For example, Yazoo Records released *Roots of Rock* in 1994, a collection of the original renditions of songs made popular by bands including Cream, the Allman Brothers Band, and Led Zeppelin. A similar Rhino release, *Blues Originals* vol. 6, includes originals of songs made famous by Canned Heat, the Yardbirds, Jeff Beck, Elvis Presley, and Led Zeppelin. There is also *Stone Rock Blues*, a CD of the originals that the Rolling Stones covered.

10. Issued as a limited-edition cassette in 1986.

11. "More insidiously perceptive than most critics, the Residents dismantle and rebuild sixteen of his standards, from 'All Shook Up' to 'Burning Love,' offering radical new ways to hear the commonplace. ...Cruelly but kindly pushing the songs to the limits of recognizability, the Residents deliberately strip away everything familiar to reveal previously hidden depths of passion, leering sexuality and gripping drama. Such dusty jewels as 'Viva Las Vegas,' 'Return to Sender' ...and 'Teddy Bear' are reborn in twisted melodies, imposed rhythms, radical rearrangements and distended vocal phrasings rendered with an exaggerated Southern drawl" (Robbins, 1990).

12. "In the best tributes the covering artist steals a song from the original artist and makes it their own, while they keep, even exaggerate, its original spirit. It's a tough trick, demanding authenticity and empathy, but Hasil Adkins pulls it off when, on Turban Renewal, he puts his seriously deranged persona all over "Wooly Bully," opening up a new understanding of the Sam the Sham sobriquet. Megadeth's Dave Mustaine literally absconds with "Paranoid." Sure Ozzy, with and without Black Sabbath, rides a crazy train, but Mustaine has hijacked it and parked it permanently in the paranoid station" (Dasein, 1995).

13. In *So Far, So Good...So What!*

14. Of course, the indexical bands are rather similar to reformed, like the Allman Brothers and Lynyrd Skynyrd, which bring together only a few of the original musicians.

REFERENCES

Dasein, D. 1994. "Tribute Bands: Respectful Imitation or Just Easy Money?" *Illinois Entertainer* 20 (12) (October): 22, 24.

———. 1995. "Tribute Albums: Looking Back in Honor." *Illinois Entertainer* 21 (5) (March): 52.

Heidegger, M. [1927] 1962. *Being and Time*. New York: Harper and Row.

Lipitz, G. 1990. *Time Passages: Collective Memory and American Pop Culture*. Minneapolis: University of Minnesota Press.

Martin, L., and K. Segrave. 1988. *Anti-Rock: The Opposition to Rock 'n' Roll*. Hamden, CT: Archon Books.

Maslin, J. 1980. "Singer/Songwriters." In *The Rolling Stone Illustrated History of Rock & Roll*, edited by J. Miller. New York: Random House/Rolling Stone Press.

Robbins, I. 1990. "Review of *The King and Eye* by the Residents." *Rolling Stone* 571 (February): 98.

Simmel, G. [1903] 1950. "The Metropolis and Mental Life." In *The Sociology of Georg Simmel*, edited by K. H. Wolff, 409–24. New York: The Free Press.

Tankel, J. D. 1990. "The Practice of Recording Music: Remixing as Recoding." *Journal of Communication*. 40: 34–46.

Weinstein, D. 1994a. "Expendable Youth: The Rise and Fall of Youth Culture." In *Adolescents and Their Music: If It's Too Loud, You're Too Old*, edited by J. Epstein, 67–85. Hamden, CT: Garland Publishing.

———. 1994b. "Ironic Youth: het heroveren van een jeugdcultuur." *Jeugd en Samenleving* 11 (November): 595–609.

———. 1995. "Alternative Youth: The Ironies of Recapturing Youth Culture." *Young: Nordic Journal of Youth Research* 3 (1) (February): 61–71.

8

— Repressive Representations —

Patriarchy and Femininities
in Rock Music of the Counterculture

Sheila Whiteley

INTRODUCTION

It is generally conceded that the sixties canon is dominated by "big books by big men about big movements" (Tischler, 1994: 26). Nowhere is this more evident than in the field of popular music where discussions about "sexual liberation" are often framed in terms saturated with male assumptions, including the rape fantasy of "dope, rock and roll and fucking in the streets" (Widgery, 1973). This chapter attempts to redress the balance and examines culturally dominant images of women in late 1960s rock from a mainly British perspective. It does not pretend to offer a comprehensive account of the music, but rather explores key groups and the ways in which their music provided specific representations of women which drew largely on mid-Victorian iconography. There are two sections. The first examines women's roles within the counterculture; the second situates women within the prevalent discourses of rock culture.

My analysis of musical style recognizes that different contextualizations produce and foreground different sensibilities. Listening to a recorded song on the radio, for example, is distinct from watching a live performance. The experience of a live performance in a concert hall is different from seeing the same group perform live on television or at a rock festival. As such, a rock group will inhabit various performing contexts and this, in turn, will affect the reception and interpretation of the musical content. The same song can be a source of sexual fantasy, aesthetic pleasure, or narrative romance, depending on the life experiences, desires, and needs of the individual listener. A consideration of rock, then, involves not only music, but equally rock culture itself.

The analysis of "meaning" in music in this chapter draws on theoretical perspectives taken from film studies, and in particular, the way in which meanings are "circulated between representation, spectator and social formation" (Kuhn, 1985: 6). Questions are raised about the nature of voyeurism and debates surrounding the construction of femininities/masculinities, power, and knowledge. More specifically, the chapter examines how femininities are constructed through representations in music.

WOMEN AND THE COUNTERCULTURE

Historical accounts of the counterculture generally point to an "intense internationalism, which was based on shared dreams, strategies, styles, moods and vocabularies" (Neville, 1971: 14). While it is equally recognized that there were divisions between the Underground, which tended towards cultural upheaval, and the New Left, which focused on political protest, these groupings were also perceived as broadly consistent in their challenge to the dominant culture. The opposition to the war in Vietnam, for example, is generally identified as the one great unifier of the counterculture in that it demonstrated a concern for the developing world and, in particular, the racial and economic exploitation of other races. While confrontation was particularly acute in the United States, where there was both an increasing rejection of parental values and a lack of commitment by draftee servicemen, European students identified the war as symptomatic of the corruptions of advanced consumer capitalism. As such, the focal activity directed against war was associated with wider social and moral issues. In particular, there was a growing recognition that a political system that perpetuated inequality and a general lack of freedom was untenable, and its institutions corrupt (Parliament, National Assembly, universities, business, the media, and leisure itself) and therefore in need of radical change.

The second half of the 1960s, in particular, produced an escalation in student protest and rebellion in most of the industrially developed countries, including Japan. These revolutionary phenomena possessed similar features which came to a head in the years 1968–9. Waves of protest swept from the United States across the Atlantic to Germany, France, Italy, and Britain. In Russia, Czechoslovakia, and Yugoslavia, students and intellectuals demanded very precise freedoms to study and to discuss, without the formal constraints of communist doctrine. In comparison, those students in capitalist countries, who were influenced by the ideas of neo-Marxism and various liberation movements, aimed at the destruction of capitalism to make a world free from war, poverty, and exploitation. There were also local grievances such as impersonal teaching and overcrowding, pedantic academicism, and bureaucratic administrations, but these were only the outward manifestations of a demand for deeper social and political changes.

While there was no single song that summed up its central values,[1] both the social and political denominations of youth protest shared a common belief that rock could articulate its concerns. Thus, through participation in the music, as either performer or audience, a common cultural and political bond could be established. As such, music had an evangelical purpose that tied it to the values of the counterculture, expressing its attitudes and providing a particular location for self-identity. John Lennon's "Give Peace A Chance," for example, assumed the role of an anthem during the anti-Vietnam marches in the United States.

The counterculture's marginalization of women in rock is therefore particularly disturbing. Apart from the occasional biting social and political commentaries from such female performers as Janis Joplin, Joan Baez, and Mama Cass, both the lifestyles and the music of the period marginalized the role of women, positioning them as either romanticized fantasy figures, subservient earth mothers or easy lays. In England, for example, there was no strong voice that could articulate the specific concerns of women within the counterculture. On the folk side there were women singers within groups (Fairport Convention, for example, had Judy Dyble in the original lineup), but as soloists women tended towards songs that prioritized traditional notions of romanticized love and feeling. Marianne Faithfull, for example, is better remembered for her relationship with The Rolling Stones' Mick Jagger than for her previous career as a pop singer, and during the period under review it is difficult to find an articulate British woman singer comparable to Grace Slick, Joan Baez, or Janis Joplin. This is not to suggest that the British counterculture listened only to British groups, but to point to the lack of a

woman singer who could set an agenda for women within the counterculture.

It would appear, then, that it was a case of men singing about women
rather than women expressing their own voices. It is hardly surprising, then,
that there was a definite positioning of women that drew on past precedents.
As Roszak points out, the struggle for liberation was seen mainly "as the
province of men who must prove themselves by 'laying their balls on the
line'. Too often this suggests that the female of the species must content herself with keeping the home fires burning for her battle-scarred champion or
joining the struggle as a camp follower. In either case, the community is
saved for her, not by her as well" (1970: 65). Musically, this was reflected in
British rock with the "love" school being represented generally by such
groups as the Beatles[2] and Donovan, and the "sex" school by, in particular,
the Rolling Stones, and Jimi Hendrix.

It could be argued that this split can be attributed to the different stylistic backgrounds of the groups themselves. But it is equally the case that it
can be correlated to the difference in motivating philosophies within the
counterculture. The concept of communality, the negation of bourgeois
materialism (including the redefinition of marriage and bonding), may have
been fundamental to all branches of the counterculture, but there was a
marked difference between the transcendent spirituality promised to the fol-
lowers of the Maharishi Mahesh Yogi and the revolutionary liberation of
Jerry Rubin and his symbolic call for patricide.

These seemingly opposing philosophies were reflected in the ethos of
rock itself at the time.[3] On the one hand, rock celebrated the present and
provided insights into the politics of consciousness – "love, loneliness,
depersonalization, the search for the truth of the person, the attempt to set
up an alternative life style" (Roszak, 1970: 156). Thus the movement
towards a communality based on love, however repressive in its attitude
towards women, seemed logical. When chaos and uncertainty, however,
were recognized as legitimate and necessary to life, and these concerns were
hinged on notions of repressed sexuality, a conjunction with sensuality and
death also seemed reasonable. The relationship between particular forms of
music and adopted philosophies is significant, then, in establishing referential points for group identification. The Beatles could project the distress of

contemporary society and set up a framework of "love, love, love" as the way to reconstituting a sense of community. For others, however, the cult of the "beautiful" was no less a sham than the vapid romantic notions of love extolled in popular music during the prerock era.

For groups like the Stones there was generally no compromise; their confrontational style equated with sexual freedom/promiscuity, relating more to hedonism and pantheism than to values connected with the spirituality of love. Adjectives like "brutal," "menacing," "erectile," "tough," "obscene," and "outrageous" can equally be applied to the Doors, the MC5, and Alice Cooper. Here, communal freedom had its darker side, and although it can be argued that the Stones had only a limited congruence with the counterculture, the fact that these other groups and performers came across as equally destructive in their attitude towards women is an important factor in an analysis of the meanings attributed by countercultural audiences to their music.

It is therefore important to determine the extent to which rock music communicates meaning. As Grossberg (1992) points out, "culture communicates only in particular contexts in which a range of texts, practices and languages are brought together." This may include "musical texts and practices, economic and race relations, images of performers and fans, social relations (for instance, of gender, of friendship), aesthetic conventions, styles of language, movement, appearance and dance, media practices, ideological commitments" (54). My own research into the counterculture certainly suggests a relationship between hallucinogenic experience and music that indicates that music was given a priority which made it an inspiration for group consciousness and practice.[4] Dick Hebdige's writings also indicate that subcultures evolve or choose cultural styles that can be made to resonate with central concerns or experiences, that there can be a homology between musical characteristics and lifestyle. Consequently music can empower individuals by constructing "moments of stable identity" that are legitimated through ideology.

A major problem in musicological analysis is discerning the extent to which music may be said to have meaning. As Shepherd points out, "music is not an informationally closed mode of symbolism relevant only to emotive, vital, sentient experiences" or "inherent psychological laws or 'rightness'"

(Shepherd, 1991: 83). Further, while lyrics and song titles may suggest a pre-ferred reading, their abstract nature allows for a mapping of individual experi-ence and meaning that provides a sense of identity and fluidity of engage-ment. As such, if there is any assigned significance to music, this significance is generally located within the commonly agreed-on meanings of the group or society from which the music originates and to which it is addressed.[5]

The symbolic fit between the values and lifestyles of the counterculture, its subjective experience, and the musical forms it used to express and rein-force its focal concerns thus relied on some form of mutual agreement between performers and listeners. Music carried with it a generally agreed-on, if often unarticulated, meaning for the members of the group identifying with it. The question of who defines, who orders, and who classifies is there-fore of vital significance. Given that some groups have more say, more opportunity to make the rules to organize meaning than others, some defi-nitions of the world may remain marginalized. An analysis of the correlation between the counterculture and the musical characteristics that were con-sidered significant in defining their oppositional stand to the dominant ide-ology, suggests that the counterculture's ideology continued to be inscribed within a patriarchal social structure. As such, the counterculture remained deeply embedded within the ideology of the dominant culture itself.

In this respect, the counterculture was very much of its time. In 1964 Harold Wilson had attempted to shift the image of the Labour Party. Under the banner of "The White Heat of Technology," there was a new emphasis on progressiveness, modernization, and youth. The rights of protest had been legitimized within limits and, allied to an expansion in the university system, had led to a student attack on pedantic teaching methods and, in particular, the lack of seminars. The building of new universities had also led to an expansion in terms of staffing and in new areas of study to include soci-ology, social psychology and, in the latter part of the sixties, a renewed interest in Marxist thought on the "superstructure" – ideas, culture, ideology – and its place within the social formation.[6] As part of this extension of higher education, there was an expansion in women's education, and while this was still limited in the ratio of male to female, there was nevertheless a greater opportunity for women to take part in formal higher education and in informal debates and meetings around, for example, the Vietnam issue and the meaning of progressiveness.

For women, the war had highlighted their problems within society, but these problems had certainly not been solved during the postwar period. The emphasis on progressiveness, which in the mid-1960s had found its voice in the progressiveness of rock, the fusion of technology, and the exploration of space did not appear to include progress towards the independence of women.[7] As Betty Friedan wrote in 1963, "there was a strange discrepancy between the reality of our lives as women and the image to which we were trying to conform, the image that I came to call the feminine mystique" (1963: 39). In England, it was evident that if the British counterculture could not provide space for the specific experiences of women, then there was no alternative but to call on the traditions of the past or look elsewhere.

There were many contradictions between the politics of the British counterculture, which stressed personal freedom, and the reality of women's roles, not only in society at large, but within the counterculture itself. In general, the British counterculture's relationship to the dominant culture was characterized by a sense of negation, disassociation, and romantic anarchy. The emphasis was on the freedom to enjoy and experience, to test alternative modes of existence for their more positive and gratifying possibilities. Characteristically, there was a blurring of the distinctions so rigorously maintained in the dominant culture between work, family, school, and leisure, but overall the stress was on the expansion of subjective awareness and creativity to be gained, for example, from hallucinogenic drugs. This definition of "freedom" continued to marginalize women. For them, the more permissive, promiscuous sexuality brought its own contradictions and pressures – how to be emancipated and yet deal with the romanticized construct of the young, single woman.

The fact that music was recognized by the counterculture as an audible signifying badge of belonging is therefore of critical importance to a consideration of the role of women. As an essential element in the underground it provided both a focus for an antagonistic relationship with the dominant culture as well as explicit links in the fusion of the mental and physical dimensions of the group. The correlation between musical and cultural characteristics was to be a unifying bond. At the same time, it provided a "commonsense" notion of the ideological framing of women which was spontaneous and repressive.

IMAGES OF REPRESSION

In many ways 1967 was a microcosm of the struggle of the decade it divided, in the interplay between action and reaction, liberalization and repression. Britain had finally passed the Sexual Offenses and Abortion Acts. The *Times* (London) had published an advertisement advocating the legalization of marijuana to which the Beatles were signatories. Even so, it must have been difficult to resist the suspicion that any doctrine that leads to greater freedoms of self-expression and individualism among the governed, but which is not sanctioned by the governors, will inevitably be repressed. Regional drug squads were formed in March 1967, and LSD and marijuana were made illegal. In August, the Rolling Stones were arrested for possessing marijuana. Pirate Radio was suppressed and raids on the *International Times*, underground music clubs, and the OZ "obscenity" trials reflected an increasingly repressive reaction by the establishment. By 1968 the counterculture was characterized by yippie anarchy and such sensationalized events as exorcising the demons from the Pentagon, nude grope-ins, and joint-rolling contests. America, like England, reacted with punitive measures and Abbie Hoffman and Jerry Rubin were tried for conspiracy, the former being sentenced to five years' imprisonment.

The Beatles' popularity throughout the sixties is well documented. The frenzied adoration by young female fans, both in Britain and America during the peak of Beatlemania, has been described by some feminists as "the first and most dramatic uprising of women's sexual revolution" in that it signaled an abandonment of control and a protest against the sexual repressiveness of female teen culture (Ehrenreich, Hess, and Jacobs, 1992: 85). Essentially, the Beatles were a mainstream band, but their ability to popularize even the most esoteric trends in British and American rock, and the extent to which their music achieved worldwide dissemination, suggests why they remain one of the most significant forces in the history of popular music. Because they were examined by sociologists and critics alike for their potential influence on the morals and attitudes of youth culture, and because their music and (especially) lyrics were subjected to extensive interpretative analysis, the release of the *Sgt. Pepper's* album, in June 1967, was awaited with an unprecedented level of anticipation. "It was the most amazing thing I've ever heard. For a brief moment, the irreparably fragmented consciousness of the West was unified, at least in the minds of the young" (Taylor, 1974: 45).

Although it could be argued that the Beatles were simply jumping on the American psychedelic bandwagon, the fact that they had become "underground converts" was significant. Their changed image and the attendant emphasis on love and drugs was newsworthy and inevitably stimulated comment and imitation. The *Sgt. Pepper's* album was in perfect harmony with the mood of the time in its LSD-influenced acid rock, raga rock, and social commentary, and its huge popularity indicates that without the Beatles, the British countercultural scene would have been far less significant. In particular, it established an agenda for the British counterculture in terms both of cultural themes and of music. Drug use had caught up with the drug orientation of rock and *"Sgt Pepper's"* had finally bridged the gap right down to suburbia" (McCabe and Schonfield, 1972: 84).

The third track on the album, "Lucy in the Sky with Diamonds," was central to British psychedelic rock in that it suggested a musical metaphor for hallucinogenic experience.[8] Musically, the gentle beat works towards a slowing down of the listener's own pulse rate, while the gradual shifting harmonies in the chromatic descent in the bass line suggest a relaxation into a comfortable and languorous dream state. The melody line of the verse is trancelike, with repetitive phrases revolving around the third degree of the scale.

For the listener, the effect is both reflective and reassuring as the gentle melodic contours respond to the dactylic meter of the words. "For No One," "And I Love Her," and "Yesterday" were also structured around rising and falling phrases and short melodies and, as such, "Lucy" evokes a feeling of trust. The listener may be entering new territory, but the guide is reliable. The use of a familiar melodic contour, juxtaposed with the exotic timbres of the celesta sound in the opening organ melody, the filtered vocal delivery, and the surrealistic lyrics are evocative of a good trip. The song elicits a sense of confidence: the Beatles have enjoyed hallucinogenic experience, they know the effects of LSD and can take the initiate through to a new and heightened sense of awareness. The foregrounding of a psychedelic environment is thus strongly supported by known musical parameters while enhanced electronic effects evoke a spatial dimension (O'Grady, 1983: 125) similar to that experienced on a trip, where heightened awareness causes the ordinary to take on new colors and dimensions. With the imagery strongly supported by musical effects, the opening sequence to "Lucy" promises a seductive route to a changed state of consciousness. It seems to say: "Follow this through to its logical conclusion...take acid, have an authentic experience, and with our guidance you, too, can meet Lucy – in the sky with diamonds."

At the same time, the song establishes a particular definition of romanticized femininity: the insubstantial and etherealized Lucy. The image of "the girl with the sun in her eyes" both reflects and constructs the preferred face of the late sixties: the "kaleidoscope" eyes, the waiflike figure epitomized by the omnipresent Julie Driscoll/Twiggy genre. Already represented as a fantasy figure, the Lucy refrain, with its brief and hypnotically repetitive phrases, inserts an element of earthy reality into an otherwise dreamlike experience.[9] "Lucy in the Sky with Diamonds" may be interpreted as a celebration of acid, but the exuberant refrain makes it equally a celebration of possession. Lucy may have a dreamlike quality, a certain elusiveness: "Look for the girl with the sun in her eyes/And she's gone," but the stereotypical and clichéd musical structures (the repetitive I–IV–V7 harmonies), and the unison vocal chant in the chorus reinstate her within the dominant catechism of rock where women are both attainable and containable.

The projection of nonreality linked to psychedelic imagery is carried further in "Julia" (1968). While the song is autobiographical, describing the mother Lennon hardly knew, Julia still retains the elusive beauty of a woman inscribed within the framework of fantasy. Sung to a slowly moving and unusually narrow-ranged melody, the shifting harmonies in the supporting chords nevertheless create an underlying tension: "Julia, morning moon, touch me." The imagery is that of the imagined woman, "hair of floating sky is shimmering, glimmering....sea-shell eyes, windy smile," drawing on the symbolic associations of the lunar goddess who stands at both ends of the silver cord of life, presiding over fertility, birth, and death. Associated with the astrological sign of Pisces, with the Druidic, the Celtic triple goddess, and the sea, she represents equally sexuality and matriarchal energies and as such, relates to the image of the earth mother, a genre that will be discussed later in this chapter. At the same time she is a symbol of the unattainable and, like Lucy, is denied the self that is human. Unlike Lennon's intense expression of love, "I Want You (She's So Heavy)," where heavy metal inscribes an earthy sexuality to Yoko Ono, Julia (like Lucy) is denied the self that is human. She is a symbol of beauty and is given no other value than to be beautiful.

By the late sixties a particular inscription of women as fantasy figures begins to emerge. Donovan carries the myth further in "Jennifer Juniper," a song in which the background combination of strings, woodwind, and cor-anglais provides a wistful and romanticized commentary on the idealized image of a woman who evokes memories of Godiva, riding "a dappled mare….lilacs in her hair….hair of golden flax." The verse suggests a certain element of fantasy, with the repetitive rhythm and melodic riffs supporting the structure of a "series of images seen in sequence" (Kuhn: 28), while the rhetorical "Is she sleeping? (I don't think so)" suggests voyeurism, "the seeing rather than the feeling of the woman" (Griffin, 1981: 122). The pleasure of both narrator and listener "depends on the object of the look being unable to see him: to this extent, it is a pleasure of power, and the look is a controlling one…. (Jennifer) can be looked at for as long as desired, because the circuit of pleasure will never be broken by a returned look" (Kuhn: 28).

Isolated by a pause, there is time for reflection before the key question – "What 'cha doin' Jennifer, my love?" – and the possibility that Jennifer "longs for what she lacks." The male singer has the power to fulfill her needs: "Would you love her? Yes, I would sir."

Lucy, Julia, and Jennifer play on the "desire of the spectator in a particularly pristine way: beauty or sexuality is desirable to the extent that it is idealized and unattainable" (Kuhn, 1985: 12). There is a sense of deceptive fascination in this particular genre, in that the image of the woman is enhanced by illusion. Women are etherealized within a dreamlike and unreal world, detached from reality, defined by the male as a fantasy escape from reality. They are "made-up" in the immediate sense in that their images are constructed by the songs and written by male singers and songwriters, but they also "occupy a place dangerously close to another tradition of representation of women, from myth to fairy tale to high art to pornography, in which they are stripped of will and autonomy. Woman is dehumanized by being represented as a kind of automaton, a 'living doll'" (Kuhn, 1985: 14).

While no reading of music can be completely objective or entirely unambiguous, there is, nevertheless, a prefacing by what has gone before which results in certain representations of women becoming so "naturalized" that they assume a taken-for-granted quality. There is, therefore, a certain element of surprise when similar fantasy figures appear in an overtly sexist band like the Rolling Stones. "Gomper," from *Their Satanic Majesties Request*

(1967) is deliberately psychedelic in musical language and, like The Beatles' "Within You Without You," uses the sitar and quasi-Indian scoring. The lyrics, however, are evocative of Donovan: "By the lake with lily flowers / While away the evening hours / To and fro she's gently gliding / On the glassy lake she's riding."

The "lily maid" draws heavily (if subconsciously) on the familiar heroines of the nineteenth century: "petite and fragile, with lily fingers and taper waists; and they are supposed to subsist on air and moonlight…wandlike, with a step so light that the flowers scarcely nod beneath it…a little too spiritual for this world and a little too material for the next, and who, therefore seems always hovering between the two, is the accepted type of female loveliness" (Dijkstra, 1986: 29). Evoking images of Elaine and Ophelia, the imagined woman is situated among water lilies, pale, and with a sweet child-like face.

With music providing an audible map of learning whereby the counter-culture could explore human relationships, such representations are clearly disturbing. As Paul Willis (1978) writes: "only specific kinds of music were chosen because they – and not others – were able to hold, develop and return those meanings and experiences which were important to the hippie culture" (46). With music given the status of a "serious" art form, lyrics and sound provided guidance in the exploration of expanded consciousness and personal freedom. What is obvious, however, is that this thrust towards personal freedom was not extended towards women who continued to be situated within a chauvinistic framework.

The Rolling Stones, for example, are generally associated with the more overt forms of sexuality as evidenced in "Parachute Woman" (1968). A strongly pulsating rhythm supports the sensual triplets in the melody line before the direct question "Will you blow me out?" where Jagger holds on to the word "out" with a characteristically suggestive vocal leer. There is little innuendo in this and many other songs by the Stones. Rather, the musical structures support the overt sexual demands in the lyrics and the pulsating rhythm leaves no doubt as to the outcome.

Songs like "Backstreet Girl", "Heart of Stone," "Under My Thumb," "Stray Cat Blues," "My Obsession," "Brown Sugar," and, in the seventies, "Negrite" and "Coming Down Again" conflate "femininity with femaleness,

femaleness with female sexuality and female sexuality with a particular part of the female anatomy" (Kuhn, 1985: 40). The women in Jagger's songs speak to the males' desire for pleasurable looking, as in "Brown Sugar": "Scarred old slaver know / He's doin' alright / Hear him whip the women / Just around midnight...." and there are again parallels with Annette Kuhn's analysis of the "Peeping Tom who separates himself in the act of looking (listening to) the object which cannot look back at him" (Kuhn, 1985: 41). By identifying with Jagger, the spectator's fantasy is given full rein: "in one sense there is no risk of disappointment"; he is quite safe because the woman in the song "will never in real life turn him down or make demands which he cannot satisfy. By the same token, of course, he can never really 'possess' her" (Kuhn, 1985: 42). Desire, however, is fueled and fulfilled: "in the final instance its object is unattainable and unthreatening" (Kuhn, 1985: 42) but, at the same time, the dominating presence of Jagger allows for positive identification for males in the audience: "You should have heard me / Just around midnight." As Jagger possesses the woman, both in the song, and, metaphorically, in live performance, the males in the audience indirectly possess her, too.

Parallel themes of sexual domination appear throughout rock history. In Jimi Hendrix's "Dolly Dagger," for example, the woman is situated as threatening, associated with the vampire figure "who sucks the blood of its victims in their sleep while they are alive, so does the woman vampire suck the life and exhaust the vitality of her male partner – or victim" (Griffin, 1981: 122). As a creature of the night she is once again associated with the moon, to become the erotic, primal counterpart of "Lucy," predatory and possessed of "a love so heavy, it's gonna make you stagger."

While hard rock and, later, heavy metal often represent women as dehumanized and degraded, fulfilling simply their role to sexually gratify the male, wanting to be humiliated, suppressed and physically harmed and objectified, the role of woman as earth mother is central to countercultural mythology. Here, the woman takes on the role of the provider, the forgiver, the healer. The image of the woman decked in flowers is common in sixties iconography. Such songs as The Beatles'"Mother Nature's Son" (1968) convey the conception of woman as the "receptive, seed-sheltering womb of a sweltering earth" (Dijkstra, 1986: 83). She is a symbol of nature, she is the earth, sexual but protective, always there for the masculine ego to inhabit when he wants to escape from the realities of life (Dijkstra, 1986: 86).

It is, perhaps, hardly surprising that the counterculture, with its emphasis on hallucinogenic experience should resurrect the nineteenth-century image of the earth mother. Earl Shimm, in 1867 had described her symbolic significance as representative of "the 'Opium Dream'...Beneath stretches a field of poppies, lifting up their stems and their shapely seed-pods, chiseled like Indian capitals; from among them, her feet disentangling themselves from their cold stems, floats up the Vision, a dim figure in human shape, her filmed eyes lifted" (Dijkstra, 1986: 90). Although the poetic language is replaced by a more declamatory rock style, the sentiments reemerge in the Rolling Stones' "Sister Morphine" ("turn my nightmare into dream") and "Dead Flowers."

The earth mother as madonna can also be traced to the nineteenth century. For Ruskin, "the path of a good woman is strewn with flowers; but they rise behind her steps, not beneath them" (Dijkstra, 1986: 269), an expression of both male sentimentality and the perception of the soul-healing power of the virtuous woman. One hundred years later, Paul McCartney expressed much the same thoughts: "To lead a better life, I need my love to be there: Here, / Making each day of the year / Changing my life with a wave of her hand."

"Lady Madonna," less naively ecstatic, nevertheless conveys some of the understanding necessary for the contemporary earth mother as her lover arrives "Friday night without a suitcase / Sunday morning creeping like a nun." "Hey Jude" conveys the sense of the woman as receptive and pliable: "go and get her," "let her into your heart," and "let her under your skin then you can make it better." It is, however, Led Zeppelin's "Stairway to Heaven" that most encapsulates the image of the etherealized earth mother: "And as we wind on down the road / Our shadows taller than our souls / There walks a lady we all know / Who shines white light and wants to show / How everything still turns to gold."

With its imagery of trees and brooks, pipers, shining white light and forests echoing to laughter, the song "is a paradigm of Spenser's 'Faerie Queen,' Robert Grave's 'White Goddess' and every other Celtic heroine – the Lady of the Lake, Diana of the Fields Greene and Rhiannon the nightmare" (Davies, 1973: 101).

At one level, the song can be read as woman's quest for spiritual enlightenment, one who has the power to determine who can enter the heavenly kingdom: "If the stars are all closed, with a word she can get what she came for" and who acknowledges that her "stairway lies on the whispering wind." At the same time, it is a fitting epitaph for the woman within the counterculture. There is a sense of nostalgia, the lyrics conjuring up images of green pastures, forests and castles, while the acoustic guitar introduction harks back to the Renaissance-like style of John Renborn and Bert Jansch. Led Zeppelin had aimed to produce "a new kind of heavy music, with slower and lighter touches, music with dynamics, light and shade, chiaroscuro" (Davies, 1973: 101), to "provide an alternative way of looking at things" (Moore, 1993: 98). Musically they succeed, and the song constructs a feeling of a musical journey in its alternation of delicate scoring and dramatic guitar breaks. Yet the representation of the "Lady" as May Queen is still firmly entrenched within sixties iconography. She is, to some extent, earthbound in her love of gold, but her sense of otherness, a figure who "shines white light," places her once again "in the sky," an etherealized earth mother... who "makes me wonder."

It is a sobering thought that feminist music critics were not taken seriously by academic institutions until 1988 when the conferences at Dart mouth and Carleton Universities in Ottawa emphasized a feminist critique. Women musicians fared slightly better. The University of Illinois celebrated the first women's music festival in 1974. But then, as this chapter suggests, the counterculture itself was male dominated in its musical agenda. There is little commentary on commitment, children, the hypocrisy of free love, or women's sexual desires and experience. Rather, women provided a fantasy escape, a focus for easy eroticism. The breaking down of old restraints ("free love"), privileged a male sexuality and autoeroticism, confirming the traditional definitions of masculinity and femininity through the dubious freedom of hallucinogenic experience. At its most oppressive, rock music in the late sixties embodied the patriarchal imaginary of the madonna-whore binary.

NOTES

1. With the possible exception of "Give Peace a Chance" and "We Shall Overcome." Otherwise songs summed up particular "moments": the

1967 Summer of Love and Scott McKenzie's "Are You Going To San Francisco?"; drugs and Bob Dylan's "Mr Tambourine Man," etc.

2.   John Lennon is somewhat outside this generalization. On the one hand he was wrestling with his own neurosis ("Crippled Inside"), and on the other, he was attempting an openly confrontational position with the political establishment. This latter position comes through strongly on the album *Sometime in New York*. Lennon was moving between the personal and the political, as instanced by the overlap between the financial support he gave to the editors of the magazine OZ at the obscenity trial in October 1970.

3.   As Grossberg points out, "rock refers to an affective investment in, and empowerment by, the cultural forms, images and practices which circulate with the music for different groups of fans, each defining its own taste culture (or apparatus). Rock is defined, for particular audiences at different times and places differently, by the affective alliances of sounds, images, practices and experiences within which fans find certain forms of empowerment" (1993: 200).

4.   See Whiteley (1992).

5.   It is possible to suggest a homology between the experience of LSD and certain forms of music. These may include:
   • an overall emphasis on timbral color (blurred, bright, tinkly, overlapping, associated with the intensification of color and shape experienced when tripping)
   • upward movement in pitch (and the comparison with an hallucinogenic high)
   • characteristic use of harmonies (lurching, oscillating and the relationship to changing focus)
   • sudden surges of rhythm (the association with an acid "rush") and/or a feel of floating around the beat (suggestive of a state of tripping where the fixed point takes on a new reality)
   • shifting textural relationships (foreground/background, collages and soundscapes that suggest a disorientation of more conventionalized musical structures and that stimulate a sense of absorption with/within the sound itself. These techniques provide a musical analogy for the enhancement of awareness, the potentially new synthesis of ideas and thought relationships that can result from hallucinogens)

In the main, musical effects were made possible by an advancement in music technology (studio effects, echo units, controlled random feedback, fuzz box, wah wah pedal, etc.)

6. While this chapter examines the importance of experience and music as expression, Althusser's examination of ideology is considered relevant insofar as he argues that human beings are constructed by ideology and that our ways of thinking about the world, of representing ourselves, becomes so "naturalized" that we take our conception of the world, for granted. See Althusser (1971: 121–73).

    As Annette Kuhn (1985) points out, "If ideology effaces itself, the process by which this takes place could explain this taken-for-granted nature of social constructs of femininity" (6). See also Kuhn (forthcoming).

7. A concern that equally interested rock musicians at the time and that is found in such tracks as Pink Floyd's "Astronomy Domine," "Set The Controls for the Heart of the Sun," etc.

8. While the Beatles denied that "Lucy in the Sky with Diamonds" was about the effects of LSD, the psychedelic coding and the lyrics in the verses suggest otherwise.

9. "Tomorrow Never Knows" (*Revolver*, 1966) is generally considered the first, and Lennon has attributed the lyrics of 'She Said She Said' to an acid trip encounter with Peter Fonda.

REFERENCES

Althusser, L. 1971. "Ideology and Ideological State Apparatus." In *Lenin and Philosophy and Other Essays*. London: New Left Books.

Davies, S. 1973. *Hammer of the Gods*. New York: Ballantine Books.

Dijkstra, B. 1986. *Idols of Perversity, Fantasies of Feminine Evil in Fin-de-Siècle Culture*. New York: Oxford University Press.

Ehrenreich, B., E. Hess, and G. Jacobs. 1992. "Beatlemania: Girls Just Want to Have Fun." In *Adoring Audience: Fan Culture and Popular Media*, edited by L. Lewis, 85–97. London: Routledge.

Friedan, B. 1963. "The Feminine Mystique." In *Feminism and the Women's Movement*, edited by B. Ryan, 77–89. London: Routledge.

Griffin, S. 1981. *Pornography and Silence*. New York: Harper and Row.

Grossberg, L. 1992. "The Affective Sensibility of Fandom." In *Adoring Audience: Fan Culture and Popular Media*, edited by L. Lewis, 63–82. London: Routledge.

Grossberg, L. 1993. "Cinema, Postmodernity and Authenticity." In *Sound and Vision: The Music Video Reader*, edited by S. Frith, A. Goodwin, and L. Grossberg. London: Routledge.

Kuhn, A. 1985. *The Power and the Image, Essays on Representation and Sexuality*. London: Routledge.

———. 1997. "Psychedelic (Acid) Rock." In *The Encyclopedia of Popular Music of the World*, edited by M. Gidley, D. Horn, J. Shepherd, and D. Tagg. City: Open University Press.

———. Forthcoming. "Seduced by the Sign: An Analysis of the Textual Links between Sound and Image in Pop Videos." In *Sexing the Groove: Gender and Popular Music*, edited by Sheila Whiteley. London: Routledge.

McCabe, P., and R. D. Schonfield. 1972. *Apple to the Core: The Unmaking of the Beatles*. London: Martin Brian & O'Keefe Ltd.

Moore, A. F. 1993. *Rock – The Primary Text*. London: Oxford University Press.

Neville, J. 1971. *Play Power*. London: Paladin.

O'Grady, T. 1983. *The Beatles*. Boston: Twayne Publishers.

Roszak, T. 1970. *The Making of a Counter Culture: Reflections on the Technocratic Society and Its Youthful Opposition*. London: Faber and Faber.

Shepherd, J. 1991. *Music as Social Text*. London: Polity Press.

Taylor, D. 1974. *As Time Goes By*. London: Abacus/Shlere.

Tischler, B. L. 1994. "Perspectives on the Sixties." *NEAA Newsletter*, 14–28. Brown University.

Whiteley, S. 1992. *The Space between the Notes: Rock and the Counter Culture*. London: Routledge.

Widgery, D. 1973. "What Went wrong ?" In *OZ* 48: 7–17.

Willis, P.E. 1978. *Profane Culture*. London: Routledge and Kegan Paul.

9

—— Popular Music and ——
the Synergy of Corporate Culture

David Sanjek

WOULD YOU LIKE TO SWING ON A GYRE?

A s the fin de siècle approaches, we find the prefix "post-" attached to virtually any noun, suggesting entropy, decay, and chaos. Certain well-worn passages from literature that address notions of closure take on the function of touchstones. William Butler Yeats's "The Second Coming" is perhaps the most quoted poetic embodiment of a master myth or grand narrative that might make sense of an exhausted and anarchic age. The opening lines – "Turning and turning in the widening gyre/The falcon cannot hear the falconer" – embody two ideas I consider germane to the current state of American popular music, the industry that supports it, and the individuals who consume as well as conceptualize it.

The first idea, enunciated in the second line of the poem, is, in effect, the metaphorical expression of an acoustic dilemma: the inability of a perceiver to apprehend an intended message. In the course of these comments, I will refer to analysts of the American popular music industry as being in a similar position: receptive, but only in a highly selective manner. The second idea finds expression in Yeats's recurrent image of the "gyre." For the poet, this image stood for a body of self-generated notions of repetition and cycli-

171

cal evolution. For me, it alludes to the current dissolution of the public sphere of American culture, the manner in which opposing centripetal and centrifugal forces virtually cancel each another out. One feels present-day American society resembles, as Todd Gitlin (1995) observes, a centrifuge in which advocacy of the *unum* that holds together the *pluribus* lacks all foundation. The future appears to hold "the same soft apocalypse to which Americans have apparently grown inured: more inequality, more punishment of the poor, more demoralization and pathology among them, the slow (or not-so-slow) breakdown of civic solidarities" (230).

Trying to make sense of one's passage through this period of time and particularly of the musical culture that accompanies it, we reflexively turn to those well-worn schemes of analysis that Robert Burnett defines as the "critical" stance and the "pluralist" position embodied by two of the most influential cultural theorists, Theodor Adorno and Walter Benjamin. To generalize, the former characterizes the "culture industry" as the producer of standardized goods constructed on the basis of "mechanical schemata," which can only "vulgarize, level, degrade and commercialize the culture of contemporary capitalist societies" (Burnett, 1996: 31). The latter counters that mass reproduction acts as a progressive force, for through it "the work of democratic artists could be shared with an audience in which everyone was able to be an 'expert' consumer" (Burnett 1996: 32).

The conceptual centrifuge that we find ourselves in when trying to establish some accommodation between these seemingly antithetical positions is reminiscent of the observation made by Ralph Waldo Emerson in 1843: "Is it that every man believes every other to be a fatal partialist, & himself a universalist?" (quoted in Gitlin, 1995: 105). The desire to discover some equipoise between the "critical" and "pluralist" stances could be said to reflect the tendency native to American culture that the historian Michael Kammen calls the "syncretistic" drive in our national character. This is not, he argues, a form of Manicheanism, the effort to divide humanity and its ideas into incompatible camps, but, instead, "the attempted reconciliation or union – by Americans historically, not by me alone – of different or opposing principles, practices, and parties" (1973: xiii). The danger, of course, in unifying contradictions is that we risk erasing all the rough edges and conceptual friction that give life and thought substance and texture.

Like Kammen, I don't want to allay the complexity and multiplicity that attends our efforts to make sense of the production and consumption of American popular music. I wish instead to inquire whether we might throw ourselves into that centrifuge and engage in the process Kammen refers to alternately as "syzygy" or its less ungainly synonym, "biformity." Both terms refer to "the conjunction of two organisms without loss of identity, a pair of correlative things, a paradoxical coupling of opposites" (1973: 89). In pursuing the possibility of a "biformal" position, I share with the Australian commentator Marcus Breen not only his feeling that "we have been too eager to be culturalists – promoters of our musical obsessions – rather than analysts and critics" but also his desire to inquire into the changing circumstances of oligopolistic ownership, global salesmanship, cross-media marketing, and the vertical integration of the means of production and consumption that now dominate the popular music industry (1995: 490). If scholars and consumers of popular music are to make any sense of the evolving music industry, they must recognize that the established structures of mass communications that Adorno and Benjamin knew are moribund. Today, the music business is but one element of a global media economy and cannot be examined apart from the other industries with which it is integrated.

In effect, what I am calling for is a new paradigm of analysis, one that not only builds upon the work of Adorno, Benjamin, and others, but also one that speaks to current circumstances and acknowledges the effects of the transformation Breen has identified. Jacques Attali has remarked that "every code of music is rooted in the ideologies and technologies of its age, and at the same time produces them" (1985: 19). To those two terms, I would add the industrial or market structures of the age. The paradigm I propose must pay greater attention to the evolving nature of the music industry and the legal and legislative regimes that support it. As Breen writes, "within the transnational conglomerates referred to as major record companies, music, or the record business, is one element of the general corporate structure and economy" (Breen, 1995: 489). The broad-based corporate structure and economy, too, infrequently find a place in either the critical or the pluralist stance. The former routinely demonizes corporate structures, while the latter assumes that individuals can, albeit limitedly, circumvent those structures' power through the process of recontextualization. Both fail to fully assess the role of industrial, legislative, and legal regimes in the creation of the meaning of popular music.

I wish to examine two broad areas. First, the corporate regime, with particular emphasis upon the recent proliferation of mergers and acquisitions and their influence upon musical production and consumption such that the material available to consumers becomes routinized and circumscribed; second, the legal-legislative regime, most notably the recent Telecommunications Bill, and how it impedes the creation and consumption of popular music as well as expands the opportunities for transnational conglomerates to dominate the marketplace.

MONEY CHANGES EVERYTHING

When we consider the corporate regime, we would do well to remind ourselves that, for many years, both academic and journalistic commentators have grown accustomed to an inflexible set of formulae for discussing the music industry. Principal among those propositions is the notion of the collision between the individual creator and the corporate producer coupled with the long-standing association of institutional size with artistic constriction. Structures of entrenched power as embodied by the "Big 6" labels – WEA, Sony, BMG, Polygram, CEMA, and UNI – are believed to vie with numerous subordinate "indies" for control of market share. Those six entities also routinely appropriate either performers under contract to the small labels or the labels themselves altogether. Geographically, corporate power in the United States is defined as entrenched in a small number of locations – New York City, Los Angeles, and Nashville – while the remainder of the North American continent must content itself with an inescapably peripheral relationship to those dominant institutional centers. On occasion, the musical culture produced in those hinterlands is accorded some value by the dominant centers when designated a "scene," as was the case most recently with Seattle, Washington, and "grunge" rock.

Like all formulae, these observations become a form of analytic shorthand, but they insufficiently illustrate the current state of the music business in two ways. First, the domination of the "Big 6" over the U.S. marketplace is steadily eroding as more and more individuals purchase independently produced and distributed musical artifacts. Their fall from preeminence, particularly in the domestic market, has been precipitous. In 1991, the "Big 6" controlled 91 percent of domestic sales, but in the last five years that figure slid to 80.9 percent (Nunziata, 1995: YE-10, YE-12).[1] The "Big 6" dominance over the international marketplace proves to be equally tenuous. It will slide from a third at the present time to roughly 20 percent by the year 2000. To be more specific, the combined US and British share of European sales has dropped from 65 percent in 1985 to a current 45 percent, while the domestic production of music in other portions of the globe bodes even worse for US-based companies. To wit, 80 percent of the music purchased in Latin America is by Latinos/Latinas and 60 percent of that in Asia by Asians. None of these statistics should erode one's belief that a "culture industry" or "leisure empire" does exist and fully intends to maintain that market share it still controls by every means at its disposal. However, they should also illustrate that notions of cultural and economic hegemony must be employed with a requisite degree of qualification as well as constant consultation of available statistics.

At the same time, the very structure and constitution of the music industry and the media industries of which it forms a portion have undergone a substantial transformation in the course of the last 20 years and particularly during the current decade. While music has inarguably always existed as a commercial form, the manner in which it becomes commodified and the systematic exploitation of those products has undergone a "sea change" by virtue of the ongoing and systematic convergence of all forms of media, the ownership of those media by an increasingly small number of corporate entities, and the government-sanctioned (certainly the legislatively overlooked) vertical integration of the means of production and distribution. This year 1995 saw this process accelerate into overdrive when the Seagram's Company purchased 80 percent of MCA for $5.7 billion; Westinghouse acquired CBS for $5.4 billion; and the Disney Corporation subsumed Capital Cities/ABC at a cost of $19 billion. In 1996, the $7.5 billion purchase of Turner Broadcasting, and its ancillary properties in cable, film, and sports organizations, was consummated by Time Warner. Marcus Breen has observed of these and other acquisitions: "This convergence has taken the historical relationship between music and other media into an altogether different realm by marrying the intensified entertainment economy to the global-telecommunications-computer infrastructure" (1995: 498).

Music is therefore no longer privileged as a unique form of intellectual property but has become, in effect, a rights package. The writers and publishers of each composition maximize its "worth" through the expected sources – record sales, moneys accrued from mechanical and performance licenses – but at the same time deploy that composition in as many contexts as possible through the means of as many media or advanced technologies as circumstances permit.[2] Metaphorically, we might therefore view any musical composition, like all forms of intellectual property, as equivalent to sourdough starter from which, the property's owner(s) hope, any number of loaves of bread might be, so to speak, baked in as many variations as possible in order to be purchased by as many consumers as the market will bear. Furthermore, the purchase of a variety of media enables conglomerates to turn those loaves into profits, for crossover marketing strategies enable recordings to sell films, films to sell video cassettes, video cassettes to sell computer games, computer games to sell printed commemoratives ad infinitum.[3]

This results in what political scientist Benjamin Barber in *Jihad vs. McWorld* calls the "infotainment telesector," which dominates the transglobal, media-dominated web of stimuli he dubs "McWorld" (1995: 78–87). Increasingly, these efforts at monopolization of all media by transglobal enterprises transform individuals from citizens into consumers and consumers alone. In the process, the managers of the "infotainment telesector" identify the ability to make purchases with human existence itself so as to make way for a proliferation of so-called democratic markets, a term espoused by President Clinton during his visit to Europe and Russia in 1994. As Barber argues, the notion that market freedom entails (if not defines) democracy inescapably leads to "imaginary communities" predicated upon the purchasing power of their members and nothing else (1995: 14). These circumstances reinforce the worst scenario constructed by Adorno and others of the social deformation wrought by the mass media and the profligate manner with which multinational conglomerates co-opt both individuals and the governments presumed to protect them from the ravages of unrestrained capitalism.

However, we might note that centrifugal forces impede the wholesale giving over of the world's citizens to the support and salvation of transglobal corporations. In addition to these institutions' increasingly tenuous domination of the marketplace, several other factors must be taken into account in order to formulate a new paradigm for analysis of the music industry. First, we must more fully acknowledge the structural volatility of corporate systems. Too often, analysts presume record companies in particular operate in a homogeneous fashion, whereas empirical examination of these institutions illustrates the amount of tension and interdepartmental combat that lies behind the recording process. As Keith Negus has stated, "whilst the production-consumption of popular music may often be experienced in terms of a conflict between commerce and creativity, it more frequently involves struggles over what is creative, what it means *to be* commercial" (1995: 316–17). Moreover, when mergers and acquisitions lead to a proliferation of disparate bodies of individuals engaged in those conflicts, more often than not the line between corporate synergy and administrative entropy proves exceedingly thin. The commercial prospects of many media conglomerates have proven to pale in light of the excessive debt connected to mergers, the inability to cut overhead or put efficiency plans in action, and the failure of much of the product placed before an oversaturated public (Landro and Shapiro, 1995). One only need attend to the widely reported stories in the popular press about the turmoil within the Warner Music Group to know self-destructive practices can lie behind the corporate facade (Masters and Fried, 1995).[4]

Second, we need to acknowledge the volatility of consumers themselves. While they may not possess as fully as some would believe the utopian potential to change their lives through the very process of consumption, they have at their command the power of the purse – the ability *not* to buy at all or fall prey to market hype. Study of the record charts indicates that, in recent years, the number of new artists who enter *Billboard*'s charts and other lists has risen, but so too has the rapidity with which those artists fall out of favor (Burnett, 1995: 111–12). One can credit this phenomenon to the public's lack of focus or restless desire for novelty. On the other hand, it may reflect an unwillingness to succumb uncritically to the blandishments of corporate advertising. A similar pattern of rejection can be observed in the motion picture industry. The failure rate of new releases has grown incrementally as have costs both of production and merchandising, the latter of which has risen 20 percent in just a single year. "The movie business," reports its preeminent investment banker, Herbert Allen Jr., "isn't bleeding to death, but it's bleeding" (Masters, 1995: 58). At the same time, the entertainment conglomerates have mitigated the decline in box office receipts by selling the music featured in films as vigorously as (in some cases even more so than) the motion picture itself. Evidence of such cross-media marketing is supported by the fact that, with a single exception, the number one song on the yearly pop charts since 1991 also appeared in a motion picture soundtrack: Bryan Adams's "(Everything I Do) I Do It for You" [*Robin Hood: Prince of Thieves*, 1991], Boyz II Men's "End of the Road" [*Boomerang*, 1992], Whitney Houston's "I Will Always Love You" [*The Bodyguard*, 1993], and Coolio's "Gangsta's Paradise" [*Dangerous Minds*, 1995]. While the success of these and other productions, both in film and on record, may tempt us to assume that the culture industry runs the marketplace and commands our range of options, we must keep in mind that each of us possesses the power of refusal, the option to opt out of the circulation of cultural artifacts. Were this not so, the number of failed recordings and box office "bombs" would not be so high.

I FOUGHT THE LAW AND THE LAW WON

Turning to the legislative regime, we again encounter both centripetal and centrifugal forces circulating about the embattled consumers of popular music as well as its overextended producers. A number of recent pieces of national legislation as well as circuit court decisions have transformed the media playing field. While not in some cases music-specific, they bear upon the operations of the popular music industry for the media they influence are synergistically allied to musical production. The parameters they create constitute the boundaries within which the creators and consumers of popular music must operate as well as define how the media of popular expression are to be exploited and when they are to be prohibited from unfettered access to the public.

The most consequential, even epochal recent legislation to affect the mass media remains the Telecommunications Bill, passed by the House and Senate in February 1996. No single bill has so irrevocably transformed national communications policy since the Communications Act of 1934, wherein the government turned over the airwaves to private interests and declared that the public interest was best served by allowing profit-making entities to possess the dominant control over the content and cost of broadcasting. Robert McChesney, the preeminent historian of the 1934 Act, has argued that if the lack of a public debate in the 1930s permitted the decision-making power over the use of the airwaves to reside in the hands of a small government-appointed body, the Federal Communications Commission (FCC), then the current bill threatens to diminish if not extinguish the power of that body and, in its place, legitimate the assumption that "competition among corporations in the marketplace will provide the most efficient and democratic communications system" (1995b: 15). The result is a media-focused version of supply-side economics whereby unhindered market forces determine and direct the course of certain vital forms of public discourse. This assumption, and the 1996 bill it supports, rests upon "the ideology of the infallible marketplace, a virtual civic religion in the United States and globally in the 1990s" (McChesney, 1996: 14).

The specific measures of the bill are wide ranging and systematic in their devolution of virtually any role on the part of the central government in the regulation of communications. At its core is the assumption that competition between the purveyors of communication will inevitably result in lower costs for consumers as well as impel those purveyors to develop new techniques and systems to improve service. These ends will be brought about principally by redrawing the restrictions over the ownership of the means of transmission as well as by allowing companies in one form of communications, the phone service (both local and long distance) for example, to embark upon another, cable television in particular. In addition, the preexistent restrictions over station ownership were amended: television broadcasters need no longer restrain themselves to owning no more than 12 stations with a maximum share of 25 percent of U.S. households, for they now can reach as much as 35 percent and acquire as many stations as they can afford. Restrictions upon cable rates will also be lifted after a three-year period and thereafter set by the marketplace. Clearly, these decisions will assure that what the public sees and hears lies in the hands of fewer and fewer corporate entities, and the cost to the public for what they consume will likely prove for many to be prohibitive.

Editorial response to this 1995 bill divides along expected lines, but even the criticism comes across as tepid, the shaking of a finger rather than the raising of a fist against the ominous threat to the public interest. Few commentators concur with Robert McChesney that "to the extent that our society, or any society for that matter, fails to examine and debate alternative policies in communications, is the extent to which our democracy is incomplete" (1995a:19). A commentary on the Disney-Capital Cities/ABC merger in *Business Week* stated, "No one can anticipate the creation of monopolistic situations in the throes of technological turmoil. In fact the best role for Washington to play is to deregulate old monopolies as fast as possible" (1995: 114). The *New York Times* waxed hot and cold, worrying that "deregulation is fine. Zero regulation is anti-competitive and anti-democratic" (1995: A12) but claiming in the end that the final bill "will, over time, offer viewers attractive new choices for entertainment and news" (1996: 22). Neither publication, nor many others for that matter, conveyed with appropriate gravity how the Telecommunications Bill reinforces the logic and practice of media mergers. At the same time, one would unwisely identify such a dereliction of investigative oversight with the knee-jerk progressive outcry over conspiracy. As Leo Bogart asserts, the synergy of mass communications entities throws together like-minded individuals as a matter of course: "Collusion is osmotic and spontaneous; it requires no deliberate or sinister intent" (1996: 17). And, one must not forget, in more than one case, both investigative entities and the objects of their investigation are owned by the same corporate bodies.

However, a proposed subsection of the Telecommunications Bill might not be said to have exhibited the malevolent intent of those who drafted it but nonetheless threatened to bring about dubious consequences, particularly for the popular music industry and all other forms of creative expression. The so-called Communications Decency Act specified that anyone who used obscenity, either written or visual, on the Internet would be subject to a $250,000 fine and an unspecified jail term. In that discourse on the Net heretofore lacked any criminal restrictions and was, if anything, self-regulating by means of "flaming" individuals whose discourse offended another participant on the system, the act stood potentially to transform one of the few genuinely accessible technologies that possesses "libertory" potential. As Steven Levy has stated in *Newsweek*, "it assumes that the Net will be treated as a medium akin to broadcast, where speech can be restricted – as opposed to a newsstand, where all sorts of discourse can thrive" (Levy 1996: 44).

Response to the act on the part of the popular music industry was swift and unsurprising. A number of companies filed a lawsuit along with the four principal commercial on-line providers (America Online, CompuServe, Microsoft, and Prodigy) that challenged the constitutionality of the law (Holland, 1996). If the lawsuit couched their criticism in constitutional language, the underlying concern amounts to consternation over the potential loss in revenues the music industry faces if access to a new and potentially lucrative forum for the merchandising of their products meets with legal impediments over lyrical content, the design of packaging, and any accompanying visual material employed on-line. The music industry's fears certainly were allayed, if not extinguished, when judges in the federal district courts of Philadelphia and New York decreed the language of the act to call for overly broad restraint on the free flow of communication between consenting adults (Lewis, 1996; McMorris and Sandberg, 1996). Both the Justice Department and various public lobbies have threatened to take the case to the Supreme Court, although many participants in the debate argue that the question of community standards remains an open issue, whether they apply to a virtual or literal context. At the same time, the prevailing wisdom appears to be that, in the instance of the Internet, the free flow of information and the free flow of commerce – specifically, the construction by record labels of web sites as forms of advertising and, eventually, points of sale for commercial recordings – will prove to be mutually supportive. In fact, many communications entities are quite pleased that the Net has become a commercial venture and will accommodate themselves to certain forms of regulation of the technology rather than wax nostalgic over the loss of the Net's iconoclastic commercial-free past. Therefore, their interest in free expression per se remains a matter of conjecture and most likely biformal to its core. The music industry's devotion to free and unfettered communication has its limit, as observed in WEA's succumbing to the criticism of former Secretary of Education William Bennett and others for their purported support of so-called antisocial forms of music, gangsta rap in particular, and subsequent divestiture of Interscope Records, the home of Snoop Doggy Dog and Dr. Dre among others.

The proponents of the Communications Decency Act, on the other hand, find themselves drawn to an equally complex position that can be defined as biformal at best and outright oxymoronic at worst. It requires a significant amount of conceptual chutzpah to label oneself, as does Senator Newt Gingrich, a "conservative futurist" and advocate at one and the same time a technologically driven free-market system along with a set of ideological presuppositions affixed to a simpler, less fragmented period of history (Rosenbaum, 1994). More to the point, the desire to extricate corporations from the impediments of government regulation potentially collides with the imposition of moral guidelines that circumscribe, if not censor, the content of and public access to the products those corporations produce.[5] At times, reactionary forces intent upon cultural prohibitions appear to engage in a peculiar form of consumption, appropriating from the dominant business culture those practices and presuppositions that conform with their social agenda and ignoring those loose ends that do not. Making sense of the public policy agenda that results from such a process requires that we attend less to the promotion of our own cultural obsessions, as Marcus Breen advocates, and focus more upon the biformal dimension of those interests our opponents pursue. Much as it might satisfy our ideological appetites, castigating them for regressive social engineering obscures the collision of complex motives that drives their activities.

YOU CAN'T ALWAYS GET WHAT YOU WANT

Consideration of these and other factors can start us on the path of the construction of a new paradigm that will address current conditions with the kind of conceptual rigor and theoretical usefulness that has characterized the work of Adorno, Benjamin, and others in the past. Meanwhile, we need not restrict ourselves merely to mental exercises over the state of the popular music industry or chastise the conglomerates who dominate it as solely an academic matter. Aside from the previously discussed choice to opt out of the equation by refusing to consume or (at least) to consume selectively, we can pursue those opportunities that permit us to investigate and thereafter agitate about the fact that, as Langdon Winner asserts, "What matters is not technology itself, but the social and economic systems in which it is embedded" (1986: 20). It is all too easy and all too common for those who support and encourage the libertory qualities of communications technologies to engage in technophilic rhetoric rather than adopt a biformal position that encompasses both the opportunities technologies create as well as the debilitating circumstances they can bring about. To that end, Winner advises, "the machines, structures, and systems of modern material culture can be accurately judged not only for their contributions to efficiency and productivity and their positive and negative environmental side effects, but also for the ways in which they can embody specific forms of power and authority" (1986: 19). Should one believe that the processes of communication, musical and otherwise, touch upon virtually all activities one can imagine, then analysts who engage in social activism would do well to heed Robert McChesney's admonition: "Regardless of what a progressive group's first issue of importance is, its second issue should be media and communication. This applies to all social movements" (1996: 16).

One avenue worth pursuing is that advocated by Mark Crispin Miller of Johns Hopkins University. He argues that the flurry of mergers and consolidations has not only contracted our "media cosmos" but also led to the reinforcement of "a *national entertainment state*" (1996: 9). The convergence of media and the supremacy of market-driven values can only be deterred, he argues, by the use of antitrust laws in order to break up and, in effect, detoxify that state and bring about a media democracy. Miller further asserts that the FCC should be impelled to put aside its lax pursuit of antitrust laws and the limited number of corporate bodies its actions have abetted.[6] More widespread knowledge of what those bodies own and how our paradigms about popular communications must be redrawn remains imperative. As Miller states: "The only way to solve the problem is to break their hold; and to that end the facts of media ownership must be made known to all. In short, we need a few good maps, because, as the man said, there must be some way out of here" (1996:10).

Extricating ourselves from this dilemma should not, as I've argued, be predicated upon an uncritiqued notion of the absolute hegemony of the corporate regime. We must reinforce, as part of a biformal vision, that the masters of that regime bear individual faces and possess human frailties. In his "Fourteen Truisms for the Communications Revolution," the communications columnist for the *New Yorker*, Ken Auletta, admonishes us to remember: "In covering the rash of mergers and firings in the communications business...we need follow more than business factors. We've got to follow the human factors – pride, greed, vanity, panic, personal comfort – behind the headlines (1996: 34). A classic example of trivial content born out of overweening pride is the lackluster MSNBC, launched as an Internet site on July 15, 1996, by Bill Gates's Microsoft in conjunction with NBC Television News, each of whom will invest $250 million during the next five years. So replete with references to the two investors is this service, a practice referred to in business school jargon as "branding," that if MSNBC were, in fact, a cow, one could not distinguish the creature's hide from the hype. For all the hoopla about the speed of downloading information over the Net, *Newsweek* commented, "There is, by the way, a more efficient way of retrieving this information. It's called a newspaper" (Marin, 1996: 77).

As each new technology launches itself into the marketplace or each new recording into the record store, we find ourselves once more enveloped by the centrifuge. It behooves us therefore to approach both those technologies and the musical artifacts they produce with as biformal a perspective a possible. Neither technophobia nor technophilia will facilitate our inquiry, and treating the music industry as a hidebound hegemonic body or a community of sensitive hipsters proves equally misleading. A new para-

digm must keep pace with the novel musical genres that continue to prolif-
erate, the mergers and acquisitions that will not abate, and the legal-
legislative efforts to maintain some manner of control over this volatile marketplace. Meanwhile, in closing, let me once more quote William Butler
Yeats, albeit in a parodic manner: those of us who contemplate and critique
the popular music industry will continue to ponder, *What rough beat slouches
toward Billboard waiting to be bought?*

NOTES

1. These and all subsequent figures are found in Nunziata (1995). For fur-
    ther information on the structure of the music industry and the relative
    dominance of the "Big 6," see Sanjek and Sanjek (1996).

2. I first came across the notion of the transformation of individual pieces
    of musical intellectual property into rights packages in Frith (1993); in
    the introduction to the series of essays on music and copyright, he used
    the phrase "baskets of rights" (ix) to characterize individual pieces of
    music.

3. While the uses of various media to merchandise music in as many con-
    texts as possible remains a time-honored process, one of the first
    instances in recent time when the practice was pursued with a
    vengeance remains Al Coury's "crossover marketing" of *Saturday Night
    Fever* (1977) for the producer of both the film and the soundtrack,
    Robert Stigwood (Sanjek and Sanjek, 1996: 597–8).

4. See Masters and Fried (1995) for a summary of the soap opera or
    tragedy (depending upon one's perspective) that ensued at the Warner
    Music Group during 1995 and led to the ousting of some of the most
    notable executives at the label and throughout the music industry, prin-
    cipal among them Robert Krasnow and Mo Ostin, and a 17 percent loss
    during the third quarter of the year by the music division.

5. A fascinating narrative account of the manner in which the social and
    corporate agendas of the Republican majorities in the US House and
    Senate collided and, in the end, derailed most of their attempts to
    reconstruct national social policy can be read in Maraniss and Weis-
    skopf (1996). It documents that allegiance to a multitude of incompati-
    ble masters, corporate and otherwise, leads to fragmentation and ulti-
    mate dissolution.

6. While I am sympathetic with Miller's campaign, it is paradoxical to note that the call for the use of antitrust laws to break up corporate hegemony parallels the arguments of the Progress and Freedom Foundation, the think tank affiliated with Speaker Gingrich's office, to dissolve the FCC and transfer its function to the antitrust division of the Justice Department or devolve them even further to state governments (Keyworth et al. 1995). While the two groups' aims differ radically, they both undermine, one directly and the other implicitly, the functions of the FCC. Might one, instead, argue that the commission needs to continue to exist and to pursue its stated (but not enacted) functions with greater vigor?

REFERENCES

"A Threat To Media Diversity," 1996. *New York Times*, July 31, A12.

"A Victory for Viewers," 1995.*New York Times*, February 3, 22.

Attali, J. 1985. *Noise. The Political Economy of Music.* Minneapolis: University of Minnesota Press.

Auletta, K. 1996. "Fourteen Truisms for the Communications Revolution." *Media Studies Journal* (spring/summer): 29–38.

Barber, B. 1995. *Jihad vs. McWorld.* New York: Times Books/Random House.

Bogart, L. 1996. "What Does It All Mean?" *Media Studies Journal* 10(2–3): 15–27.

Breen, M. 1995. "The End of the World as We Know It: Popular Music's Cultural Mobility." *Cultural Studies* 9(3): 486–504.

Burnett, R. 1996. *The Global Jukebox. The International Music Industry.* New York: Routledge.

"The Expanding Entertainment Universe." 1995. *Business Week*, August 14, 114.

Frith, S. 1993. "Introduction." In *Music & Copyright*, edited by S. Frith. Edinburgh: Edinburgh University Press.

Gitlin, T. 1995. *The Twilight of Common Dreams: Why America Is Wracked by Culture Wars.* New York: Metropolitan Books/Henry Holt.

Holland, B. 1996. "RIAA Among Decency Act Opposers." *Billboard*, March 9, 5.

Kammen, M. 1973. *People of Paradox: An Inquiry Concerning the Origins of American Civilization*. New York: Vintage.

Keyworth, G. J. Eisenbach, T. Lenard, and D. E. Colton. 1995. *The Telecom Revolution – An American Opportunity*. Washington, DC: Progress and Freedom Foundation.

Landro, L. and E. Shapiro. 1995. "Entertainment-Industry Outlook Is a Tear-jerker." *Wall Street Journal*, July 9, B1–B6.

Levy, S. 1996. "Now for the Free-for-All." *Newsweek*, February 22, 42–4.

Lewis, P. H. 1996. "Judge Blocks Law Intended to Regulate On-Line Smut." *New York Times*, February 16, D1, D16.

Maraniss, D. and M. Weisskopf. 1996. *Tell Newt to Shut Up!* New York: Touchstone/Simon & Schuster.

Marin, R. 1996. "Rebooting the News." *Newsweek*, July 29, 77.

Masters, K. 1995. "Hollywood Fades to Red." *Time*, August 5, 58–60.

Masters, K. and S. Fried. 1995. "The Precarious Throne. " *Vanity Fair* (October): 90, 94, 96, 99, 100, 104, 106, 115–18.

McChesney, R. 1995a. "Public Broadcasting in the Age of Communication Revolution." *Monthly Review* 47(7): 1–19.

———. 1995b. "Telecon." *In These Times*, July 10, 14–17.

———. 1996. "The Global Struggle for Democratic Communication." *Monthly Review* 48(3): 1–20.

McMorris, F. A., and Jared Sandberg. 1996. "Indecent-Material Curbs Are Struck Down Again." *Wall Street Journal*, July 30, B6.

Miller, M. C. 1996. "Free The Media." *The Nation*, June 3, 9–12, 14–15.

Negus, K. 1995. "Where the Mystical Meets the Market: Creativity and Commerce in the Production of Popular Music." *Sociological Review*: 43(2): 316–41.

Nunziata, S. 1995. "The Year In Business." *Billboard*, December 23, YE–10, YE–12.

Rosenbaum, D. E. 1994. "Republicans Like Both Previews and Reruns." *New York Times*, December 11, 1, 16.

Sanjek, R. and D. Sanjek. 1996. *Pennies from Heaven. The American Popular Music Business in the Twentieth Century*. New York: Da Capo Press.

Winner, Langdon. 1986. *The Whale and the Reactor. A Search for Limits in an Age of High Technology*. Chicago: University of Chicago Press.

10

Fields of Practice

Musical Production,
Public Policy, and the Market

Holly Kruse

An area of neglect in popular music studies – most noticeably in popular music studies in the United States – has been the relationship between popular music studies, the market, and the state. This is unfortunate, because much research taking place on popular music (including my own work) cannot be separated from questions of the influence of market factors and state policies on musical practices and scholarly agendas. In this chapter, I want to look in particular at the central role of the state in helping to create the conditions in which popular music is produced, circulated, and studied. I will first describe concepts from the work of sociologist Pierre Bourdieu that can be applied to the study of intersections between popular music studies, economic relations, and the state; I will then examine various state-imposed national and local popular music policies; and finally, I will raise questions about the role of popular music scholars in this web of state and market relations.

FIELDS OF PRACTICE

In order to better conceptualize the relationship between the market, the state, and popular music studies, I found it useful to turn to the work of Pierre Bourdieu. Although Bourdieu's work is limited by his inability to account for fundamental changes in society and his failure to outline in explicit terms the roles played by both the state and individual actors in various social, political, economic, and cultural processes, his notion of "fields" of practice that comprise social space is quite useful. As noted by Bourdieu scholar Richard Jenkins, Bourdieu's work is important because of its "systematic exposition of the inter-relatedness of education, cultural consumption, and stratification patterns in modern society" (1993: 180). The intersections of popular music practices, popular music studies, and economic and political forces are of increasing interest to popular music scholars, and Bourdieu's notion of fields is particularly valuable in understanding these interrelationships.

Bourdieu notes a number of fields that structure social space. For purposes of this chapter, the four key fields to examine are the field of cultural production, the economic field, the educational field, and the field of power. Each field is a specific, hierarchically structured domain defined by particular forms of capital in which individual agents struggle over capital and other resources. For example, in the economic field struggles occur over control of economic capital; in the educational field, struggles take place over educational capital – essentially, school-imparted knowledge; and in the field of cultural production, struggles occur over, in Bourdieu's words, "the power to impose the dominant definition of the writer [or artist] and therefore to delimit the population of those entitled to take part in the struggle to define the writer [or artist]....it is the monopoly of the power to say with authority who are authorized to call themselves writers [or artists]"(1993: 42).

Because the stakes over which struggle takes place are different in each field, each field is relatively autonomous from other fields, yet fields are structurally homologous; and they are linked by sets of practices, or logics of practice, enacted across fields. Moreover, all fields exist in relation to the field of power. Richard Jenkins states that "the field of power it to be regarded as the dominant and preeminent field of any society; it is the source of the hierarchical power relations which structure all other fields" (1992: 86). None of the other fields, including the field of cultural production and the educational field, can be understood without consideration of power relations.

Besides describing the field of power's dominant relationship to the educational and cultural production fields, Bourdieu also outlines the relationship between these two subordinate fields, noting that the educational field, through its power to incorporate the study of specific cultural products into mainstream academic study, plays a crucial role in validating certain products of restricted cultural production; the educational field and the field of power are where struggles over culture and its legitimation are played out (R. Jenkins: 120). There is, of course, a time lag between the emergence of new cultural products (jazz, rock and roll, etc.) and their acceptance as legitimate objects of academic study. Once accepted into academia, however, cultural products become more explicitly linked to the state, for, as Bourdieu notes, "the state, after all, has the power to orient intellectual production by means of subsidies, commissions, promotion, honorific posts, even decorations, all of which are for speaking or for keeping silent, for compromise or abstention" (1993: 125).

I will turn to the educational field and the field of power (primarily the state) in a moment, but first I want to look more specifically at the relationship between cultural production and the economic field. Within capitalist societies, the field of cultural production always exists in some relationship to the market. Independent rock/pop production is an obvious example of a point at which cultural production and the market converge. If we look at cases of cultural production that fall into the subcategory Bourdieu calls the "field of restricted production," where profit is disavowed (and which he at times defines as "production for producers," as opposed to the field of large-scale production), we find that even a tiny, independent label that puts out small pressings of 7-inch vinyl singles and sells them through mail order and in independently owned stores through independent distributors participates in a market defined and structured by major labels. Furthermore, it has become extremely difficult for independent labels to maintain their status as sites of record production and distribution entirely outside of or in opposition to mainstream music production and distribution. This is demonstrated by recent examples of major labels using independent distributors – rather than their in-house distribution arms – to market some "alternative" releases, distributing some singles as 7-inch records only after small, independent rock labels had enjoyed success with the 7-inch format that had been deemed obsolete by the mainstream record industry a few years earlier.

Even less obvious examples point to the pervasiveness of the market in seemingly noncommercial musical production. Musical fan texts (such as songs about television shows written by their fans; for instance, the fan-

"filked" *Star Trek* – based songs of which Henry Jenkins writes) and sampling are dependent on commercial products from which sounds and ideas are appropriated. Similarly, bluegrass music aficionados who gather together to jam are dependent on the market. That is, many jams take place at festivals, where one must pay to get in; and even when players gather in homes to jam, the songs they play have most likely been learned from records or at festivals, rather than through an oral tradition. Such practices exist at the margins of musical production, yet they are influenced by the market and its forces. It is indeed quite difficult to imagine modes of cultural production in a capitalist society that exist entirely in a noncommercial public sphere.

The importance of the economic field in relation to popular music practice is reflected, to a degree, in popular music studies. While it cannot be said, at least in the US, that the music industry sets the agenda for popular music studies, there are clearly forms of academic research, particularly social scientific analyses, that are useful to, and may even be commissioned by, record companies. Yet there are certainly subtler ways in which the agenda of popular music studies has been influenced by market forces. For example, genre classifications generated, at least in part, by the music industry through its promotional, retail, and radio apparatuses – like alternative, country, techno, and so on – provide the parameters for much scholarly work. While academics may take up industry categories and labels, I think many of us are also generally careful to critique them and recognize them for what they are. Still, we need to be much more self-reflexive about our acceptance and reproduction of generic categories, and about our positioning and roles in relation to the economic field, the field of cultural production, the educational field, and, ultimately, the field of power.

NATIONAL POLICIES

The overlap of market categories with those used in critical and academic discourse reminds us of the usefulness of Bourdieu's schema in popular music studies. As Bourdieu points out, the field of power dominates and permeates all fields, and we must therefore remember that both the education system and the market always exists in relation to the state. In this section, I want to further examine the relationship between the market and the state, which, in terms of music production, is not as obvious in the US as it is in countries like Canada, Australia, Denmark, or the United Kingdom, where the relationship between music-making and national policy making is explicit. Canada and Australia, for instance, have airplay quotas that require radio broadcasters to devote a specified amount of airtime to music originating within that nation. Since 1970 Canadian law has required that 30 percent of AM radio content be produced, written, or performed in Canada, and similar regulations requiring significant programming of Canadian content apply to FM radio. Included in the phrase "Canadian content" is not only music made and recorded in Canada, but any music written or performed by a Canadian (Shuker, 1994: 63). During the mid- to late-1980s, policy makers in New Zealand debated a similar law, which would have established a radio airplay quota often to 20 percent of "music composed, arranged, performed or recorded by New Zealand citizens or residents" (Shuker, 1994: 65), but such a quota was never adopted.

Airplay quotas are attempts to counter the market dominance of foreign-owned (and predominantly US-based) multinational record companies; they are intended to help maintain national identity in the face of American cultural imperialism through greater circulation of native cultural forms and products. Yet the efficacy of quotas in creating and maintaining coherent national identities is called into question by Simon Frith, who observes that under quotas: "It doesn't matter what Canadian or Australian music sounds like, as long as it meets certain criteria of production (written by Canadians, produced by Canadians, performed by Canadians, produced in a Canadian studio). Cultural industry policy makes no reference to the expressive values of music, only its economic potential....As a Soviet state official once said to me (New Music World was negotiating to bring Soviet musicians to Glasgow), 'We've got rock, punk, reggae, heavy metal, jazz. Just tell us what sort of groups you want'" (1993: 23). Not only is the effect of quotas on the promotion of national culture questionable, but as Jody Berland points out, in the case of Canada, airplay quotas had no significant effect on the structures of ownership and distribution within the Canadian record industry (1991: 321).[1]

Content quotas, however, are not the only means by which national governments intervene in popular music. State-funded broadcasting services like the BBC have played important roles in shaping popular music. Frith argues, for instance, that John Peel's show on the BBC's Radio 1 helped determine the direction taken by independently produced British pop music

in the years after punk (14). The British government has also indirectly promoted pop and rock through its funding of performing arts colleges, which
have been central in the development of popular music in Britain (Frith,
1993: 14–15) in a way unparalleled by any performing arts schools that
receive some form of national and/or state funding in the US. In the Netherlands, national funding of popular music has been more direct than in the
UK; since the late 1970s, the Dutch government has provided funding
through the Ministry of Culture, Recreation, and Social Work for pop-collectives that have been central in rock education programs and musicians'
union issues (Shuker, 1994: 58–9). Roy Shuker notes that, unlike other
national governments, in the Netherlands "the central government...shifted
from the traditional State relegation of rock music to the commercial market to consider rock music as a cultural form like any other, and thereby worthy of a similar level of support" (59).

The US government of course has no such history of funding rock and
pop music, and even its funding of "high culture" has been under attack in
recent years and is now decreasing. Furthermore, broadcasters in the US
face no content quotas, and National Public Radio (NPR), the broadcasting
service that receives government funding, is not widely listened to relative
to commercial radio. NPR is formatted by local affiliates, who may choose
to program classical, folk, bluegrass, jazz, or any other music of their choos-
ing – or they may choose not to program any music at all and air only news
and talk shows. NPR certainly does not fill the central role in setting (or
attempting to set) a national pop music agenda that the BBC fills in Britain
or the CBC fills in Canada.

These examples, however, are not meant to suggest that there are no
national policies pertaining to popular music in the United States. Through
trade policies, the US is able to exercise a great deal of control over cultural production in countries with which it trades, and thus further US interests. Agreements like the General Agreement on Tariffs and Trade (GATT),
the North American Free Trade Agreement (NAFTA), and the pre-NAFTA
bilateral US-Canada Free Trade Agreement (FTA) give the US power to
retaliate against countries that engage in "unfair trade practices" in a wide
variety of areas. Such agreements, for example, enabled the US to force
British Columbia to discontinue a governmentally funded tree planting program on the grounds that the program constituted an "unfair subsidy" to the
Canadian timber industry (Barnet and Cavanaugh, 1994: 351).

Pressure of this sort under bi- and multilateral trade agreements occurs in the culture industries as well. In her article "Free Trade and Canadian Music: Level Playing Field or Scorched Earth?" Jody Berland argues that the US-Canada Free Trade Agreement is detrimental to the Canadian music industry because it requires the Canadian government to cut back or eliminate funding that may appear to subsidize the recording industry. Berland cites a US study done in 1984 – five years prior to the adoption of the FTA – that

> identified Canada ("among other countries to a lesser degree") as committing a number of "unfair trade practices," including import quotas, restrictions on US-produced commercials, state-owned production and distribution facilities which are "unfair competition" to private companies, foreign ownership restrictions, discriminatory tax rules, and unfair customs practices. The US position was that government subsidies and other interferences with free-market trade practices had to be abolished; the position of Canadian critics of the Agreement was that such abolition would lead to the elimination or radical curtailment of the independent communications/cultural industries within Canada. (1991· 320)

The FTA as adopted allows retaliation, in the form of tariffs, against a trading partner who is seen as engaging in protectionist practices. So, for instance, if the Canadian government gives a one-million-dollar subsidy to the Canadian recording industry, the US can retaliate with one million dollars in tariffs against Canadian exports. In Berland's words, under the FTA, "the specific protection of cultural products, practices, and traditions within a country (in this case, Canada) is thereby legally abolished as a right of government" (320).

In theory, as Berland points out, since retaliatory tariffs can be levied by either party in the agreement, the public policy disadvantage is equal for both sides. In the realm of popular music production (and mass entertainment in general), however, the US has no vehicle for funneling government subsidies to the recording industry, while Canada, through the Sound Recording Development Program (SRDP) established in 1985, has used government funds to support Canadian popular music production and distribution. Programs like the SRDP, and even Canadian content quotas on radio and television, therefore put Canada in a position to be retaliated against by the US because such programs and policies work against the creation of a "level playing field" and a "free flow" of information between the two countries (Berland: 320–2; Alleyne, 1995: 50).

Terms like "free flow" of information and "level playing field" are ironic when used by US trade officials in this context, since culture industry subsidies and content quotas have arisen because of the dominance of US mass culture all over the world. Yet when the US employs these terms, it is using them to refer only to the economic conditions of trade; cultural rights, as Mark Alleyne observes, are not a major concern of exporters of mass media products, but they are a central concern of those countries that import more music, movies, television programs, periodicals, and books than they export (54). From the US's perspective, if one country provides subsidies to its recording industry and another country doesn't, then the playing field is not level, even if the subsidized record companies are dwarfed in size, profit, and power by the unsubsidized ones.

To therefore argue that the United States, which is home to many of the most powerful producers of mass culture in the world, does not have a national policy supporting its recorded music industry is misguided. Through trade agreements, the US government attempts to ensure the continued well-being of its music industry by restricting the cultural-economic policies of its trading partners.

LOCAL POLICIES

As with national policies, local policies supporting popular music production and circulation at first glance appear virtually nonexistent in the United States but can be found in other countries, primarily European countries. For example, Dutch pop-collectives, while receiving funding from the national government, operate primarily at the local level. Perhaps the most striking examples of governmental support for local popular music can be found in the United Kingdom, where in the past decade there has been a significant move towards local council funding of rock and pop. The Greater London Council (GLC) and the Sheffield City Council were the first local government bodies in the UK to directly promote pop music production in their cities, but by the late 1980s and early 1990s city councils in Liverpool, Norwich, Glasgow, and other localities were pursuing pop music policy initiatives (Street, 1993; Frith, 1993; Cohen, 1991).

John Street sees the move by local councils into programs promoting pop and rock as an extension of the traditional role of localities in support-ing local cultural events and venues (1993, 43). Yet while British cities and towns have long histories of supporting theaters and arts centers, it was only in the 1980s that local governments saw popular music as worthy of support. Why? Sara Cohen observes that in Liverpool, the driving force behind public-sector involvement in local popular music production was a desire to stimulate the economy. Liverpool's goals, according to Cohen, have been to keep successful local bands in Liverpool, to make the local music industry more profitable, and to use the local music scene's success to regenerate other areas of the local economy (1991, 334).

Indeed, every local council in the UK involved in popular music promo-tion appears to be inspired largely by economic motives. For instance, as described by Cohen, the Labour-dominated council that came to power in Liverpool in 1987 strongly advocated a central role for culture industries, including popular music, in helping the city shift from an economy based in the declining manufacturing sector to one based in the service sector (1991, 334). The city published an Arts and Cultural Industries Strategy in which, according to Cohen: "[The] key objective was 'to maximize the contribution which the arts and cultural industries make to the economic *and* social well-being of the city,' thus placing the emphasis upon business and employment development, and upon community involvement, the provision of services, and more general quality-of-life issues"(1991, 334). Such goals seem to place a rather unwieldy burden on local culture industries, including popular music.

However, many music scenes in the UK have not merely welcomed involvement by local councils, they have lobbied for it. In Sheffield, the genesis of the Music Factory project – a plan for a combined practice and recording facility drafted by the City Council's Employment Department – was lobbying by local music industry participants (Frith, 1993: 15). Similarly, in Norwich it was a coalition composed primarily of local musicians who banded together under the name of the Norwich Venue Campaign (NVC) and lobbied the council to fund a local performance venue (which became the Waterfront) (Street, 1993: 45).

Attempts at cooperation between councils and local music industries have worked to some degree, but they have also created relationships of considerable tension. Such tensions are understandable, of course. In the

case of Norwich's Waterfront, the city council owns the building that houses the venue; it leased the building to a trust composed of council members
and others, which in turn sublet the building to members of the NVC who
manage the Waterfront. The different interests of parties involved – the
interest of the council in promoting Norwich and creating jobs versus the
interest of the management in providing a place for practice, performance,
and education – have led to a great deal of conflict (Street, 1993: 47–8).
Cohen describes similar tensions in Liverpool resulting from council-gener-
ated music initiatives, including concerts, plans to develop a cultural district,
and plans to build the Liverpool Institute of Performing Arts (Cohen, 1991:
336–8). Many in the Liverpool music scene are skeptical of the council's
ability to effectively oversee music programs and events (and apparently
with some justification); they are unhappy that the council's initiatives have
been directed primarily at visitors rather than residents; and they are concerned that both public and private bodies involved in city development initiatives lack an aesthetic appreciation of popular music and/or an understanding of how the music business operates (Cohen, 1991: 338–9).

So far, city council involvement in local music production and circulation in the UK has had mixed results. Some programs beneficial to music
scenes have been created; however, many of the policies have been disad-
vantageous to local scenes. In her discussion of cultural policy initiatives,
Cohen goes so far as to state that the Liverpool case study "reveals that, in
trying to encourage growth within the music industries, the city council,
along with other agencies in the public and private sector, has, unintentionally, been impeding it" (1991, 340–1).

In the United States, a similar degree of intervention by local governments in local music production and performance does not yet exist. However, as with national pop music policies, it would be naive to assume that
there are no policies in US localities that affect popular music. In fact, of the
four forms of control British city councils have exercised over local popular
music production – regulation, finance, cultural policy, and industrial/eco-
nomic policy (Street, 1993: 44) – three are common in the United States.
Local authorities exercise control over liquor licenses, noise ordinances,
event permits, and obscenity statutes, all of which can impact what kinds of
live music get played and what kinds of recorded music get sold. Local
authorities may also have power over rent levels and taxes[2] for businesses,

and localities may offer arts festivals or other events that include popular music and that are in part underwritten by city governments.[3]

Local scenes in the US are expected to make a name for themselves without the help of local governments. If anything is seen as enabling scenes to emerge in certain localities, it is some combination of low costs of living and making music and of the proper sort of social and cultural environment. As an indie pop musician who played in bands while living in the college town of Davis, California, put it: "Davis is a town that doesn't have really high rents, and you can actually rent houses and practice in the houses. There are a couple of little clubs around town – just enough so you can play. A college radio station right in town, so you can walk down with your little band tape and give it to them and get it played on the radio…Those are the ingredients for a scene." (Miller: 1990)

It is perhaps because of this laissez-faire notion of how music scenes develop that local popular music policies have not been of interest to American scholars or policymakers. However, it is important to note that a specific sense of music as something that can be performed and produced locally within a "music community" exists in the US; this notion of a local music community (in opposition to a centralized, nonlocal music industry) was important in the development of popular music promotional policies by local councils in the UK (Frith, 1993: 16). In the wake of early 1990s media hype about the Seattle music scene (and earlier waves of publicity about music scenes in Athens, Georgia; Minneapolis, Minnesota; Austin, Texas; and elsewhere), it is certainly conceivable that local governments in the US might consider investing in music scenes in order to create outside interest in their localities.

Should this happen, popular music scholars in the US might find themselves in a position similar to that of many popular music scholars in the UK: namely, involved in the policy-making process. Popular music researchers in Sheffield, Liverpool, and other cities have conducted surveys on the status of local music industries and on the success of various music-related public policies (Frith, 1993: 18; Cohen, 1991: 341–2). In the final section of this chapter, I would like to problematize the involvement of academics in such a process – one in which both the market and the state have vested interests.

FIELDS OF CONVERGENCE

I have not yet discussed the role of the educational field in detail, although Bourdieu's concept of fields makes clear the relationship between cultural production, the state, and education. Zygmunt Bauman argues that the relationship between these three entities has changed markedly in recent centuries. Whereas intellectuals were once central to policy formulation, that role has been turned over to bureaucrats and lobbyists as society has moved towards encouraging consumption and away from trying to develop ways to maintain state control over subjects (Bauman, 1992: 15–17). Intellectuals are no longer in the position of making and remaking culture, but instead their task is to study and try to better understand it (Bauman, 1992: 25) – which is indeed the primary role of academics who are part of popular music policy processes.

Nevertheless, Bauman's statements are obvious generalizations, for one can point to numerous examples of scholars who have had significant policy impacts: futurists Heidi and Alvin Toffler, whose work has had an impact on policies proposed by United States Speaker of the House of Representatives Newt Gingrich; Vaclav Havel, who became the first president of the Czech Republic; and popular music scholars in Europe, who have been involved in various stages of musical production and performance policy making.

Yet because scholars, including popular music scholars, are already part of policy apparatuses elsewhere, we need to ask whether it should be the goal of pop music scholars in the United States to influence policies, both national and local. With the media focus on specific US music scenes (such as Seattle, Austin, Columbus, Athens, etc.) and the likely concomitant desire of communities to find ways to economically benefit from these local music scenes, as well as with the increasing impact of national and international trade agreements on musical practices in the US (and elsewhere), it is reasonable to assume that there will be both a desire on the part of those who study popular music to become involved in the policy-making process, and a desire on the part of policymakers to solicit input from pop music scholars. The expertise of many popular music scholars would certainly be useful in developing policies and assessing their impacts.

However, I also think such involvement is problematic. Popular music studies are hardly univocal and certainly could not (and indeed *should* not) present a united front on the national level. Interventions could perhaps be more successful on the local level, even though at this time there does not seem to be a demand on the part of US localities for music policy proposals or evaluations from academics. I would also argue that because the bulk of popular music research in the US has focused on textual analysis, genre history, and technology, it is ill equipped to address, much less legislate, pop music policy.

Yet if there was ever a time for American popular music studies to examine its role in policy debates, it is now, not only when there is increasing state involvement in popular music-making on the national level, but also when conflicts over mass-mediated culture have largely divided cultural observers into two camps: one that celebrates individualism and the "democracy of public culture" and another that argues for the greater collective good of protecting families and society as a whole from debasing influences. What gets lost in this polarization is both the fact that there is no real "democracy of public culture" in a society where markets are controlled by a handful of conglomerates and the fact that this debate is being framed by institutions (media companies, political bodies) whose leaders are, in Bourdieu's terms, products of the same class habitus.

Positing a role for popular music scholars in this interaction is further complicated if one takes into account Bourdieu's argument that pedagogy is central in reproducing social relations and reflecting the dominant interests in society. Those of us who teach are engaged in what Bourdieu calls "pedagogic action," which he argues is a form of symbolic violence, always tending "to reproduce the structure of the distribution of cultural capital among these groups or classes, thereby contributing to the reproduction of the social structure" (Bourdieu and Passeron, 1990: 11). Educators are already part of a hierarchy that is in turn part of the power structure of society as a whole; becoming more explicitly involved in furthering the interests of the market and the state would require that we more closely examine the implications of our pedagogic actions and our research.

Bourdieu's work, his "exposition of the interrelationships between education, cultural consumption, and stratification patterns" (R. Jenkins, 1992: 180), provides an important starting point for self-analysis by popular music scholars. If after such self-reflection, US pop music scholars decide to take up the gauntlet of policy making, likely places to start might include articulating relationships between national debates and local practices and policies, questioning what roles the state and the market play in supporting or defining or research, and critiquing the effects of the confluence of the fields of cultural production, economics, politics, and education within the field of power.

NOTES

1. When discussing Canadian airplay quotas, it is important to note that these exist not only at the national level, but at the regional level as well. Line Grenier (1993) describes in detail Canada's French-language vocal music policy (FVM). Adopted in 1973 largely to combat the homogenizing influence of dominant American music on Canadian radio program, the FVM required (and continues to require) that 65 percent of songs on privately owned Francophone radio stations be in the French language (120). Interestingly, from the start this rule met with opposition from individuals in the music industry, who feared that the need to supply radio stations with French-language music would limit the development and production of other forms of musical products in Quebec, and thus further marginalize record companies based in Quebec.

2. Greg Mountain, a booking agent and promoter in Philadelphia during the 1980s and 1990s, believes that Philadelphia's amusement tax and liquor-by-the-drink tax have been detrimental to the local music scene, especially since clubs do not receive any additional city services for these taxes.

3. Of course, like British municipalities, many cities in the US have helped to fund local "high culture" – symphony orchestras, opera companies, ballet companies – but while British councils have begun to include popular music in their arts provisions, this has not generally happened in the US.

REFERENCES

Alleyne, M. D. 1995. *International Power And International Communication*. New York: St Martin's Press.

Barnet, R. J., and J. Cavanaugh. 1994. *Global Dreams: Imperial Corporations and the New World Order*. New York: Simon and Schuster.

Bauman, Z. 1992. *Intimations of Postmodernity*. London: Routledge.

Bennett, T., et al. 1993. *Rock and Popular Music: Politics, Policies, Institutions*. London: Routledge.

Berland, J. 1991. Free Trade and Canadian Music: Level Playing Field or Scorched Earth? *Cultural Studies* 5(2): 317–25.

Bourdieu, P. 1993. *The Field of Cultural Production*, edited by R. Johnson. New York: Columbia University Press.

Bourdieu, P., and J.C. Passeron. 1990. *Reproduction in Education, Society and Culture* (2d ed.) London: Sage.

Cohen, S. 1991. "Popular Music and Urban Regeneration: The Music Industries of Merseyside." *Cultural Studies*. 5(2): 332–46.

Frith, S. 1993. "Popular Music and the Local State." In *Rock and Popular Music: Politics, Policies, Institutions*, edited by T. Bennett, et al., 14–24. London: Routledge.

Grenier, L. 1993. "Policing French-Language Music on Canadian Radio: The Twilight of the Popular Record Era?" In *Rock and Popular Music: Politics, Policies, Institutions*, edited by T. Bennett, et al., 119–41. London: Routledge.

Jenkins, H. 1992. "'Strangers No More, We Sing': Filking and the Social Construction of the Science Fiction Fan Community." In *The Adoring Audience: Fan Culture and Popular Media*, edited by L. A. Lewis, 208–36. London: Routledge.

Jenkins, R. 1992. *Pierre Bourdieu*. London: Routledge.

Miller, S. 1990. Personal Interview.

Shuker, R. 1994. *Understanding Popular Music*. London: Routledge.

Street, J. 1993. Local Difference? Popular Music and the Local State. *Popular Music* 12(1): 43–56.

Part III

Location and Movement in the Spaces of Popular Music

11

—————— Crossing Over ——————

Selena's Tejano Music
and the Discourse of Borderlands

Ramona Liera-Schwichtenberg

> The 23-year-old woman driving in her pickup
> down the flat, empty Corpus Christi highway
> past warehouses and Wal-Mart had a life
> bubbling with plans and possibilities. After
> years of performing in the honky-tonk clubs of
> South Texas' Tejano music circuit, her career was
> soaring: Not only was she the undisputed queen
> of Tejano, she was emerging as one of the
> brightest new stars on the Latin pop-music scene...
> Three hours later she lay dying in the arms of a
> stranger on the motel floor, shot dead by the hand
> of a woman she'd trusted with her life.
> —D. McLane, "The Double Life of Selena," 88

The life and death of tejano music superstar Selena Quintanilla Perez seems to have all the ingredients of "Dos Mujeres, Un Camino" (Two Women, One Destiny), a Mexican soap opera in which she appeared. Since her shooting death on March 31, 1995, Selena (as star icon) and her music have enjoyed a mainstream popularity not achieved in her lifetime. At the time of her death, sales of *Amor Prohibido* (Forbidden Love) tripled, reaching 1.5 million copies as the best-selling tejano album (Richmond, 1995); and in July 1995, her posthumous album, *Dreaming of You*, debuted at number one on *Billboard's* album chart. The album has the distinction of being, after Janet Jackson, the second-fastest selling release by a female vocalist in the history of popular music (Patoski, 1995). Two weeks after Selena's death, five of her albums, all in Spanish, appeared on *Billboard's* 200 album chart, signaling her "arrival" in the mainstream (Lemieux, 1995). Selena has not been forgotten by the Mexican American entertainment industry either; in December 1995, the National Council of La Raza Bravo Awards named *Dreaming of You* album of the year.

Called the "queen of tejano music," Selena was well known (since the age of 14) on the tejano circuit ranging from Texas to Mexico; she also gained fame from her appearances on Univision's *Johnny Canales Show* and other Spanish-speaking media outlets that broadcast her performances to many Latin American markets (Richmond, 1995). Selena was a favorite performer among many different Latino cultures from Colombia to Queens, bridging tejano music and culture across the Rio Grande to northern Mexico. During her career, she garnered 22 Tejano Music awards, among them a 1994 Best Music Video Award for "No Me Queda Mas," and was named 1994 Female Entertainer of the Year (for the eighth consecutive year). Not only did she represent success for Tejanos (Texans of Mexican Ancestry) and tejano music, but her achievements also symbolized advancement for *la raza* (the people).

Though Selena's success was understood as success for Mexican Americans, her success was also understood in commercial terms, which is not exclusive from, but rather a part of, the "advancement of a people." She was seen by EMI-Latin executives as the key to crossover success for tejano music's entrance into the Anglo mainstream market. Shortly before her death, Selena signed with SBK Records, the parent company of Capitol/EMI-Latin, for an English-language album due out in 1995 (Richmond, 1995). Ironically, only in death did she achieve crossover success. As a result, tejano music, which is the variously accented expression of a borderland culture, moves from a community-based "in-between-ness" to the media-hyped, capitalist center stage as a marketable commodity. Given these shifts, it is important to investigate the function of the "Selena phenomenon" in relation to cultural identity, which I take to mean "the points of identification, the unstable points of suture which are made in the discourses of history and culture" (Hall, 1989), and the politics of location (Hall, 1991).

In what follows, I examine the "crossover" and "borderlands" metaphors defining Selena's tejano success in the context of renegotiating the identities of Mexican Americans as a historical phenomenon. In other words, these are "lived" metaphors, grounded in a history of the migratory dispossession and internal colonization of Mexican Americans. Further, I argue that these are useful metaphors in explaining the movement and translation of an oppressed group's musical expression from the borderlands of South Texas to Anglo mainstream diffusion. In this regard, the "Selena phenomenon" provides an exemplary case for the dialectical interplay of forces, located between life/death, Texas/Mexico, and Tex-Mex Madonna/Virgen de Guadalupe, framed by the master tropes of borderlands and crossover.

Cultural studies scholars have been questioning and interrogating the explanatory power of certain theoretical concepts such as "difference" and its synonyms (indicating sexual or racial minorities) that attained popularity during the "postcolonial/multicultural boom" of the early 1990s (cf. M. Morris, 1988). This is not to say that the "boom" was a "bust"; for example, a second wave of postcolonial critics and theorists have emerged to productively challenge the earlier groundwork laid by Gayatri Spivak and Edward Said. Moreover, multiculturalism is currently being retheorized in relation to postmodernism and postcolonialism, as well as in relation to the globalization of culture and ethnicity.

But, given the trendiness of university scholarship, which is involved in circulating knowledge as cultural capital, many scholars who earlier allied themselves with notions of "difference" appear to be stepping back. For example, David Theo Goldberg (1994: 7) argues convincingly that the globalization of ethnicities has created "corporate muticulturalisms" and "differences" that are, among other things, "part of the centrist academy." Such appropriations, he argues, drain terms of their referential and political efficacy. He notes that the failure to theorize a nuanced understanding of multiculturalism has sometimes resulted in "politically naive theoretical sloganeering," including the mantra of "difference" (Goldberg, 1994: 14). Lawrence Grossberg (1995) has also questioned the adequacy of too easily accepting "difference as a critical moment," suggesting a theory of otherness, rather than a theory of difference. This is all well and good.

However, we must be careful in too easily debunking (as well as too easily deploying) those terms used in theorizing the experiences or subjectivities of others, lest we forget the thick, layered description of a people's history. As Malcolm X (1992) reminds us, "History is a people's memory." Moreover, it is hard not to note that those appropriating terms that name the marginal are typically white men in the centrist academy who have always had the privilege to do so. Speaking to such cavalier appropriations, Rafael Pérez-Torres (1995: 170) coins the term "migratory readings" as a strategy that steals from the lived practices of the dispossessed; yet, he concedes, such a strategy is double-edged for it "also evokes within its discursive strategies the same process of negotiation undertaken by migrant groups caught between poverty and repression in their homelands, and cultural dislocation and oppressive marginalization in the centers of power to which they flee."

The "Selena phenomenon" suggests the complicity of a migratory reading in which location is literal as well as figurative. The borderlands of South Texas/Mexico is a place of historical oppression and migration, but it is also the space of a people's music. Selena's music invokes the complexities of Mexican American identity as her pop-version of tejano, imprinted with the migrant *conjunto* of 150 years ago, crosses over to the metaphoric space of the dominant – the mainstream. Thus, from the outset, we are confronted with the metaphor "mainstream," commonly used to describe the demographics of the dominant culture: amorphous, whitewashed, blended, middle class, and above all, assimilated.

This assimilationist inflection is also present in the concepts of "crossing over" and its correlate, "passing," both terms which suggest movement towards winning acceptance by the white power elite (e.g., "crossing over" the color line or "passing" as white). But besides referring to a case of mistaken racial identity, "passing" also refers to death. For instance, in her discussion of Nella Larsen's short story, "Passing," Judith Butler (1993: 183) notes how Clare, who passes as white, also passes out the window to her death. According to Butler, who cites Henry Louis Gates, Jr., "passing carries the double meaning of crossing the color line and crossing over into death: passing as a kind of passing on." In this sense, Selena (as signifier of her music) embodies a double meaning of the term "crossover" as 1) a boundary – crossing movement into the Anglo music market; and 2) a passage from life to death, signifying a transcendent movement to the "other side." "Passing" is also appropriate in this regard, since it suggests a racial blending into the mainstream as well as death. Thus, we have the spectre of "crossover" signifying a literal death, and a metaphoric death by whiteout.

"Mainstreaming" exacts a stiff price in the associative linkage of money and death. Indeed, if capital functions in the service of difference (Grossberg, 1996), what could be more "different" than a dead brown woman with a "new" sound? Selena is figured at the site of capitalism's central contradiction between private ownership and socialized production, in which she is both *del pueblo* (of the people) and a "phenomenon," a multinational money-making venture, particularly (and exclusively) in death. As John Morthland (1995: 22) notes, "Selena has crossed over but it took her death to do it; the only thing missing from the flourishing Selena business is Selena herself." Capital infuses her with renewed life. Thus, we have the perverse spectacle of a dead Chicana (described as a "sleeping corpse" as her body lay in state) animated by the "invisible hand" of market economics. Here, the opportunities for dead Mexican Americans in the white musical mainstream seem endless. Death may be the ultimate assimilation. As EMI-Latin president José Behar points out, "We are actually developing an artist in the Anglo market that isn't with us" (Morthland, 1995: 21).

Selena and her music have been memorialized at the altar of big business. Although she initiated commercial product endorsements prior to her death in 1994 – signing a six-figure deal with the Dep Corporation, and agreeing to promotional tours for Coca-Cola, AT & T, and Southwestern Bell (Richmond, 1995) – Selena was further commemorated through the corporate farewells in *People* magazine, which included her photos, words expressing love and sorrow, and a Coke or Dep or AT & T logo. Coca-Cola announced its intentions to market a Selena commemorative Coke bottle to Latino youth throughout the world. And, in a macabre twist, there has been talk of using some of Selena's previously recorded concert and television footage to create "new commercials." As Geraldo Ruiz (1995: 110) ruefully notes, "Coke has the intention of bringing Selena back to her beloved public with a message: 'Buy Coca-Cola.' In this day and age when we can bring people back from the dead with computer graphics and old footage, we can only imagine the huge rise in sales of Coca-Cola when Selena's fans see her face again and hear her voice again."

On the other hand, Selena's success has led the way towards the current mainstreaming and development of tejano music. Since 1990, sales figures for tejano artists have jumped from $10–12 million dollars and to more than $50 million in 1994 (Lannert, 1995). Although the mainstream acceptance of songs of the disenfranchised do, to some extent, produce a "whitening effect," Selena's brand of tejano music has come to represent the borderlands region of South Texas and the low-income Molina barrio where she lived.

However, between borderlands and mainstream there is contested terrain. Greil Marcus (1991: 65–6) suggests this dynamic interplay when he observes that, "there is no greater aesthetic thrill than to see minority culture aggressively and triumphantly transform itself into mass culture. The mainstream absorbs, it breaks down, it spits out, it buries, and it destroys – and it is also changed." Thus, both the culture negotiating the mainstream from the borders, as well as the mainstream itself, is transformed by this interaction; and central to the whole notion of musical incursion from one location to another is the metaphor of liminality: borderlands.

In "The Space of Culture, the Power of Space," Grossberg (1996: 178) criticizes the "proliferation" of spacial metaphors – such as "margins, boundaries, homes, voyages, and destinations," of which borderlands is a ready example. His criticism is well taken given the transcultural abstractions of some of the new postcolonial and cultural studies scholars; however, his own turn to the global follows suit. The function of summarily dismissing "border" metaphors paves the way for Grossberg's Deleuzian-Guattarian theory of "the abstract machine," which is itself a metaphor that "produces a particular configuration of reality" (1996: 180–1). Though he himself figures the global, Grossberg criticizes other scholars for their return to a colonial past as a means of privileging the location of such a history as "the 'proper' figure for identity." Yet, figures always fall short of representing the complexities of identity; they function, rather, as shorthand for the geopolitical ruptures and liminality of a particular historical site of conquest. "Borderlands" should not be a fashionable buzzword, nor should it be automatically discarded just because *some* scholars cannot see their own histories mirrored in that metaphor. In this regard, the lure to figure "the global" (at the expense of the local) is indeed seductive as a totalizing and omniscient gesture.

Instead, I propose that we move from the stratosphere towards the materialist conditions of an oppressed people's history, which is a construction forged in struggle – Hegel's "slaughter bench" of history (Smith, 1983: 255).

As Rosa Linda Fregoso (1993: 65) notes, "for Chicanas and Chicanos and also for Mexicans living on the borderlands, the concept has a longer history and a more politically charged meaning, referring to geopolitical configurations of power and to power relations within a cultural process." The "borderlands" metaphor captures an affective sense of the literal borderlands between the United States and Mexico, created through US invasion and conquest in the mid-1830s and 1840s (Acuña, 1989). Shaped by a history of United States colonization and occupation, the "borderland experience" most closely resembles the colonial experience of "Australia and/or South Africa, where colonizers relegated indigenous populations to fourth-class citizenship or non-citzenship" (Acuña, 1988: 20).

The border dividing the United States from Mexico, established in 1848 along with the Treaty of Guadalupe Hidalgo, sealed the fate of 100,000 Mexicans on the Texas side of the border (Anzaldúa, 1987). Annexed by conquest and thrown off of their land, these tejanos lived in the interstices, straddling two worlds as bicultural and bilingual, never quite Mexican and never quite recognized as American. To this day, with the rabid Right discussing the merits of erecting a 30-foot wall at the border (or a 200-mile fence) and deploying the US military as border guards, "the borderlands remain a site of rupture: economic disempowerment, racial categorization, sexual stratification, cultural marginalization" (Pérez-Torres, 1995: 245).

But the borderland also represents a porous, fluid field that bears the lasting traces of numerous conquests and migrations. The border has been the transitory space of many musical confluences and racial/ethnic identities. Such diversity complicates any singular notion of *a* Mexican American identity. As Carlos Muñoz Jr. (1989: 8) indicates, "Mexican Americans are among the most racially mixed nonwhite people in U.S. society. They are indeed a *rainbow people* difficult to define in traditional race and ethnic relations terms." In fact, the radical *mestizaje* constituting Mexican American identity is wide-ranging, including: Spanish conquistador, Black Moor, American Indian, European, Asian, Aztec, or Mayan – a mix that has been further complicated by Mexican American intermarriages with African Americans, Asian Americans, and European Americans.

While this multicultural and multiracial "mix" defining Mexican Americans may suggest random dispersion, there are strong regional differences between tejanos, Los Angelinos, Hispaños, and those Chicanos in rural and urban areas. Here, the regional cannot be stressed enough, as Muñoz (1989:

8) puts it, "In contrast to the experience of other nonwhite groups, the question of Mexican American identity has been rooted in regional cultural contexts." The internal cultural differences that distinguish Mexican Americans in South Texas from those in other parts of the state or the border from urban or rural areas "have been reflected in cultural forms, [most] notably musical forms" (Muñoz, 1989: 9). Thus, South Texas establishes a sense of place for *conjunto*, a musical form that has functioned historically as a resource for migrants, and that has survived in the various strains of contemporary tejano music.

Conjunto music developed sometime after 1850 from "North Mexican border music," which was a kind of folk music originating in the border regions of northern Mexico and southern Texas, including parts of Texas defined by the Rio Grande (Peña, 1985). Not surprisingly, this Tex-Mex music was communal in nature, similar to Cajun ballads or bluegrass as "poor people's music." Traveling minstrels would often entertain migrant workers, accompanying them to their work in the cotton or strawberry fields. It is out of this milieu that *corridos* (ballads about Mexican heroes and Anglo villains) originated along the South Texas/Mexican border in response to Anglo aggression against Chicanos. One of the early corrido musicians was Lydia Mendoza who was known as the "singer of the poor" during the Depression (Anzaldúa, 1987). Thus, from its inception, conjunto was a mixed-race, border-people's music – a mixture of Spanish, Mexican, and European influences.

By the 1860s, the European accordion was added to the mix. At this time, the central instrument in conjunto (which means ensemble) became the button accordion, introduced into northern Mexico and South Texas by German immigrants, some of the first colonists in Texas who settled farms and built breweries there. Borrowing from the German oompah bands, tejano musicians combined an accordian-driven polka with traditional instruments such as the *tambora de rancho* (goatskin-head drum) and *bajo sexto* (12-string Spanish guitar). In the 1890s conjunto developed as dance music and continues to function in that manner as a community resource for Mexican Americans, particularly for those of the working class (Peña, 1985).

Conjunto is the basis for contemporary tejano music, which from the late 1950s to the 1970s incorporated *orquesta* (orchestra) with horns and synthesizers as *orquesta tejana*, a sound associated with cultural assimilation and upward mobility. Later, orquesta was combined with rock and other types of Mexican music (Peña, 1985). Over the years, tejano has undergone a "layering" of sounds and influences that, like a palimpsest, bears the traces of musical combinations, migrations, trends, and rearrangements. For example, González and Flores (1994) note the Spanish guitar, Mexican horns, country-western, and pop combinations in tejana ranchera, as well as the *cumbia*, which is dance music with a polka beat.

Yet, though musical genres may shift, leaving behind their tonalities and rhythms in the region while in transit, the borderland region remains marked by the geopolitics of an invasive border. The border bears witness to a history of violence and death, economic opportunity, conquest, desire for the American Dream, discrimination, exploitation — in other words, it too has multiple meanings, grounded in a location that is scarred by occupation and dispossession. The complexity informing a history of conquest and a culture of differences impinges on how Mexican American identity is conceived.

Mexican American identity, which finds an avenue of expression through tejano music, has always negotiated the multiple layerings of mixed-race "difference" from the baseline of a shared history — shared, in part, through the knowledge that one's "race" came into being through conquest, the rape of Indian women by Spanish conquistadors. While Anglo-European identity unconsciously presumes the centrality and effaced history of the victor (the imperialist assumption), Mexican American identity is learned through a history and culture that is handed down from one generation to the next (a people's memory).

In this respect, the colonization of a place and a people is a form of cultural inheritance that provides continuity to the mixed-race, multiple identities of the Chicana. Like the accordian in the original conjunto, which carries with it the German polka to cheer up the migrants in their misery, a people's history of oppression is the recurring motif that informs the constitution of identity, later complicated through migrations and intermarriages (like the musical mixtures that inform contemporary tejano). Though lately, identity has become a suspicious location as a site of struggle, it is difficult to imagine Mexican American identity in any other terms. It is, at the very least, a site of cultural struggle and negotiation, and many such negotiations around identity take place through music.

Thus, it would seem that Selena has "crossed the border," figuratively, geoculturally, and musically through tejano music, renegotiating Mexican American identities in the mainstream. Though not consciously, she expanded the range of tejano, thereby contributing to the process of historical layering. Selena's trademark sound – combining Mexican cumbia rhythms with hip-hop, reggae, polka, tropical, country-western, R & B, and techno-pop – synthesizes (and samples) types of music, each with its own complex genealogy. For instance, among Selena's songs, the "Techno Cumbia" names its techno beat and driving rhythm, and her pop hit "Bidi Bidi Bom Bom" combines rap, salsa and disco; whereas "Commo la Flor" is pop-Mexican, and "Baila Conmigo" has a heel-clicking Spanish sound. Incorporations such as these address the fluidity of influences in refashioning a mass culture version of tejano. Arguing against the use of a mythic past that essentializes Chicana identities, Fregoso and Chabram (1990: 206) assert that "cultural identities have histories, they undergo constant transformation, and far from being etched in the past, cultural identities are constantly being constructed."

This is especially true of Selena, whose expansive musical repertoire articulates the mestizaje of identities within the borders of South Texas and beyond. Moreover, in the borderlands, her homeland, she is figured with the star iconography that crosses Tex-Mex Madonna with Virgen de Guadalupe: both virgins of complexity, converging from either side of the border. Thus, Selena's figuration borrows the sexy bustiers and the penchant for musical grazing from Madonna Ciccone, the Italian American superstar who critiques the religious icon (her namesake) in a celebration of the body. However, unlike Madonna, Selena has distanced herself from scandal and maintained close ties to her family and community, even while adopting Madonna's flashy fashion sense.

In death, Selena has acquired the other powerful virginal association, the Virgen de Guadalupe, which is an important religious, cultural, and political symbol, uniting Indian and Spanish influences in one image. Throughout Mexico, Central America, Puerto Rico, and the Southwest, the Virgen de Guadalupe is worshiped in shrines as the patron saint of Mexico as well as emblazoned on United Farm Workers' banners, tattooed on the arms of *pachucos* and painted on the hoods of low-riders. As a part of the sacred and the secular, the Virgen is an icon woven into daily life, on keychains, on posters, and elsewhere. As Gloria Anzaldúa (1987: 30) points out, "La Virgen de Guadalupe is the symbol of ethnic identity and of the tolerance for ambiguity that Chicanos-Mexicanos, people of mixed race, people who have Indian blood, people who cross cultures, by necessity possess." Whereas in life Selena assumed the title of the "Latina Madonna," an ethnic version of a white pop-star, in death she is represented as Mexicana in a move that places her closer to the Mexican side of the border as the Virgen de Guadalupe. Indeed, fan-created, makeshift shrines to Selena dot the places where she lived and died in Corpus Christi. Thus, one could, in effect, enact a popular version of the "stations of the cross" in a trek beginning at Room 158 of the Days Inn where she was shot, proceeding to her boutique, and ending at her home in the Molina barrio. For people of Mexican ancestry, who combine Indian beliefs with Catholicism, death is dealt with performatively, through building homemade shrines, lighting candles, covering mirrors, and talking about it. In Selena's personification as the Virgen de Guadalupe, "people ask for her protection, assured that she is ever-present and watching over them. Flowers and candles are laid out to keep her memory alive" (Ruiz, 1995: 120). Thus, the memory of Selena, revered as "the voice and soul of the Mexican American community" (Martinez, 1995: 18), passes into history as a shining moment for *la raza*. For Mexicanos, the chasm separating life and death is not so great – the crossover, merely a step away. As a result, Selena has been deified as a folk saint since her death, much as César Chávez has been.

Though Selena's passing was mourned in the Anglo marketplace, nowhere more than in South Texas was there such an outpouring of grief, punctuated by candlelight processions throughout the region (and even a release of white balloons into the heavens in Wichita, Kansas). Selena's identity as a tejana was rooted firmly in the borderlands, and one gets a sense of that border culture through the numerous condolences expressed in the small-town, South Texas newspapers where area businesses, friends, neighbors, teachers, school children, and disc jockeys all bid farewell to Selena and attest to her identity as *raza*, "one of us." For instance, John Hernandez asserts that "[she] definitely took our culture into a national and international spotlight" (Del Valle, 1995: 8). Reflecting on why Selena was important to her, 17-year-old Lydia Guzman of McAllen, Texas, states, "She inspired us to be proud of our heritage and express it in the best way possible" ("Selena," 1995a: 3). Pat Garza of Brownsville, Texas, put it simply: "She's our music" ("Selena," 1995b: 1).

Selena, who came from the lower-income Molina barrio, did not forget her community or her culture, and continued to live in the barrio. Rogelio

Botello Rios, a program director in McAllen, remarked that although Selena knew she had a bright future ahead of her, "she was always conscious of where she came from" (Del Valle, 1995: 8). Before and after Selena's funeral on April 4, 1995, hundreds of grieving fans called the Diocese of Corpus Christi seeking explanations for the tragedy, and asking for guidance. Reverend Eduardo H. Garcia of Our Lady of Guadalupe Catholic Church reflected on Selena's community-based identity: "No one can explain death, and the Hispanic [sic] and black children from Selena's neighborhood – our kids, feel a sense of possession in her loss because she was one of them. She never forgot where she came from" (Flores, 1995: 12A).

Thus, we return to the place we started from, the politics of location that is, in this case, the ground for cultural identity – a multifaceted, precious possession that connects past, present, and future. Selena didn't forget who she was or where she came from: her identity and location intertwined, and were expressed through the electrified beat of her pop-tejano, a wild mix spiked with the conjunto and *norteño* of long ago. I make no claim to musical authenticity here nor do I move to essentialize the identity of a people in a trope – with Mexican Americans, that would be impossible.

However, my "migratory reading" that appropriates figures from the dispossessed (my people) has returned the figure, "the borderlands," back home from where it came. It is Selena who has taken tejano music elsewhere with strains of the *cumbia* seeping through porous borders. In yet another farewell to Selena, the Narcisco Martinez Cultural Arts Center in Harlingen, Texas, provides this homage: "'El Huracan Del Valle,' and the father of Texas Mexican Conjunto, made our music an integral part of our community and left an everlasting legacy. Selena, you took the music throughout all of the Americas and continued the legacy, proving our music has no borders" (Narcisco Martinez Cultural Arts Center, 1995: 6). Clearly, music migrates and passes through on its way somewhere else. But it is from somewhere. So too Selena, the tejano queen from the borderlands, was just passing through and crossing over, leaving us with one more layer to the musical palimpsest called tejano. In reference to the place and space of music, a fan's graffiti sums it up best: "Selena, Rock the Heavens like you did the Earth!"

Muchas gracías, Nora López and Yolanda Cruz-Orozco
for sharing the borderlands with me.

REFERENCES

Acuña, R. 1988. *Occupied America: A History of Chicanos* (3rd ed.). New York: HarperCollins.

Anzaldúa, G. 1988. *Borderlands/La Frontera: The New Mestiza*. San Francisco: Spinsters/Aunt Lute.

Butler, J. 1993. *Bodies that Matter*. New York: Routledge.

Del Valle, F. 1995. "Sweet Siren." *Selena, Para Siempre, Harlington (TX) Valley Morning Star*, April 7, 8.

Flores, J. 1995. "Vaya Con Dios, Selena: Hundreds Grieve as Star Laid to Rest," *The McAllen (TX) Monitor*, April 4, 1A, 12A.

Fregoso, R. L. 1993. *The Bronze Screen: Chicana and Chicano Film Culture*. Minneapolis: University of Minnesota Press.

Fregoso, R. L., and A. Chabram. 1990. "Chicana/o Cultural Representations: Reframing Alternative Critical Discourse." *Cultural Studies* 4(3): 203–14.

Goldberg, D. T. 1994. "Introduction: Multicultural Conditions." In *Multiculturalism: A Critical Reader*, edited by D.T. Goldberg, 1–41. Cambridge: Blackwell Publishers.

González, A., and G. Flores. 1994. "Tejana Music and Cultural Identification." In *Our Voices: Essays in Culture, Ethnicity, and Communication*, edited by A. González, M. Houston, and V. Chen, 37–42. Los Angeles: Roxbury Publishing Company.

Grossberg, L. 1995. Respondent for the panel, "Post-Colonial Theory and the Possibilities for Communication Studies: Four Positions," Speech Communication Association, San Antonio, TX, November 20.

———. 1996. "The Space of Culture, The Power of Space." In *The Post-Colonial Question: Common Skies, Divided Horizons*, edited by I. Chambers and L. Curti, 169–88. New York: Routledge.

Hall, S. 1989. "Speaking for the Subject." Speech delivered at UC-Santa Barbara, May 26. (Cited in Fregoso and Chabram, "Chicana/o Cultural Representations.")

———. 1991. "Old and New Identities, Old and New Ethnicities." In *Culture, Globalization, and the World-System*, edited by A. D. King, 41–68, SUNY-Binghamton, Department of Art History.

Lannert, J. 1995. "Selena's Sound," *People*, spring, 49–50.

Lemieux, J. 1995. "Selena's Legend Grows: Slain Tejano Star an Icon for Border Residents Wanting Heroes." *The McAllen (TX) Monitor*, April 16, 1A, 12A.

Malcolm X. [1964] 1992. *Malcolm X Speaks Out*, edited by N. Richardson, C. Chermayeff and A. White, 88. Kansas City, MO: Callaway Editions.

Marcus, G. 1991. *Dead Elvis: A Chronicle of a Cultural Obsession*. New York: Doubleday.

Martinez, L. B. 1995. "Always & Forever." *Selena, Para Siempre, Harlington (TX) Valley Morning Star*, April 7, 18.

McLane, D. 1996. "The Double Life of Selena." *US*, March, 88–97.

Morris, M. 1988. "Banality in Cultural Studies." *Discourse* 10 (2): 3–29.

Morthland, J. 1995. "Selena, Born Again." *Entertainment*, August 18, 18–22.

Muñoz, Jr., C. 1989. *Youth, Identity, Power: The Chicano Movement*. New York: Verso.

Narciso Martinez Cultural Arts Center. 1995. Advertisement, *Selena, Para Siempre, Harlington, (TX) Valley Morning Star*, April 7, 6.

Patoski, J. N. 1995. "The Sweet Song of Justice." *Texas Monthly*, December, 102–5, 132–6.

Peña, M. 1985. *The Texas-Mexican Conjunto: History of a Working-Class Music*. Austin: University of Texas Press.

Pérez-Torres, R. 1995. *Movements in Chicano Poetry: Against Myths, Against Margins*. Cambridge, UK: Cambridge University Press.

Richmond, C. 1995. *Selena! The Phenomenal Life and Tragic Death of the Tejano Music Queen*. New York: Pocket Books/Simon and Schuster.

Ruiz, G. 1995. *Selena, The Last Song*. New York: El Diario Books/Latin Communications Group.

"Selena: Fotos y Recuerdos." 1995a. Special Section. "Why Was Selena So Important to You?" *The McAllen (TX) Monitor*, April 7, 1.

"Selena: Fotos y Recuerdos." 1995b. Special Section, "Why Was Selena So Important to You?" *The McAllen (TX) Monitor*, April 7, 3.

Smith, T. 1983. "Performing in the Zone: The Presentation of Historical Crisis in *Gravity's Rainbow*," *CLIO* 12 (3): 245–60.

12

—— "Yo Quiero Mi MTV!" ——

Making Music Television
for Latin America

Robert Hanke

This chapter considers the transnationalization of music television, focusing on the introduction of MTV: Music Television in Latin America.[1] As part of a new transnational media order in Latin America, MTV Latino raises old questions about the political economy of music television and its impact on Latin American popular music as well as the cultural identity of Latin American youth. However, it is also important to consider new communication technologies and emerging transnational networks within the context of globalization (Morley and Robbins, 1995) and to theorize music television in relation to the process of transculturalization and hybridization (Lull, 1995). Only with such a dual focus can we begin to address what implications the diffusion of what Columbian-born MTV Latino producer Raul Estupinan calls "a new language, an MTV language" may have for Latin American popular music and everyday life (quoted in Lorente, 1994).

To begin, I describe the development, corporate strategy, and programming flow of this new network. My description of the making of music television for Latin America highlights the network's pan-Latin approach, "localization" strategy, and "Latin American" structure of feeling. I go on to discuss the place of the Latin sound/vision mix within the context of Latin American popular culture. Here I draw on work in Latin American cultural studies (Barbero, 1993a, 1993b; Rowe and Schelling, 1991). This work on the history of cultural mixing in Latin America, alongside other engagements with postcolonialism and world music, suggests that the Latin presence on MTV Latino is a marginalized yet productive local margin of a US-based global network – a "Latin" audiovisual space of juxtaposition, transculturization, and hybridization. In this sense, MTV Latino might be forging a new, electronic landscape that may be less culturally homogeneous than we often assume. Formed out of the interaction of homogenizing and heterogenizing forces, MTV Latino thus constitutes an imaginary "Latin" audiovisual space "in which common sounds, languages, syntax, materials and institutions are occupied and articulated in diverse directions" (Chambers, 1994: 83). This line of reasoning puts into question any simple linkage between the monopolization of music television, the commodification of global music culture, the televisual mediation of Latin popular music, and its place in Latin American everyday life.

In mapping the Latin audiovisual space constructed by MTV Latino, my approach presupposes that the study of the texts and practices of MTV Latino requires not only an eye for images but an ear for music. Indeed, Berland has claimed that music television's visual images "never challenge or emancipate themselves from their musical foundation" (1993: 25); "the rhythm of the song, both first and primary, anticipates and conquers the eye" (40). Such claims, buttressed by Goodwin's (1992) critique of many critics' neglect of the soundtrack, require us to rethink earlier arguments about postmodern MTV. However abstract, nonnarrative, or televisual the field of MTV Latino's representation, "melody itself is a sonorous landscape in counterpoint to a virtual landscape" (Deleuze and Guattari, 1991: 318). In my riff on Deleuze and Guattari, the work that Latin American musicians do can be described as a "territorial assemblage" of Latin styles. With their different timbres, tempos, rhythms, melodies, harmonies, arrangements, lyrics, motifs, and counterpoints, Latin popular music can be heard and seen to "express the relation to interior impulses or exterior circumstances" (318). MTV Latino's flow and juxtapositioning of Anglo and Latin sounds and visions no doubt participate in the movement towards cultural homogeneity, but Latin popular music is best understood as a force that creates a "consolidation of coexistence and succession," which is not homogeneous. So as co-motion music television, MTV Latino has differential economic effects upon the cultural mobility of international Anglo and Latin rock. However, the Latin margin of this network, which mediates a Latin style of "holding together heterogenous elements," may have a cultural effectivity that is not entirely directed by, nor reducible to, the logic of worldwide capitalism. This line of inquiry makes mapping MTV's Latin beat a more complicated task; for in this telemusical, cartographically dense space, Latin rock and the cultural identity of musicians and fans take place in transient and transnational ways.

YO QUIERO MI MTV!

MTV Latino, a 24-hour, Spanish-language network, was launched on October 1, 1993.[2] The cable service is owned by MTV Networks, a division of the entertainment conglomerate Viacom International Inc.[3] The network's programming is produced by Post Edge, a production and satellite-signal distribution company.[4] When it was launched, MTV Latino was MTV Networks' fourth global affiliate, joining MTV Europe (launched 1987), MTV Brazil (1990), MTV Asia (1991; relaunched 1995), and MTV Japan (1992). More recently, MTV Networks has launched MTV Mandarin (1995) and MTV India (1996).

The worldwide audience for MTV Networks is currently estimated to be about 265.8 million households in 75 territories on five continents. At its launch, MTV Latino's estimated audience was 2.3 million households in 21 "territories"; by June 1996, the network claimed to reach 6.9 million households. Such estimates, provided by MTV Latino, do not merely reflect the size of the actual audience; they are part of the production of the audience commodity that is sold to advertisers of global brands.[5] The estimated audience for MTV Latino is very small compared to MTV US, which is available in over 62.6 million households, and MTV Europe, which is available in 53.6 million households. Nonetheless, MTV Latino quickly established itself. By October 1994, MTV Latino was reported to be the number one cable network in South America (Faiola, 1994b).[6]

MTV Latino is distributed via satellite reportedly to every South American country. Brazil, however, is the territory of MTV Brazil, a Portuguese-language network based in Sao Paulo and hosted by Brazilian VJs that is estimated to reach more than 14 million households. MTV Latino is also not available in Cuba, and there are no plans for distribution there until "Castro's gone, or when it's politically correct to be there" (Friend, 1994). As a foreign-owned cable service, the network does not have to deal with government regulations, except in Mexico.[7] In some countries, like Ecuador, MTV Latino is also offered by broadcast stations that pay for the programming; however, MTV Latino's reach is primarily dependent on the diffusion of cable television in the region.[8] In the US, MTV Latino is carried by cable operators in Miami Beach and Hialeah, Florida. Further US distribution is limited to nine cable systems in southern California, and one in Boston, but other cable operators, such as Tucson Cablevision, have been adding the network to attract new cable subscribers (Saralegui, 1994).

Network revenues are derived from sales to panregional advertisers of global brands and affiliate sales.[9] At its launch, Coca-Cola and EverReady were the only "charter" advertisers; by 1995 the network had contracts with over 30 advertisers, including Kodak, IBM, Budweiser, L.A. Gear, Master-Card, Nike, Philips Electronics, Warner Brothers, Sony, and Miller (Whitefield, 1995c).

MTV Latino is MTV's only global affiliate based in the United States. Miami was chosen as its headquarters because it is both a transfer point between many capital cities in Latin America and close to MTV US in New York, which provided "leverage" and talent in launching the service (Friend, 1994). Taking advantage of "synergy" in a geoeconomic sense was another reason.[10] While synergy may operate between the various divisions of a conglomerate like Viacom International Inc., there are also benefits to the media firm that are believed to accrue from being located in close proximity to other media industry firms, such as talent agencies, recording studios, advertising agencies, or Spanish-language television networks. South Florida has continued to develop a television and film production infrastructure that would make Miami the nonunionized "Hollywood" of Latin America (Arrarte, 1994; Whitefield, 1995b; Bell, 1996). In recent years, many major record labels with Latin music operations have established Miami as a national and international production center for Latin popular music. Five major recording labels (Sony, Warner, BMG, EMI, and PolyGram), multinational labels Fonovisa and Rodven, and a number of independent labels (Karen, Biscayne Europa, MPI, Cubaney, and Velvet) are located in Miami (Tarradell, 1993). Finally, a consideration for the Talent and Artist Relations department was proximity to Latin American popular music stars, especially those who visit Miami during concert tours.

Sara Levinson, an executive vice president of MTV US who was involved in the planning of MTV Latino, also emphasizes a cultural factor in the location of the network's headquarters: "Miami seemed to be very much a music and cultural center for Latin America and the US.... The studio could be anywhere in some remote area in the world, and you would never know where we were broadcasting from. But we often go outside the studio, and we felt you could find a lot of the Latin culture right in the streets of Miami" (quoted in Rodriguez, 1993b). In addition to this connection to the pan-Latinity of the Miami streets, Richard Arroyo, network president, observes that "South Beach was a compatible place. It kind of captures the trendy, hip culture that we're in touch with" (quoted in Lorente, 1994). Since the television show *Miami Vice* first appeared in 1984, South Miami Beach and the Art Deco district have become a center for the international fashion industry. MTV Latino's connection to this culture industry is visible in the mix of designer, funky and vintage fashions worn by MTV VJs, provided in exchange for on-air fashion credits.

PUTTING THE "PAN-LATIN" CONCEPT INTO PRACTICE

MTV Latino is building on the "pan-European" concept developed for MTV Europe. In the case of MTV Europe, where the relationship between music television and transnational advertising was first developed, one major problem was "that European youth is not a homogeneous entity, and [MTV's] aim must therefore be to combine global marketing with targeting regional consumers" (Sturmer, 1993: 52). The largest pan-European advertisers (Coca-Cola, Levi-Strauss, etc.) turned to rock 'n' roll as an "international language" in order to overcome linguistic and cultural "barriers." In this way, advertisers began to pursue the European youth audience, and to use music television to constitute pop audiences as a social group whose "lifestyle" was expressed through rock sounds, stars, and styles (Frith, 1993).

In the European testing ground for MTV-as-world network, MTV executives were concerned about possible accusations of "cultural imperialism"; thus, MTV's international operating maxim became "Think globally, act locally." According to William Roedy, London-based president of MTV Networks' international operations, MTV Europe was 80 percent American or British music when it began; but by 1995, when the network began to turn a profit, Roedy would claim the programming was 80 percent "local

European." As Roedy sums up the operating logic: "it's not like McDonald's or one-size-fits all. Really, it's the antithesis of homogeneity" (quoted in Whitefield, 1995a). In this way, MTV could enter the new, transnationalizing media order of Europe as a stateless transnational corporation, bypassing both historical fears about "Americanization" and debates about the role that television would have in forging a distinctive European identity in a transnationalizing Europe (see Morley and Robbins, 1995).

MTV Latino represents an extension of this global strategy into the Latin American context. While MTV Latino is based in the United States, and Hispanics represent a growing proportion of the US population, distribution to US cable operators has been a low priority; rather, "the network was established to capture the growth of Latin America" (Arroyo quoted in Lorente, 1994). The lack of attention to the US Hispanic market is also due to two additional factors: recent federal cable regulations placing limits on rates have made the US market less lucrative and almost all US households with cable already receive MTV US (Banks, 1995). Second, within the network's pan-Latin strategy, there is much more attention to Mexico and Argentina than any other countries in the region. These two countries are not only where the majority of MTV Latino's current viewers live, but they have also developed their own Latin pop/rock traditions and represent the largest markets for this form of popular music.[11]

MTV Latino, like its other global affiliates, aims to appeal to viewers from 12 to 34. The network clearly seeks to address and construct its young Latin American viewers as consumers. As Friend (1994) elaborates: "...they want Levis jeans and they want Reebok sneakers. They want the global brands that are big and it sort of gives the teen culture its own identity. But teens tend to look to America to set the trends, and we are sort of the voice of the MTV generation, of the teen generation." In this statement, the locus of cultural identity appears to be completely circumscribed by global marketing interests.[12] Whatever sociocultural or historical differences there may be between geographically dispersed Latin youth, "there are things the audience shares in terms of their concerns and feelings that link them to a generation" (Levinson quoted in Silver, 1993). MTV Networks' search for Latin youth, as a transnational segment, thus involves the effort to define the sociocultural mentality of this "generation," to give them a "voice," and to help define their desires and sense of well-being or satisfaction through an international discourse through and about musical and nonmusical consumer goods (Leiss, Kline, and Jhally, 1990).

Programming a transnational music television network to fulfill these commercial ambitions entails a strategy of "localization." As Tom Hunter explains: "While we have a huge advantage of a common language, the diversity within the territories we're talking about – I mean, just in South America, there are so many differences, and then you throw in Central American countries and the Caribbean countries, and the US Hispanic market, and you have a huge, wide range of experiences and tastes and appeals. Putting all that together is one of our greatest challenges, but it's not a matter of finding the lowest common denominator. If you're gonna do that, then you really could do only one MTV for the whole world. We think that localization is everything" (quoted in Rodriguez, 1993b).

How, then, does MTV Latino try to establish a presence in, and be a part of, local Latin American culture? We can begin to address this question by examining how the network reaches into the local through its production and programming practices. These include segments shot on location from South Beach, Miami; a daily viewer request program (*ConeXion MTV*), during which excerpts from viewers' letters are read; specials taped in Argentina, Chile, Colombia, Ecuador, Mexico, Peru, Venezuela, and Uruguay; or programs devoted exclusively to videos by lesser-known acts that are popular in a particular country. In music programming, the playlists of local rock radio stations in Latin America are continually reviewed. In music videos, a local sense may be expressed by iconographic elements that signify particular cities or landscapes. In nonmusic programming, *Aufera* (Outside) and *Semana Rock* (Rock Week) highlight Latin American places or newsworthy events. *Playa MTV* – a series being developed to present the best beaches in Latin America – presents these places in Latin America as sites of international tourism and leisure. As the network "regionalizes" its programming, there are plans to develop more programming devoted to local contests, events, and specials (e.g., *Ski MTV*).

At the same time, the meaning of "local" is not without boundaries that limit MTV Latino's menu of music videos. Since the majority of the network's current viewers are in Mexico and Argentina, more attention is paid to local music tastes and markets in these countries. As far as local popular music in Miami is concerned, the most common complaint is that MTV Latino's selection of Latin music video clips excludes one of the most popular, and local musics of all – salsa – even though salsa music videos are available.

Here it is important to note that MTV Latino has defended its ratio of about 80 percent Anglo to 20 percent Latin videos as being due to the small pool of Latin videos to choose from. But Latin music industry executives have been critical of this ratio and the network's pop-rock formula (Lannert, 1994). Since Spanish-language artists comprise about 60 percent of album sales for most record companies in Latin America, Francico Nieto, regional management director of EMI Music International Latin America, asserts that "this indicates that the network should broaden its musical lineup" (quoted in Lannert, 1994). Obviously, "localization" in the selection of music videos involves MTV Latino's definition of "hip" Latin American pop-rock – a definition that, at least in the beginning, somewhat conflicts with record companies' interest in marketing salsa, merengue and other regional genres. According to Baptiste (1996), the pool of Latin videos the network selects from has increased, so that by June 1996, Latin videos were estimated to comprise about 35–40 percent of the total. Despite this increase, the musical lineup continues to emphasize Latin pop-rock music.

How then does a "global" format like MTV Latino claim to provide popular and culturally relevant "local" offerings? MTV Latino "adheres to the overall style, programming philosophy, and integrity of the MTV trademark while promoting local cultural tastes and musical talent" (MTV: Music Television Global Fact Sheet). As Friend (1994) elaborates:

> the format is global...after that is everything is local. The only reason why the format is global is because ... music transcends culture. It transcends just about every socioeconomic boundary or niche you can find. So music is sort of a universal language and we are a music channel first and foremost, in spite of what you read. That's the global position and that gives us global strength, obviously, in doing any type of global promotions or global tie-ins. Obviously, the music video music awards is a global event now and that's something that's fed to all the affiliates. We can literally reach all of our subscribership with this one event....I think what distinguishes us on the local side is that we

make an effort – well, yes we do go in there with Guns N' Roses and Aerosmith and those bands – we make an effort to find out what's going on locally with the local music. It's not just...MTV US imported.

Such statements echo MTV Latino promotional spots enjoining its audience to "Think globally, act locally." The role attributed to popular music is the decisive link between the global and the local, but the network's rhetoric rests upon the assumption that Anglo music is more "universal" than Latin music. MTV Latino's commitment to "local" Latin American popular music would be a source of new, and different, sounds; at the same time, MTV's format constructs a more homogeneous global vision. One MTV Latino network ID segment, a collage of sounds occurring at the same time in different places (Moscow, Lubbock, Nairobi, Tokyo, etc.) proclaims "One Sound, One Time, One Place." Another ID segment anchors its stream of images with the slogan "One World, One Image, One Channel."

In March 1996, MTV Networks International announced a new stage in its international development, one that suggests a limit to MTV's pan-Latin ambitions. According to Bill Roedy, "MTV has been a great unifier. Our research shows that young people like to hear about other countries, travel more than their parents and are much more open-minded. Still, there's a tremendous passion for cultural diversity" (Roedy quoted in Whitefield, 1996b). Accordingly, the network plans to "regionalize" its programming model in Europe, Asia and Latin America by creating new local production centers, utilizing more regional talent and VJs, and "localizing" playlists. Digital compression technology and an increased supply of satellite transponders enables an affiliate to maintain a core of international and pan-regional programming and to provide more local offerings.[13] However, Roedy also acknowledges that regionalization will bring each affiliate closer to particular regional and national markets. So, on June 1, 1996, MTV Latino began the process of splitting into a northern service based in Mexico City, providing programming tailored to Mexico, Central America, and the Caribbean, and a southern service, based in Buenos Aires, which will focus on South America. As Baptiste (1996) comments: "One of our initial goals was to unite the area in music as much as possible. We've accomplished that with some things while also uncovering the differences between the two markets. Sometimes it's a question of timing, sometimes it's a question of taste, sometimes it's a question of cultural influences. And this just permits us to go in there and, instead of trying to make the whole area one..., I think the dedication to really coming up with programming that works – more targeted – is even a better idea." So MTV Latino moves into the future by recovering the original meaning of marketing, refining its pan-Latin programming model to adapt to regional time zones and to provide a televisual environment that would also attract advertisers bound by national creative licensing agreements or whose budgets are allocated to achieving regional advertising goals.[14] Goodwin (1992) has suggested that MTV US, in order to successfully deliver viewers to advertisers and record companies, "must promote countercultural and antiestablishment points of view" (154). This is not the place to assess the political stance of MTV Latino; it must suffice to say that the central issue is not "countercultural" credibility but how to program a credible Latin structure of feeling and sound/vision mix – one that allows for young viewers to identify with Latin American VJs and rock stars.

Programming the "Latin American" Feel

One of the obvious ways in which MTV Latino constructs an imaginary "Latin America" is by employing Spanish-speaking VJs. The original VJs were 25-year-old Alfredo Lewin, from Santiago, Chile, 24-year-old Ruth Infarinato, from Buenos Aires, Argentina, and 27-year-old Gonzalo Morales, from Mexico. Cuban American Daisy Fuentes hosts *Top 20 MTV*, as well as cohosting MTV US programs like *Beach MTV* and *Rock N' Jock*, making her the only VJ who appears on both networks.[15]

A sign on one of the MTV Latino sets reads: "Spanish Spoken Here. Se Habla Español." MTV Latino VJs are not required to change the inflection of their native dialects, although there is an effort to avoid idioms that could be confusing or obscene in other parts of Latin America. The VJs use Spanish to introduce videos; however, when speaking to Anglo guests, they use English, and Spanish subtitles are added, since a large percentage of MTV Latino's viewers are assumed to speak English.

While Latin music videos are interspersed throughout the music programming schedule, the network's Latin music feel is most strongly expressed in shows like *In Situ*, a one-hour program of "all the Latin music that you can ask for," and *Raisonica*, a twice-weekly half-hour program devoted to *rock en español*.[16] The promotional spot for *In Situ* announces that this particular program is MTV Latino's answer to the dilemma of traditional and modern sounds of Latin music. During *In Situ*, Latin music that may not go into "heavy rotation" will appear, including the occasional salsa or merengue music video.[17]

Comparing MTV Latino's programming grid for June 27–July 3, 1994, to the grids for June 1996, we get a better idea of the network's programming flow at these two points in the network's development. The former programming flow resembles MTV US during the first stage of its history, which was built upon narrowcasting and flow. However, it is evident the latter that MTV Latino is not just a 24-hour flow of music videos, but that it exhibits the "dayparting" and "stripping" practices that MTV US turned to in 1988 (Goodwin, 1992). Regular programs included *ConeXion MTV* ("Most Wanted" videos); *Headbangers* (hard rock and heavy metal); *In Situ, Lado B, MTV Clasico* ("classic" music videos); *Rockumental* ("Rocumentary"); *Top 20 MTV* (Top 20 video countdown); *Unplugged* ("acoustic" concert series); and *XPO* (premieres of new videos and new acts). By mid-1996, the schedule also included *Aufera* (a daily "road trip" through Latin America), *Fashion MTV, Gustock* (cooking and video show hosted by rocker Fabian Quintero), *Hora Prima* (spotlighting live performances from MTV Latino's studios, as well as interviews, news, sports), *Mastermix* (dance music), *Nación Alternativa* ("alternative" music from established and breaking bands), *Raizonica* (*rock en español* from "underground" and established groups), *Semana Rock* (weekly news and reports on music, pop culture, fashion, concert tours, "up-and-coming" bands, politics, movies, and social issues), and *Top Ten US* (best of MTV's Top 20 from the United States).

MTV Latino's playlist would be familiar to North American viewers of MTV US, but it is not a replication of the MTV US playlist. Gabriel Baptiste, director of music programming, reports that 45–50 percent of the playlist is influenced by US charts, 25 percent is influenced by European charts, and 25 percent is influenced by releases in Latin American markets (Baptiste, 1994). The network's musical emphasis is on rock, Anglo-American and Western European performers, "superstars" like Bon Jovi, Madonna, and Aerosmith, or international stars like Green Day, Red Hot Chili Peppers, or Ace of Base. As for the predominance of Anglo performers, Baptiste (1994) explains: "I think the one thing that there's perhaps a misconception about is that it would be a lot more Spanish than it is, but the problem that we have is that the international stuff – the Guns N' Roses, Nirvana – is the glue that holds the whole region together. There's a common denominator there in terms of rock radio. They're playing those artists. The thing that has not spread from one place to another are the artists from any one particular country. Like Argentina, the artists have traditionally not gotten a lot of play in Mexico, and vice versa." Salsa and merengue, while immensely popular forms of Latin music, are regarded as incompatible with MTV Latino's core sound. As Baptiste (1994) explains: "The problem is that it clashes with what tends to be the unifying factor there, which is Nirvana and Guns N' Roses and Ace of Base...Aerosmith for example. I mean...you can't go from an Aerosmith, which is really the center of the channel, to merengue or salsa, and expect not to have a train wreck." Similarly, there is very little Afro-Caribbean presence in the music programming, even though music videos by UB40 and Big Mountain are presented, as well as Bob or Ziggy Marley. According to Baptiste, MTV Latino would program more reggae "but the videos are so atrocious" and "they're not the center of attention of powerful, top-rated radio stations" (1994).

In light of these exclusions, it appears that particular Latin musicians and singers are getting heavy rotation and beginning to typify MTV Latino's vision of pan-Latin popular music. These are groups like Mano Negra (which first gained international exposure through MTV Europe), Los Fabulosos Cadillacs, Los Pericos, and Soda Stereo from Argentina; La Les, Los Tres, and Lucybell from Chile; Los Caifanes, Café Tacuba, and Maná from Mexico; Los Aterciopelados from Colombia; or Héroes del Silencio and Marta Sanchéz from Spain. Most of these groups and performers are on major record labels. Baptiste also observes that bands like Paralamas from Brazil are very big in Argentina so that "if you take somebody from outside the region, you have a better chance of making them work across borders than somebody who's inside the region" (Baptiste, 1994).[17] So while MTV Latino may give US, UK, or western European-based performers the ability to penetrate Latin America music markets, it also offers Latin performers some capacity to penetrate into the everyday life of young Latin Americans.

It is not possible for me to offer textual or ethnomusicological analysis of Latin music video clips here, but based upon my viewing of programming from June 1994 and April 1996, I can offer a few observations. The vast majority of Latin music videos feature male performers and all-male bands. Videos featuring female performers and singers (e.g., Alajandra Guzman, Cecilia Toussant, Claudia Puyot, Marta Sanchez, Soraya) are directed by men. As one might expect, love and male-female relationships are a standard theme; it is also evident that some music videos employ the codes and conventions for representing women as part of an adolescent male "dreamworld" (see Jhally, 1995). There is a range of moods, themes, and styles, but there is a tendency towards performance-centered choreography, intercut with a pastiche of images that emphasize the central performer. The visual style may range from social realism to romanticism to surrealism or parody. While many Latin videos feature urban settings, some have featured performers in nature settings, intercutting shots of performers with panoramic shots of the landscape.

A few music videos in the Latin mix have expressed sociopolitical themes or can be seen to address specifically Latin American issues. Mano Negra's "El Señor Matanza" (Mr. Killer), one of MTV Latino's nominees for Latin Video of the Year, is a case in point. Shot surreptitiously in Bogotá, it is set in the city's main square, and is composed of shots of Indian and African children, urban adult migrants, and the central performer, juxtaposed with shots of para-military forces. The video for "Matador," by Los Fabulosos Cadillacs, "is definitely addressing the same kind of situation as a (El) Señor Matanza, of some of the people who were killed and disappeared in the Argentine situation" (Baptiste, 1994). Even when music videos do not specifically reference Latin American political affairs, the contemporary urban life of Latin American cities comprises the mise-en-scène of some music videos. For example, the video for "Solin" by Maldita Vecindad (bad or cursed neighborhood) and Los Hijos Del 5to Patio intercuts concert footage with scenes of neighborhood street life.

A more detailed analysis of the Latin music video texts remains to be done; it does appear, however, that some directors who have adopted the visual aesthetic of MTV have not had their creativity stultified. Nor does it mean that music videos featuring Latin rock stars cannot serve as a vehicle for popular memory, an expression of social consciousness, or as a means of organizing popular pleasures and/or desires. Indeed, the rapid editing rhythm may inhibit any preferred decoding of the stream of visual images, thereby privileging music, noise, and co-motion over linear narrativization and closure. As Walter Benjamin, reflecting on the Dadaist quality of motion pictures, wrote, 'The spectator's process of association in view of these images is indeed interrupted by their constant, sudden change" (Benjamin, 1969: 238). Latin rhythms and styles thus provide a sonorous counterpoint to, and foundation for, this fragmented flow of images.

BEYOND THE REFRAIN

For all of the ambiguities and contradictions that appear in implementing a strategy of "localization," it appears that MTV Latino serves mainly as a vehicle for promoting US, UK, and western European international rock music and as a one-way vector of transnational advertising campaigns. From the perspective of US political economy, it has been argued that MTV Networks' near-monopoly on music television and its programming emphasis may "intensify the one way flow of music and popular culture from these Western nations to other countries, eclipsing and marginalizing indigenous music" (Banks, 1995: 43). Banks (1995) concludes that "MTV's programming is permeated by a relentless commercialism that attempts to nurture international youth culture based on ideals of consumerism…contributing to an erosion of indigenous culture, values, traditions" (49). In this refrain, MTV Latino does not appear to articulate with anything other than consumer culture and consciousness. The new language of MTV, even if it speaks or sings in the native tongue, is regarded as the same old imperializing one, producing a convergence of international musical taste that marginalizes Latin music, or standardizes *rock en español* as a segment within a homogeneous international style of popular music.

One could easily extend this general argument by drawing upon Attali's (1992) historical analysis of the production of Western music, and contend that MTV is an extension of the recording technologies that made the mass production and consumption of musical commodities possible. In the "age of repetition," MTV operates as a televisual model for replication – "the mold within which reproduction and repetition take shape" (Attali, 1992: 118). As a form of musical reproduction and repetition, MTV Latino functions as a mode of accommodating Latin popular music to the control of Warner, Sony, MCA, BMG, EMI, and Polygram (see Burnett, 1996). In this general argument, the molding of music and musicians according to the logic of commodification and ideological normalization results in a homogenized, Euro-Americanized popular music culture, even though the profits from these performers now flow to US, Japanese, West German, Dutch, or British stockholders. Along with the loss of musical variety, the commodification of musical desires and pleasure results in silence, for people only "hear the noises of commodities into which their imaginary is collectively channeled, where their dreams of sociality and transcendence dwell" (Attali, 1992: 122).

It is undeniable that MTV Latino represents and reproduces a popular music culture that no longer means what *cultura popular* means in Spanish or

Portuguese, which is the "culture of the people" (Lull, 1995, 72). At the same time, the inadequacies of the cultural imperialism thesis (see Tomlinson, 1991) with reference to popular music (see Laing, 1986; Goodwin and Gore, 1990; Robinson, Buck, and Cuthbert, 1991) have become apparent. It seems to me, therefore, that the question of MTV Latino's cultural effectivity must move beyond the cultural imperialism refrain, with its tendency towards reductionism, ethnocentricism, and fatalism. For in this refrain, all cultural flow between the transnational corporation and the national are one-way and any history of cultural mixing is either disregarded or only regarded as a form of desecration or deformation of some authentic, indigenous musical form. Recent work on world music reveals just how problematic such a standpoint on authenticity has become (see Davies, 1993; Barrett; 1996; Erlmann, 1996); in the de- and reterritorialization of musical styles and genres composing popular music today, there is no singular moment of authenticity in terms of sound, instrumentation, or lyrics (Davies, 1993).

In the Latin American context, the cultural imperialism refrain ignores the historical specificity of the constitution of the "popular" and the complex and ambiguous relationship between popular classes and mass culture. To use Barbero's (1993b) words, "Mass culture does not occupy a single position in a system of social classes, but simultaneously embraces heterogeneous practices and products" (19). Historically, popular cultures in Latin America have had an "interpenetrative relationship" with mass culture, so the space of the popular is one of dispersed sites, rather than a homogenous space of European, bourgeois hegemony, or US capitalist hegemony. As Rowe and Schelling (1991) also observe, "Almost all cultures in Latin America are now mediated to some extent by the city, both in the sense of the massification of social phenomenon and of the communication technologies which make it possible" (97). So within an internationalizing, neoliberal Latin American political context, the Latin urban popular is a complex site of hybridization and deterritorialization in which cultural forms can be "separated from existing practices," and recombined "with new forms in new practices," and can be translated (i.e., travel) from one location to another. So while MTV Networks' expansion beyond the United States has been read as a "symptom of an expanding American media world order" (Goodwin, 1992: 179), from the perspective of the continuous history of transculturization, it becomes problematic to describe the cultural impact of MTV Latino only in terms of a national discourse of imposition and assumed acculturation to US consumer culture. This disregards the process of "massification" as well as Latin forms of social modernity. Notwithstanding the economic facts of the Latin American geoeconomy, it becomes problematic to see the effects of one-way flow of Anglo-Euro-American popular music as a displacement or degradation of indigenous Latin music when *rock en español*, a tradition invented in the 1960s in response to imported American rock 'n' roll, is an indigenized form of popular music.

The cultural effectivity of MTV Latino will remain an open question until the dynamics of MTV Latino's uses and interpretations are investigated. Beyond the mediacentric framework of reception analysis, Barbero calls our attention to the places of "mediation," such as everyday family life, "where the social materialization and the cultural expression of television are delimited and configured" (Barbero, 1993a: 215). In this approach, the daily life of the family is seen as a primary place of transactions with television and a space of negotiations with, and resignifications of, Latin televisual genres. So in contrast to the *telenovela* and its melodramatic emphasis upon kinship identity, we may assume that MTV Latino will draw its young viewers into the international world of rock music and its less familial, youth-cultural repertoire of objects, practices, and messages.

Beyond the framework of television in everyday life, any further analysis of the dynamics of consumption must also consider how MTV Latino's foreign musical or iconographic elements may encounter cultural conversion or resistance. González (1994b) comments that "there is a rich history in the continent of sturdy local cultures resisting, recycling and subverting foreign elements, remaking them to their own image." This local culture, with its pre-Columbian roots, remains resilient in the face a growing number of North American networks that are providing foreign cultural information and ready-made popular culture icons.

The enduring popularity of regional musics and the influence of radio broadcasting also render any general propositions about the impact of MTV Latino upon Latin American popular music undecidable. John Lannert, Latin American/Caribbean bureau chief for *Billboard Magazine*, observes that: "the flagship acts that really sell for the labels in Mexico, for instance, are much too regional in appeal to make it in, say, Argentina. You're talking about a market that is still dominated in large part by rural, domestic, folkloric groups that often don't meet MTV's hipness quotient" (quoted in Faiola, 1994). The popularity of regional musics explains why Latin American record companies, whose global strategies have even greater reach into local music than music television, would like to see MTV Latino accommodate salsa, merengue, and other regional genres even more (Lannert, 1994). As Baptiste (1996) observes in retrospect: "There are certain artists [from Argentina], try as we might to make them popular in Mexico, that just haven't broken through." Interestingly, MTV Latino executives claim that the network has begun to show signs of influencing radio programming. Baptiste (1994) observes that: "Our Top 20 is becoming, because we publish it, we send it on in fax, basically to anyone who asks for it,...the de facto Top 20 for the area." To which Corcoran adds: "Throughout the region, artist managers tell us that they're getting added to radio (playlists) because the radio programmers are watching their music on MTV Latino. And radio station DJs in Santiago, Buenos Aires, Mexico City and Miami confirm it" (quoted in Faiola, 1994b). Indications are that MTV Latino programming appears to extend the movement of homogenization that already exists within the Latin American radio and recording industry, a movement that began over three decades ago (Rowe and Schelling, 1991). Today, each Latin American country's popular music charts may be read as featuring the "same, top 20 artists," and thus, a "common musical ground" (Saralegui, 1994). But this does not mean that MTV Latino's selection of Latin popular music is uniform in musical motifs, styles, rhythms, and preferred genres. To the contrary, as Barbero (1993b) writes, the "standardization of products and the uniformatization of gestures require a constant struggle against entropy and a periodic renovation of patterns of differentiation" (19).

Rock en español is clearly an evolving hybrid cultural form of expression. As Gonzalez (1994a) notes, a new generation of musicians, responding to Anglo-American rock and inspired by such international superstars as Bob Marley, have been recreating the sound of Latin popular music. Fashioned in their own image, this new music is "worldly but rooted in local tradition. It takes its attitude from rock 'n' roll but its sound from a neighborhood party. It comes MTV-friendly but speaks the language of home. And it is finding a surprisingly large, avid audience" (González, 1994a). As part of Latin American "mass" culture, *rock en español* is a remix of the foreign and the national, made by young musicians that are not only bilingual but bicultural (González, 1996).

Latin American musicians have been working on this remix for some time however. "For 30 years, two generations of musicians and audiences in Latin America have been reinventing rock, mixing Delta blues and Chuck

Berry with corridos and zambas, mimicking high-tech means with low-tech imagination, inventing their own faces out of old family photos, Hollywood movies and MTV clips" (Gonzalez, 1996). Rising, and sometimes falling, local *rock en español* scenes also have their own geohistorical specificity. For example, in response to the sounds of imported Anglo US and UK-based rock, two types of new rock appeared in Chile. Imitations of Anglo rock were sung in English for middle-class consumption, while "rock national" or "rock subterráneo" was sung in Spanish and produced in the urban periphery (Rowe and Schelling, 1991: 121).

From the perspective of Latin musicians, it is important to note, as Robinson, Buck, and Cuthbert (1991) have pointed out, that imitation is only the first stage of reaction to the dominance of Anglo-American rock (e.g., English covers of Chuck Berry and Little Richard, or Spanish remakes of Elvis Presley songs). Their research shows that a variety of factors lead musicians to pass from the stage of imitation to the stage to indigenization, writing and recording original material in Spanish in a way that preserves traditional musical styles. During this stage, imported music is not just a format for repetition; rather, "sound and textual motifs are resemanticized in terms of the local" (Rowe and Schelling, 1991: 121). This new form of popular music first emerged in the 1970s in Argentina with figures like Charly Garcia, and in Mexico in the 1980s with bands like Los Caifanes, Maldita Vecindad, and Café Tacuba. In Argentina, there was a greater receptivity to native rock following the Falklands War with Britain in 1981 that allowed bands like Los Dividodos and Los Fabulosos Cadillacs to become established (Moore, 1994).

Transculturalization, writes Lull (1995), "produces cultural hybrids – the fusing of cultural forms" that are "popular almost by definition" (155). For example, the Mexican band Los Caifanes released its first album in 1981; their hit single "La Negra Tomasa" was an update of Cuban *cumbia* music. Today, they blend ska, rock 'n' roll, and Mexican folk rhythms.[18] Another band, Café Tacuba, mixes influences as diverse as classic Mexican boleros, *norteño*, ska, punk, and others. So the term *rock en español* refers to many sounds; it fails to characterize and to classify the vastly heterogenous popular music of Latin American recording artists. For example, contrast Dominican singer-songwriter Juan Luis Guerra, who has reinvented merengue and *bachata* by using jazz harmonies and borrowings from South African choral singing, with Fito Paez, a band that could only be from Buenos Aires with their allusions to the Beatles and nuevo-tango. *Rock en español*, like American rock 'n' roll seen from a multicultural perspective, is a hybrid form of music that may be more dialogic than derivative (see Lipsitz, 1994).

While much of this music may never enter MTV Latino's playlist, the network does open up a new and important space for those who are successful in getting "heavy rotation." As musicians continue to work on the Latin mix and extend their praxis to the making of music videos, they gain access to an important means of representing the "rock and roll apparatus" (Grossberg, 1984) and are able to achieve a kind of affectivity they could not otherwise have. The practice of making music videos is an aesthetic, expressive practice of translating the infinite possibilities of mutating, hybrid sounds into images that travel across time and space. Los Fabulosos Cadillacs, Los Caifanes, Charly Garcia, El Tri, Los Tres, Café Tacuba, Soda Stereo, and Illya Kuryaki y los Valderramas exemplify the mix of transcultural sounds and visions that are crossing ethnic, cultural, and national boundaries to create a new cartography of Latin popular taste.

MTV Latino's 1994 Latin Video of the Year "Matador" by Los Fabulosos Cadillacs no doubt helped the group's Japanese-owned record company Sony, whose Latin American division is based in Miami, sell 400,000 recordings by the Argentine "alternative music" band. As their music video indicates, this band has not abandoned politics. Nor does it sound like they or some of the other featured Latin bands have abandoned the more complicated rhythms of their own mixed culture. In the long history of interaction with American rock 'n' roll, they are reconstituting a dynamic dialogue of Latin musics and American rock within a new, televisual and transnational space. This space may be occupied by various bands and performers, so as to articulate common sounds in various directions; for example, the *Unplugged* performance of Illya Kuryaki y los Valderramas constitutes a dialogue of Argentinean rock and African American rap music while the performance of Café Tacuba resonates with traditional Mexican musical styles.

Yet, as Lipsitz (1994) has pointed out about world music and global commerce, the paradox is that many Latin performers may only gain access to broader audiences when they conform to Anglo rock 'n' roll and its Euro-American scales and tunings, harmony, electronic instruments, dance rhythms, and musical intonations (Lipsitz, 1994: 62). The exclusion of other local musical styles reveals the limits of MTV Latino's vision of pan-Latin popular music. To emphasize only conformity and constraint however would be to deny Latin American recording artists some agency to make their own rock musical history, even if Anglo-American music is the dominant influence and the relationship between the US core and the Latin American periphery is best summarized as one of "asymmetrical interdependence" (Colista and Leshner, 1996). In reflecting on the territorial assemblage of the Latin margin of an Anglo, Euro-American-centered music television network, we need new ways of mapping the Latin beat, without neglecting the political economy of globalizing music television, or reverting to cultural populism and reinscribing a romanticized cultural aesthetics. The challenge is to describe MTV Latino's distinctive Latin sound/vision pastiche and to map a new kind of space, one in which the juxtaposition and the coexistence of "folk," "popular," and "world music" refrains remain "tied to the song of the people according to variable relations of crowd individuations" so as to "bring into play affects and nations" (Deleuze and Guattari, 1991: 347).

NOTES

1. This chapter would not have been possible without access to MTV Latino executives. I am grateful to Richard Arroyo, senior vice president and managing director, for allowing me to arrange interviews. Personal interviews were conducted by the author with Bruce Friend, vice president of strategic planning and research, and Gabriel Baptiste, director of music programming. Additional media relations material was provided by Nelson Benedico, vice president of marketing communication. Earlier versions of this chapter were presented at the 12th Annual Intercultural/International Communication Conference, February 2–4, 1995, Miami, Florida; at the Drake Conference on Popular Music, March 29–30, 1996, Des Moines, Iowa; and at the International Communication Association Convention, May 23–27, 1996, Chicago. This chapter also benefited from the thoughtful comments of Tom Schumacher and editorial guidance from Thom Swiss and L. DeLana Browning.

2. MTV's first foray into Latin America came in the form of an hour-long, weekly program called *MTV Internacional*. Launched on July 15, 1988, it was seen in the United States (distributed by the Telemundo network) and sold by MTV Networks Syndication Sales Worldwide to Argentina, Bolivia, Chile, Costa Rica, the Dominican Republic, Ecuador, Pana-

ma, Paraguay, Uruguay, and Venezuela. Produced in the United States (currently at the South Miami Beach studios of Post Edge), the weekly Spanish-language hour-long program of music videos, interviews, and news was and continues to be hosted by Cuban American Daisy Fuentes. By August 1991, the program – which began playing 70 percent English and 30 percent Anglo but evolved into a 50-50 mix – was reaching 10.6 million homes (Banks, 1995). The program had a twofold purpose: first, to change younger Latin viewers' perceptions of television as a medium only of interest to older audiences, and, second, to reach young, second-generation Hispanics raised in the United States who may be more familiar with US, UK, and western European popular music than Latin American (Spanish) popular music. For some observers, *MTV Internacional* became the most popular music video program in Spanish because of its host. Daisy Fuentes's "neutral accent" and "hard-to-place" looks enabled diverse audiences within Latin America – young Mexicans, Venezuelans, Paraguayans, or Brazilians – to identify with her (Rodriguez, 1993a). However, less visible to viewers, was how the program increased the awareness among Latin labels of the importance of music video as a promotional tool (Seralegui, 1994). And, as John Duff, MTV Latino's affiliate sales director points out, by the time the network was launched, "local distributors and viewers were already familiar with the product, as were local governments, which did not flinch at MTV's sometimes sexually suggestive content" (quoted in Silver, 1993: C6,n).

3. Viacom International Inc. is an entertainment conglomerate that also owns cable networks VH–1, Nickelodeon/Nick at Nite, and half of Comedy Central, as well as Madison Square Garden, Paramount Communications, and Blockbuster Entertainment Corporation. For the April–June quarter of 1994, Viacom announced $244.2 million in earnings, up from $41.6 million from the previous year. This enormous growth in profits was led by its cable networks, which saw a 20 percent increase in revenue (McCash, 1995). However, MTV Latino had yet to turn a profit by the end of its first year of operation (Faiola, 1994b).

4. In March 1995, Post Edge was purchased by the post-production conglomerate International Post Limited (Lorente, 1995).

5. Due to difficulties of audience measurement in Latin America, Friend (1994) admits that the number of subscribers is routinely doubled for advertising sales purposes. Only Mexico, Chile, Argentina, and Brazil

have ratings systems to assess viewership. Whitefield (1995d) reported the formation of an industry group of 15 cable channels, including MTV Latino, to standardize audience research and ratings for the Latin American cable market.

6. However, by 1995, it was reported that GEMS, worldwide audience made it the number one Spanish-language cable network. MTV Latino's US audience of 570,000 subscribers is about one quarter of GEMS' US audience (Rabin, 1995).

7. *ConeXion MTV*, a program hosted by a Mexican VJ, is a coproduction between the network and Services Especializados de Television Por Cable de Mexico.

8. Subscriber charges range from $28.00–$45.00 in Argentina, to $15.00 for basic cable service in Mexico (Variety, 1994). According to the first major survey of cable television in Latin America, released in February 1995 by New York–based Audits and Surveys, 47 million consumers (or 13.4 million households) have access to cable programming. Whitefield (1995b) notes that the internationalization of Miami's Latin media industry entered a new phase in the early 1990s because of four factors: (1) more satellite capacity, (2) US government pressure to stop the pirating of satellite signals, (3) the opening up of Latin American cable companies to US investors, and (4) the rapid construction of cable systems in Latin America.

9. Total revenue for MTV Latino breaks down as follows: (1) about 60 percent from advertising sales (commercials, sponsorships), (2) about 40 percent from affiliate sales (cable systems and syndication), and (3) about 2 percent from new business, which includes *Unplugged* licensing and merchandise. In addition, local cable system operators are offered two minutes of time every hour for local advertising.

10. "Synergy" is a term used in the media industry, and by some media scholars, to describe the possible benefits that might accrue to media conglomerates through the greater coordination of activities (see Turow, 1992).

11. MTV Latino is not the only provider of music television in Latin America; in Argentina it competes with Canadian music video network MuchMusic and domestic channel Music 21, and in Mexico, it competes with Tele-Hit, owned by Televisa (Lannert, 1994).

12. A *Fortune* feature article provided to me by Bruce Friend sums up MTV Latino's view of its teen viewers-as-consumers, as a valuable portion of "the most global market of all": "In a world divided by trade wars and tribalism, teenagers, of all people, are the new unifying force. From the steamy playgrounds of Los Angeles to the stately boulevards of Singapore, kids show amazing similarities in taste, language, and attitude. African Americans and Asians, Latinos and Europeans are zipping up their Levi's, dancing to the Red Hot Chile Peppers, and punching keyboards of their Macintosh PC's. Propelled by mighty couriers like MTV, trends spread with sorceress speed. Kids hear drumbeats a continent away, absorb the rhythm, and add their own licks. For the Coca-Colas and the Nikes, no marketing challenge is more basic than capturing that beat. There are billions to be earned" (Tully, 1994: 90). In such formulations, we see how advertisers of youth-oriented global brands are utilizing rock music. Through market research, teenagers are produced as valuable global commodities, and rock's universal beat and its affective power are harnessed to the expansion and unification of international markets.

13. For South America, a new satellite became operational in March 1996, allowing MTV Latino to move to its own transponder and to utilize up to eight different channels.

14. According to Baptiste (1996), the process of splitting the service began on April 15, 1996, with the ability to deliver commercials that abide by the creative licensing agreements of its advertisers. On June 1, 1996, they began splitting up the programming for a six-hour period Monday through Thursday to address the problem of programming across regional time zones and to begin to customize the playlists for northern and southern services. So from MTV Latino's operational time of 7:00 p.m. to 1:00 a.m., those two services can operate independently of each other. MTV Latino plans to continue to expand the hours within which the network can regionalize its music and nonmusic programming. Among the programs deemed "localizable" are *Top 20 MTV*, *Aufera*, a daily show from Mexico or Argentina, and a possible series of weekly shows.

15. In March, 1996, the original VJs were joined by four others: 29-year-old Javier Andrade of Trenque Lauquen, Argentina, 24-year-old Alejandro Lacroix of Buenos Aires, Argentina, 25-year-old Arturo Hernandez of

Mexico City, Mexico, and 25-year-old Edith Serrano of Veracruz, Mexico.

16. Originally, *In Situ* was a half-hour program hosted by a guest VJ, usually a Latin American musician. As Baptiste (1994) explains: "Because the music is so radically different from what we do, we didn't feel comfortable attaching any of our 24-hour-a-day VJs to the show." The current hour-long version does not have any host.

17. The MTV Latino playlist has four categories, which determines how frequently, and what position in the hour, music videos are aired. While plays a day may be affected by special programming or the rotation they are in, the "Buzz Bin" category (for new videos) is five plays a day, the "Power" category is five plays a day, the "Heavy" category is four plays a day, and the "Medium" category is three plays a day. These categories relate to MTV Latino's territories in the following way: "The highest positions that we have are reserved for the things that are working across the board. Then the medium category are for things that are working in quite a few of the territories, but not all of them. And then the category that comes up three times a day are things that are working in any one area that we think have an opportunity to break through, that sound and look good, but aren't proven successes yet" (Baptiste, 1994).

18. In the case of Paralamas do Sucesso, MTV Latino may provide a forum free from government efforts to censor their live performances ("Brazilian Rock Band Censored for Criticizing Congress," 1995).

19. Reeves (1993) notes that while modern and commercial forms have been used for social criticism and political mobilization, there is also a long history of folk forms being adapted for such purposes.

REFERENCES

Arrarte, A. 1994. Hollywood in the Tropic? *Miami Herald*, February 7, 12BM.

Attali, J. 1992. *Noise: The Political Economy Of Music*. Minneapolis: University of Minnesota Press.

Banks, J. 1995. "MTV and the Globalization of Popular Culture." Paper presented at the Intercultural/International Communication Conference, Miami, FL, February.

Baptiste, G. 1994. Personal interview, August 5.

————. 1996. Telephone interview, June 25.

Barbero, J-Martin. 1993a. *Communication, Culture and Hegemony: From the Media to Mediations*. London: Sage.

————. 1993b. Latin America: Cultures in the Communication Media." *Journal of Communication* 43(2): 18–30.

Barrett, J. 1996. "World Music, Nation and Postcolonialism." *Cultural Studies,* 10(2): 237–47.

Bell, M. 1996. The Hispanic Hollywood. *Miami Herald*, March17, 1F, 5F.

Benjamin, W. 1969. "The Work of Art in the Age of Mechanical Reproduction." In *Illuminations*, edited by H. Arendt (trans. H. Zohn), 217–51. New York: Schocken Books.

Berland, J. 1993. "Sound, Image and Social Space: Music Video And Media Reconstruction." In *Sound and Vision: The Music Video Reader*, edited by S. Frith, A. Goodwin, and L. Grossberg, 25–43. London: Routledge.

Besas, P. 1994. "Latin America at a Glance." *Variety*, March 28–April 3, 52.

"Brazilian Rock Band Censored for Criticizing Congress." 1995. *Sun-Sentinel,* July 5, 11A.

Burnett, R. 1996. *The Global Jukebox: The International Music Industry*. London: Routledge.

Chambers, I. 1994. *Migrancy, Culture, Identity*. London: Routledge.

Colista, C. and G. Leshner. 1996. *Traveling Music: Following the Path of Music through the Global Market*. Paper presented at the International Communication Association, Chicago, IL, May 23–27.

Davies, C. 1993. "Aboriginal Rock Music." In *Rock and Popular Music: Politics, Policies, Institutions*, edited by T. Bennett, S. Frith, L. Grossberg, J. Shepherd, and G. Turner, 249–65. London: Routledge.

Deleuze, G., and F. Guattari. 1991. "[1837]: Of the Refrain." In *A Thousand Plateaus: Capitalism and Schizophrenia*, translated by B. Massumi, 310–50. Minneapolis: University of Minnesota Press.

Erlmann, V. 1996. "The Aesthetics of the Global Imagination: Reflections on World Music in the 1990s." *Public Culture* 8: 467–87.

Faiola, A. 1994. "Now Youngsters Are Demanding Yo Quiero Mi MTV." *Miami Herald*, October 9, 1K.

Friend, B. 1994. Personal interview, June 23.

Frith, S. 1993. "Youth/Music/Television." In *Sound & Vision: The Music Video Reader*, edited by S. Frith, A. Goodwin, and L. Grossberg, 67–83. London: Routledge.

Goodwin, A. 1992. *Dancing in the Distraction Factory: Music Television And Popular Culture*. Minneapolis: University of Minnesota Press.

Goodwin, A. and J. Gore. 1990. "Worldbeat and the Cultural Imperialism Debate." *Socialist Review* 20(3): 63–80.

Gonzalez, F. 1994. "Out Of Colombia Hillbilly Goes Pop." *Miami Herald*, June 19, 1I.

———. 1994b. "Flick of TV Switch Establishes Shared Memories." *Miami Herald*, December 5, 42SA.

———. 1996. "*Rock en Español*." *Miami Herald*, March 8, 20G–21G, 22G.

Grossberg, L. 1984. "Another Boring Day in Paradise: Rock and Roll and the Empowerment of Everyday Life." *Popular Music* 4: 225–58.

Jhally, S. 1995. "Dreamworlds 2: Desire, Sex, and Power in Rock Video." Northampton: University of Massachusetts.

Laing, D. 1986. "The Music Industry and the Cultural Imperialism Thesis." *Media, Culture and Society* 8: 331–41.

Lannert, J. 1994. "Labels Assess Impact of MTV Latino: Channel Draws Mixed Reviews from Execs." *Billboard*, July 2, 4(2).

Leiss, W., S. Kline, and S. Jhally. 1990. *Social Communication in Advertising: Persons, Products, and Images of Well-Being*. New York: Routledge, Chapman and Hall.

Lipsitz, G. 1994. *Dangerous Crossroads: Popular Music, Postmodernism, and the Poetics of Place*. New York: Verso.

Lorente, R. 1994. "MTV Latino Pulsates from South Beach." *Miami Herald*, March 24, MB1.

———. 1995. "N.Y. Firm to Buy Post-Production Company Here." *Miami Herald*, March 17, 1C.

Lull, J. 1995. *Media, Communication, Culture: A Global Approach*. New York: Columbia University Press.

McCash, V. 1995. "Viacom Reports $244 million profit." *Sun-Sentinel*, August 16, D1.

Moore, D. 1994. "Latin Rockers Seek Global Roll." *Variety*, March 28–April 3, 48, 64, 67.

Morley, D., and K. Robbins. 1995. *Spaces of Identity: Global Media, Electronic Landscapes and Cultural Boundaries*. London: Routledge.

Rabin, A. 1995. "Gems' Cable Growth Shines: Network Says It's No. 1." *Miami Herald*, August 24, 1C.

Reeves, G. 1993. *Communications and the 'Third World.'* London: Routledge.

Robinson, D., E. Buck, and M. Cuthbert. 1991. *Music at the Margins: Popular Music and Global Cultural Diversity*. Newbury Park: Sage.

Rodriguez, R. 1993a. "Daisey Fuentes: MTV's Export Leader." *Miami Herald*, May 29, 1G.

———. 1993b. "Yo Quiero Mi MTV!" *Miami Herald*, September 30, 1G.

Rowe, W., and V. Schelling. 1991. *Memory and Modernity: Popular Culture in Latin America*. London: Verso.

Saralegui, M. 1994. "MTV Latino Attracts Viewers in the U.S. and Abroad." *Wireless International*, March, 14, 18.

Silver, V. 1993. "For MTV, A Leap to Latin America." *The New York Times*, September 27, C6(N), D6(L), col. 1.

Sturmer, C. 1993. "MTV's Europe: An Imaginary Continent?" In *Channels of Resistance: Global Television and Local Empowerment*, edited by T. Dowmunt, 50–66. London: British Film Institute.

Tarradell, M. 1993. "Miami Latin Music Scene Awards Show Spotlights Area as Hispanic Home Base." *Miami Herald*, May 14, 20G.

Tomlinson, J. 1991. *Cultural Imperialism: A Critical Introduction*. Baltimore: Johns Hopkins University Press.

Tully, S. 1994. "Teens: The Most Global Market of All." *Fortune*, May 16, 90–97.

Turow, J. 1992. "Globalization of Mass Media Ownership." *Communication Research*, 19(6): 677–81.

Whitefield, M. 1995a. "As History Marches Forward, So Does the Reach of MTV." *Miami Herald*, April 9, 1K–3K.

———. 1995b. "El Nuevo Hollywood." *Miami Herald*, April 17, 22BM.

———. 1995c. "Cross-Country Ads." *Miami Herald*, April 23, 1K, 2K.

———. 1995d. "15 Cable Channels Team Up to Promote Latin Focus." *Miami Herald*, October 21, 1C.

———. 1996. "Dancing to Their Own Beat." *Miami Herald*, March 23, 1C.

13

—————— Studying Rock ——————

Toward a Materialist Ethnography

Tony Kirschner

Popular music is, behind television, the second largest revenue-generating mass medium. Rock has become ubiquitous in the American cultural milieu, from television ad jingles to presidential campaign anthems. As a subject of scholarly inquiry, rock music has increasingly become the topic of much discussion from a variety of disciplinary perspectives. But academics sometimes dive into one rock concern or another without seriously considering the nature of the object in question. This analytical haste has tended to skew the bulk of rock scholarship towards certain issues that stem from the legacy of research habits developed and sedimented in more established traditions of popular culture study such as television, film, or literature. For example, Andrew Goodwin (1992) demonstrates how academics, excited by the rise of music videos in the eighties, raced to examine this supposedly new medium with a host of methodologies borrowed from psychoanalysis, film theory, and television studies, to name a few, without really considering music videos in terms of straightforward popular music practices and norms.[1]

In order to partially redirect the trajectory of current rock scholarship, it is necessary to problematize rock itself and attempt to understand how it operates materially – in its historically constituted field of power relations – before moving on to other (typically interpretive) matters. In this chapter, I will begin by talking about rock music in its specificity, comparing and contrasting it to other popular culture forms. From this discussion, I will comment on some of the common methods of studying popular music, and propose a strategy that allows the analyst to investigate neglected dimensions of rock in light of recent theoretical developments. Most of the assertions I make about rock music and methodology in this chapter are the result of the (literal) tension between my dual lives as rock musician and researcher. I play guitar, write songs, book shows, and perform managerial duties for a touring and recording rock band called The Slips. In addition to my musical endeavors, I am a doctoral candidate in Communications and Cultural Studies focusing on popular music and critical theory. I trust this piece will demonstrate that the simultaneous production and analysis of popular music has been a mutually enhancing experience.

WHAT IS ROCK?
THE NOT-SO-OBVIOUS, OBVIOUS QUESTION

Marcus Breen (1995) has attempted to understand popular music and the evolving nature of its status as a commodity, according to the recent consolidation and internationalization of the entertainment industry, wherein music plays a key role in a wider multimedia deluge. He uses the term *cultural mobility* to describe how "music is moving rapidly into fresh areas" (Breen, 1995: 497). Breen demonstrates how the rise of entertainment conglomerates has changed the way music presents itself to its audience and altered its relation to other media. He suggests that multimedia corporations use music strategically to penetrate new markets. Nevertheless, in spite of recent shifts in popular music's position in the global entertainment nexus, rock music still exists as a somewhat distinct cultural form, and must be grasped properly on its own terms if one seeks to understand rock's place in larger entertainment networks.

Breen's usage of cultural mobility suggests that we examine rock via its relation to international capital and "institutional economics." But I want to start at a more basic level with three characteristics of popular music – its textual mobility, its large amateur realm, and its spatial mobility. These three attributes, which distinguish rock from other mass media, are not all-encompassing essential features of rock music, but instead, fairly obvious structural tendencies that are usually overlooked, or inadequately theorized, in rock research.

First, popular music texts, unlike film, television, or other domains of popular culture, exist in a multitude of interrelated configurations. That is, rock presents itself to us in many different forms: live performance, recorded commodity, radio broadcast, music video, commercial jingle, movie and television soundtrack, and background music in public spaces.[2] These forms, of course, can be consumed in a variety of contexts and settings, either in the forefront or background of other activities. Consider how this differs from television, film, or literature, all of which offer a limited range of textual manifestations and consumption alternatives. The term, "textual mobility," is a mutation of Breen's notion of cultural mobility. It implies that rock music is textually chameleonic, always changing its appearance to suit the context. Understanding the interplay and dynamics of rock's different textual forms is a necessary precursor to understanding popular music in general since the rock world embodies the totality of these different textual styles.

Second, while television and film are, for the most part, big corporate ventures intended for massive audiences, popular music often is not (though this is hardly apparent when reading the literature on rock). In fact, the lion's share of rock music production occurs at the amateur level. One could point to cable access television, and independent/student/home films as examples of amateur or independent movie and TV production, but these instances constitute at best a tiny niche within the larger domain of television and film. The production costs for these media are simply too high (independent film budgets are usually far beyond the reach of the amateur film maker). Additionally, these niches do not have an established infrastructure for dissemination because of the regulatory mechanisms that govern the respective industries. Other than art theaters and university settings, where does one go to see homemade/student movies? Where could one buy videos of these texts? There is little exchange between cable access and big-time television; the former rarely serves as a stepping stone or "farm league" for the latter. Because of the configuration of the television and movie industries, and the accompanying standards and available technologies of production, the vast majority of movies and television shows are big-budget productions intended for mass audiences (whether or not they succeed).

Rock, on the other hand, has a huge amateur[3] and quasi-professional[4] realm supported by a well developed production and distribution infrastructure – an infrastructure that, as Frith (1981) has noted, is closely tied to the big time. With the exception of "sensational discoveries," all rock begins at the amateur level, and there is an intimate and undertheorized reciprocal relationship between small-time and big-time rock music. Even though most popular music consumption revolves around major label star acts, there are far more bands, venues, record labels, support personnel, etc., that exist at the low end of the spectrum. Popular music, unlike movies or television, can have extremely low production costs (used gear is cheap, effective, and omnipresent), can be performed anywhere where noise is tolerated, and can be recorded and duplicated at increasingly inexpensive rates (think of Nirvana's *Bleach* ,which was recorded for $600). My personal experience in music-making has located me in the endless stream of small-time bands (there are said to be 10,000 functional bands in the greater L.A. area alone!), all slugging it out night after night in a never-ending cacophony of competition, strategic positioning, and reconfiguration.

The immense amateur realm of rock music is responsible for the staggering amount of rock texts that continuously flood the marketplace, especially if one factors in all the textual forms in which rock presents itself. In small-time rock music, there are numerous bands (horizontal dispersion), each with few fans (vertical dispersion). The opposite horizontal versus vertical relationship is found for big-label, mass-oriented popular music: there are relatively few acts, each with many fans.[5] This horizontal versus vertical relationship is best seen as a continuum that spans between megastars (REM, U2, the Rolling Stones, etc.), of which there are a finite number – each enjoying vast international audiences – and the countless ranks of garage bands who play to their friends.

The third attribute of popular music that differentiates it from other forms of mass-mediated popular culture is its spatial mobility. Spatial mobility refers to the unique ways in which rock travels across geographical space, borrowing from and influencing other music in a subtle process of cultural diffusion. The technologies of rock are highly transportable and difficult to regulate. CDs and tapes, from major-label superstars to unsigned garage bands, are distributed locally, nationally, and internationally. Radio broadcasts operate in similar formats across the nation. Bands tour constantly, and the rock press and fanzines keep producers and consumers up to date on regional and national musical trends. Therefore, while the local band or "scene" phenomenon occurs in virtually every city, small or large, it is misleading to talk about the music of particular locales apart from larger global processes. No musician is raised in a void, free from the lurking effects of, say, Mötley Crüe. Sounds travel relentlessly at every level of the rock world. However, we must also acknowledge the power of local trends and invention; there is some degree of sonic and stylistic unity within a given scene, but this unity should be regarded as a specific articulation of cosmopolitan cultural flows (see Mark Olson, chapter 14). Understanding the diffusion and interplay between international major label rock and local musics remains an inadequately addressed issue in rock scholarship.[6]

Further, rock's spatial mobility is linked to its largely amateur nature and textual mobility. A band's small-time status ensures that its music will have a limited geographical range and influence. Different forms of rock texts have different patterns of spatial diffusion: a touring band will only reach the people who attend its shows, whereas a CD can be circulated more efficiently since its reception is not dependent on a scheduled appearance, and videos can be sprung on anyone who turns to the channel at a given time. The nature of musical diffusion varies according to the textual form – one gets a more distinct, but no less important, sonic experience from an engrossing club show than one does from a radio broadcast played quietly while studying. Television and film, while undoubtedly having profound social effects, are for the most part evenly distributed across a given country, and usually produced by large corporate professionals, thus engendering a sharply different process of spatial effectivity.

THE SUCCESS CONTINUUM

The three differentiating features of the rock formation – its textual mobility, widespread amateurism, and spatial mobility – can be better understood along a "continuum of success." Virtually all rock bands that produce original music desire success in one way or another. Otherwise, playing covers is far easier and more lucrative.[7] Success, however, is not a simple issue. It can be measured in terms of number of fans or record sales (such as Hootie and the Blowfish), cultural influence (wherein a particular type of music and its associated styles impact broad sections of youth/music culture, e.g., Gangsta Rap), or peer influence (wherein other musicians and rock critics, but not necessarily large sections of the public, are inspired by bands, e.g., the Velvet Underground). Bands like Nirvana are quintessential successes since they flourish in all of these categories. Moreover, the continuum of success organizes more than just band activity. It operates in a homologous way, with the same vertical and horizontal dispersion, for record labels, recording studios, clubs, engineers, managers, etc.; the ranks of the unsuccessful far outnumber the lucky few who are at the top of their game.

Regardless of how one measures success, it should be seen as a central trope in popular music, informing and motivating the entire domain of rock culture. Analyzing popular music along this continuum complicates the traditional academic framework of analysis based on an outdated, linear model of communication. As Herman, Swiss, and Sloop note in chapter 1, the linear model of communication forms rock scholarship's discursive apparatus along a tripartite division between the analysis of music production, texts, and consumption. In fact, these three divisions of popular music study are intertwined in a manner far more complex than can be accounted for by the linear model of communication. Modes of consumption are the end result of production processes; at the same time they are an integral part of music-making since audience approval and commodity consumption are tied up with most people's definition of success. Even the most vehemently anticorporate band needs some sort of income and approval to sustain its existence.

Nevertheless, I feel it is helpful to begin with questions of production, for if we want to understand the rock process materially, issues of production are crucial. Frith feels that "the relations of cultural production determine the possibilities of cultural consumption" (1988, 5). Frith is not implying that we view rock through the lens of a reductionist Marxism wherein the interests of capital dictate rock content and activity. Instead, Frith suggests that the way in which rock functions in society, to its fans and detractors alike, is intimately and reciprocally connected to the conditions that structure and regulate its production – conditions that are often oversimplified if not overlooked.

The conditions of rock music-making involve much more than matters of political economy, governmental policy, or music business practices, though these are important concerns. Conditions of production are a constellation of forces that also include powerful ideological and mythmaking machines acting on positions of gender, race, and class, as well as intangibles like talent, charisma, desire and luck, all of which are entwined and

enacted in music-making apparatuses that function along the success continuum. For example, discursive machines, which mobilize myths such as
rock authenticity or authorial invention/originality, have tremendous influence in the entire domain of the rock world, from production to consumption. These forces shape the way people make and experience music. A good
case in point is demonstrated by a personal songwriting experience. One of
the members in my band adheres strongly to the notion that good rock
music must be "original" and not reminiscent of past texts, especially if the
new music conjures up associations with undesirable rock styles. When I
presented a new song to the band to learn in practice, he complained about
the fact (unrecognized by me) that the song's bridge, which I was very proud
of, sounded like the main riff from Rush's old song "The Spirit of Radio." I
had to scrap the bridge, since it is not "cool" for an *indie-rock* band to sound
like Rush, and write a new part. This microexample of the way discourses
and myths have real effects in the songwriting process occurs continually in
a myriad of ways in all facets of rock making and consumption. As analysts
of rock music, we must understand how these forces shape rock practices
differently as we move along the success continuum.

What makes the continuum of success a particularly useful tool in theorizing popular music for the cultural studies practitioner is that it is governed
by the logic of *access*. Progress along the continuum is not available to the
vast majority of those rock music-makers seeking upward mobility. The
logic of access guarantees that the production of music is completely bound
by relations of power. Jacques Attali (1985) describes how the power struggles that organize sound into the categories of music and noise mirror, and
even forecast, material conditions of society. Examining the rock formation
via a continuum of success is a perfect method for operationalizing Attali's
theory within a smaller scale because each popular music style can be seen
as a place of music, marginalizing those musical practices (noise) that fall
outside of its generic codes ("If it's not punk, it's crap!"). The continuum of
success points us to the convergence of forces that dictate what gets to be
music and what is relegated to noise. This becomes more apparent when we
examine the issues of textual mobility, amateurism, and spatial mobility
along the success continuum.

First, textual mobility is not achieved by most rock producers. We take
for granted that pop groups make videos and play stadium tours without
understanding that these commonplace occurrences are only available to

bands after considerable achievement. Anyone can be in a garage band, but progress from there into clubs, fanzine reviews, record deals, radio play, video production, etc., is the result of incremental victories of music-making access. Simply, the more forms a rock band's music appears in, the more successful it is. Regional club acts don't get onto movie soundtracks and are only tangentially related to international media conglomerates.

Viewing rock's textual mobility as a situation of controlled access reframes music production in political terms. What are the factors that allow an act to enter into an indie recording deal (one of the first measures of "real" success)? Mapping paths of textual mobility point us towards networks of exclusion based on rhetorics of talent and generic elitism, which may be quietly complicitous with racist, sexist, classist, or homophobic practices. If a band comprised of women proves itself as a successful local live act in a given town, what obstacles (or shortcuts) must it face to procure a record contract or make videos?

Second, rock's vast amateur realm is obviously directly related to the continuum of success. Every upwardly mobile band seeks to be more successful (according to what they consider to be success), but only a lucky few achieve mass popularity or influence. It is in focusing on the *road* to mass popularity and stardom that we uncover how the rock process works, not only because this is where the majority of rock activity occurs, but also because we direct our analytical energy towards understanding the panoply of forces that govern and propel success.

Nevertheless, most rock scholarship begins with the premise that popular music is mass-mediated music, music intended for mass audiences. Yet if we look at the complete field of rock music, we find this to be only partially the case. According to Frith, "it is only pop music whose essence is that it is communicated by a mass medium...Pop music is created, however successfully, for a large audience and is marketed by the record industry" (Frith, 1981: 6). Frith's analysis only tells half the story. In fact, most pop is produced with modest intentions – most bands dream of, and work toward getting signed, but know they are lucky if they sell more than 500 copies of their CD or tape before they break up. I am not making the common argument that small-time rock is somehow free from the corrupting effects of capitalism while corporate rock is an empty commodity manipulated by profit-seeking international conglomerates. The relationship is far more dynamic and complex. Instead, I am arguing that the rock process simply functions differently at low-success levels.

For example, the realities of commerce affect the rock process in ways that may seem paradoxical to the art versus commerce binary. The members of an aspiring band usually have to work day jobs to sustain themselves. If the band is lucky enough to get money from an independent record label, the band usually makes do with substandard, rushed recording situations even though they are usually granted creative autonomy. Conversely, virtually all bands that enter into major label contracts are given enough money to quit their day jobs, buy new gear, and focus on music. They are sure to be granted a comfortable and professional recording situation, but they realize that if their album does not please the company they will be dropped. Flaming Lips frontman Wayne Coyne, in an interview with critic Jim DeRogatis about moving to a major label, illuminates this situation nicely: "We never called it punk rock, that was just all the money and time we had…We really liked the idea of breaking free of that whole thing where independent bands spend fifty dollars making shitty-sounding records…It wasn't like dreading going into the recording studio. We'd wake up everyday, and ideas would be flying out of everybody's heads. We could set up an amp and put a mike sixty feet down the hall just to see how it sounded. After that we didn't want to make a record ever again if we had to do it the old way" (DeRogatis, 1996: 230). It is a myriad of subtle differences like these that ensure amateur rock is not a microcosm of megarock, or a uniform activity for all participants.

Although I feel that writing about rock as mass culture tends to simplify and obscure the diversity of small-time popular music production practices, this body of work is obviously important. Most bands with significant cultural clout operate at a level of wide dissemination. Simon Frith and Lawrence Grossberg have been particularly effective at conveying how rock functions as a mass medium connected to youth with political possibilities. But these perspectives function with a degree of abstraction that can only grasp rock's effects and processes at the most general level. They generally turn a blind eye to small-time production within the dramatically varied popular music terrain. The many little worlds of popular music are not mere microcosms of mass-mediated rock, but neither are they distinct,

autonomous zones of authenticity. Grafting the full spectrum of rock practices onto the continuum of success allows the rock analyst to avoid setting
rock up in terms of the weary art-versus-commodity binary. Instead, we see
the discourses pertaining to art, commerce, authenticity, talent, etc., as
material forces that shape rock practice *differently* as one follows the continuum.

The concept of spatial mobility can be understood as two related features of popular music. First, there is the question of straightforward mobility, which refers to rock's capacity to move across geographic space. But
globality is a rite of passage, where the ability to move one's music signals
increasing levels of prominence. The success continuum raises political
questions then: who and what gets to move where? There have been, for
example, several instances where my band's music has traveled because we
are from a city noted as having a "hot scene." My band has landed out-of-
town shows using our home city, Champaign, Illinois, as a major selling
point to otherwise indifferent promoters. Other local bands that align themselves with generic styles seen as different from the "Champaign scene" (e.g.,
heavy metal) may as well be from any Midwest small town. But what are the
real constraints to touring, to getting one's CD distributed and played in
wider geographical radiuses?

Another feature of spatial mobility is related to issues of intertextuality,
and is one of the most difficult matters to confront in rock music. By intertextuality I refer to the process of textual "dissemination" and diffusion that
renders no text "free" from the effects of other texts (in this case musical).
That is, within every rock song is contained, in varying degrees, elements of
and references to previous songs and generic styles. The more success a
band has, the more spatial reach its music will have, thus increasing the
potential for cultural influence. If sounds travel continually through radio
waves, nationally distributed discs, television videos, and touring live performances, how does one make sense of this wide-ranging distribution of
sound? If no one is "free" of mass-marketed music, how can one claim
"garage authenticity" when a small-time band's music is as saturated with Led
Zeppelin influences as is, say, Guns N' Roses? Understanding intertextuality
does not involve unmasking authorial intent, but rather attempting to make
sense of the *effects* of the bewildering number of rock texts that circulate
across space, and grasping those mechanisms which control circulation.

MATERIALISM VERSUS ETHNOGRAPHY: A METHODOLOGICAL DEBATE

We have seen that rock music contains several differentiating attributes that are in constant flux and struggle along a continuum of success traversed by relations of power. Understanding rock – or any social formation – means understanding the forces that regulate its operation. We have also seen that rock functions differently as it travels along the success continuum – small-time rock has a connected yet distinct modus operandi from its big-time cousin. Thus, we must devise a research strategy that can account for internal differences in rock music, and also be able to identify the underlying constitutive power structures.

There is a debate in cultural studies (and elsewhere) between ethnographers, who advocate hands-on interaction with the cultural domain in question, and materialists, who are generally social theorists, less concerned with empirical matters. My concurrent roles in the academy and "on the road" have led me to find merit and limitations in both areas. Close contact with the real workings of many dimensions of rock culture has moved me to question the value of analyses based solely on high degrees of abstraction and theory; some claims, as I hope I have shown, just do not seem to ring true to my experience. But I also realize the limits of personal experience; intimate knowledge of the rock world alone is not sufficient for the kind of contextual, interdisciplinary analyses required by cultural studies. A closer look at the basic claims made by materialists and ethnographers will clarify what I learned intuitively.

From the camp of the materialists, Grossberg (1988, 1992, 1994) has questioned the usefulness of ethnography in cultural studies: "While it is not my intention to deny the "reality" of effectivity of experience, I do question its status – its place and effectivity with the material relations of social life and power. One needs to ask what we know when we know how someone experiences material relations" (1988: 380). Grossberg contends that material conditions produce experience. Therefore, we will have little chance to develop adequate strategies for critique and struggle unless we enter the material realm, the realm that produces the possibilities of experience. Grossberg calls this project "radical contextualism," wherein links are made between " points, events or practices…within a multidimensional and multi-directional field" (1992: 50). Grossberg uses the term "radical" to modify context because he feels it is misleading to isolate a cultural practice outside the historical structures and networks of everyday life in which it is embedded; context is the necessary means by which we make sense of social life for political academic work. Radical contextualism involves the construction of a *map* of power – a map that offers ways of recognizing and combating oppressive hierarchical regimes within a field. The materialist project can be accomplished through various available techniques such as cultural studies' notion of articulation and radical contextuality (Hall, 1986; Grossberg, 1994), Foucauldian genealogy and discursive analysis (Foucault, 1972, 1977, 1978), or, for the bold, Deleuzian rhizomatics (Deleuze and Guatarri, 1987). Radical context, in Grossberg's sense, is only realized at the end of an analysis – it is the product rather than backdrop of intellectual work.

On the other hand, material abstraction, devoid of any empirical detail, also has its problems. If one focuses only on theorizing the power dynamics of the social, one is susceptible to overgeneralizing or trivializing the real day-to-day workings of lived life. If we apply high theory to an inaccurate, simplified, or incomplete illustration of the rock world, then our results will be weakened if not worthless. Radway claims that "production of a useful map, then, necessitates at least some firsthand familiarity with the environment acquired through the temporary assumption of an inhabitant's point of view" (1988: 366). Ethnography allows us to participate in the nuances and eccentricities of popular music as lived experience in order to "get it right."

Several recent books (Cohen, 1991; Finnegan, 1989; and Shank, 1994) have attempted to study popular music-making at the amateur level. Sara Cohen's ethnography of Liverpool rock bands and Barry Shank's account of the Austin, Texas, popular music scene are two such works that provide ethnographic detail of local/amateur music-making practices. Unfortunately, this work may suggest that there is some distinctive nature to a local scene, as if Austin punk was absolutely unique, beginning and ending at the city's limits. Territorially bound ethnographies, especially Shank's, fail to link intimate accounts of local practices to the bigger picture, reducing complex flows of popular culture to a sort of local determinism.

So this leaves us with a dilemma. On the one hand, mass music approaches, like those of Grossberg and Frith, are effective at explaining rock music's working at the most general, abstracted level. These materialist approaches have been particularly powerful in describing rock's political possibilities and constraints, while avoiding banal claims of universal resistance, or pessimistic outlooks of rock sterility. However, these methods ignore the internal differences of popular music production (and consumption) practices, collapsing the multifarious field into the realm of mass media (of course, there are great variations found in big-time rock culture in itself). They rarely offer empirical precision in a field defined by its wild variances. On the other hand, ethnographic portrayals of rock music provide us with detailed analyses of local rock practices. They can account for differences within the ever changing, varied rock terrain. But ethnography, as it is traditionally conceived, is performed in a bounded territory – the field – making it difficult for the ethnographer to connect his or her findings to wider global influences. The rest of this chapter will present a brief sketch of a methodology – materialist ethnography – that retains ethnography's sensitivity to the empirical breadth of the rock formation, and materialism's ability to explain the reality of the conditions that produce it.

Toward a Materialist Ethnography

It is popular music's relentless movement across space that poses the biggest challenge to the ethnographer. Typically, ethnographers have approached the "field" as a local manifestation of a particular culture – one goes to location "x" to study culture "y" – but this premise has become less tenable as global notions of culture gain more currency. Although there is a diverse and often antagonistic spectrum of positions packaged under the rubric of "globalization," few would deny that the degree of cultural interconnectedness and exchange has dramatically changed in nature and intensity in the last few decades.[8] This is especially the case in rock music.[9] Ethnography, which in the past has drawn its epistemological authority from its supposed ability to provide rich and accurate pictures of the lives of localized peoples, will have to be reconfigured in the wake of globalization arguments.

Arjun Appadurai (1990, 1993) has written about the effects of globalization in a manner that is at once responsive to the impact of worldwide, "disorganized" capitalism and sympathetic to the material effects of culture. Rather than equating globalization with homogenization, or in our case local musics as direct microcosms of mass musics, Appadurai points to the uneven relations and antagonisms – the disjunctures – between different intercontinental "flows" as the site for analysis: "The new global economy has to be seen as a complex, overlapping, disjunctive order, which cannot any longer be understood in terms of existing center-periphery models (even those which might account for multiple centers and peripheries)... The complexity of the current global economy has to do with certain fundamental disjunctures between economy, culture and politics which we have only begun to theorize"(1990: 6). These global flows are represented by the never ending movements of people, capital, commodities, information, and ideas. Culture, according to Appadurai, is in motion, and must be examined through the difficult procedure of identifying the articulations of global flows transterritorially from one's particular position, depending on the task at hand.

Appadurai identifies five dimensions of global flow for analysis: ethnoscapes, technoscapes, financescapes, ideoscapes, and mediascapes,[10] though we could surely identify others. What is relevant is his usage of the suffix "-scape" to denote two features of global flows. First, "scape," taken from landscape, denotes irregularity and fluidity, which fits nicely with the ever evolving rock world. Second, as in a painting of a landscape, the term "scape" alludes to the perspectival nature of global flows. The picture one gets depends entirely on how one looks at the given phenomena. Champaign, Illinois, the obvious "natural" domain of much of my ethnographic work, is better construed as a perspective, rather than a demarcated site of analysis.

Appadurai's work implies that the most pressing problem for contemporary ethnography is adopting a cosmopolitan stance. But how can a method that is based on the bodily interaction of the researcher and the researched apprehend articulations and disjunctures of global flows? If we perceive the object – popular music – in motion, dispersed along different trajectories, then we must devise a method that can document rock life moving across space. Bands and support personnel travel constantly, music moves through different media, money travels, as does information and ideas. I suggest a version of ethnographic data collection, which I will call "cosmopolitan ethnography" to respond to Appadurai's critique of research practiced in bounded territories. The cosmopolitan ethnographer does not approach the field from a prioritized site, although one's situatedness will necessarily lead him or her to spend more time in some places than others (analyzing one's ability to travel becomes central). So the fact that I live in Champaign, Illinois, suggests that a good part of my ethnographic experience will stem from there. But priority is given to those (very frequent) instances when my experience takes me elsewhere. How does a pop group's recorded music travel through media and commodity flows? What is involved in the movement of people, money, information, and technology by a touring rock band? And in turn, how do "foreign" instances of rock production flow into our lives where we live *and* when we travel?

While traditional ethnography might focus on the occurrences in a particular city, cosmopolitan ethnography concentrates on the motion of music-making, seeking to understand the common paths, the routes that "pull" and points of blockage – understand, that is, how "centers" or alliances get constituted. The field of small-time rock is characterized by constant reconfiguration and instability. As Joe Carducci testifies, "A band is a tough thing to be a part of. Every band is, in a sense, doomed to fail...Good bands must survive about four years of poverty trauma to get to where they are getting by, rather than scraping by" (1990: 7, 14). In three years, my band, The Slips has had 13 members! Our first drummer moved to Chicago and is in a new band. Our second drummer moved to Nashville with his family and is now in a band that got signed to a major label. Our third drummer moved to England on an academic scholarship and plays over there. Our current drummer moved to Champaign because it is regarded as a fertile site for rock...and I haven't even mentioned bass players or singers yet. Cosmopolitan ethnography urges the researcher to concentrate on change and movement, and the spatial effects of these transformations, as opposed to traditional ethnography that tends to construct an unintentionally deceptive picture of localized uniformity.

Cosmopolitan ethnography also draws attention away from issues of self and identity, and toward broader movements and engagements across space. The body of work that describes self-transformation and identity formation (e.g., Kreiger, 1991), while powerful and valid for certain research questions, is less useful for a materialist project that is concerned with the forces that structure daily life.[11] The cosmopolitan ethnographer uses personal involvement (in my case playing in and managing a rock band) to create accounts of different cultural experiences across an uncentered field. Unlike Clifford (1992), whose *traveling ethnography* model connects centers to peripheries, other centers, or wider (global) contexts, I begin with a premise of uncentered transport and trajectory, and trace patterns and discrepancies – disjunctures – between flows. How do different media travel in different situations? What is the relation between the travel of people and ideas and commodities? Clifford operates in a logic of local/global, where the point of ethnography is to produce a "comparative cultural studies." The cosmopolitan ethnographer acknowledges localized centers of activity but does not attempt to compare these centers to other areas. The local is taken up as a point of convergence (articulations of power) between various flows and mobilizations.

The territorial field of cosmopolitan ethnography is created through the work of the ethnographer who must reflect on the conditions of travel, and the reasons for points of convergence. Travel in this sense means literal movement (in all its forms) and ethnography provides access to the *experience* of this movement. Notice that the questions being asked by the cosmopolitan ethnographer relate directly to conditions of access along the success continuum, since rock success is defined by accessing different forms of mobility. As one attempts to travel in the rock world, this travel will be constantly thwarted (and enabled) by a variety of factors that will become readily apparent during research. For example, as part of my research, I helped out at a small record label that marketed a variety of bands from different rock genres, from heavy metal to rootsy pop. All the bands on this label were competent, professional, and upwardly mobile within their various genres. When trying to book shows for these bands, it became apparent how the "key" rock clubs in Chicago adhered to a strict "indie-rock" format where talent and musical quality were far less important than aesthetic compliance to indie-rock rules. In this capacity I was able to see firsthand how networks of exclusion (good or bad) restrict and facilitate movement in the rock world. To put it differently, the cosmopolitan ethnographer maps the rock terrain, looking for constellations of power to be used in subsequent material analyses – it is strategic ethnography in a shifting field.

POWER GEOMETRY

While Appadurai's work sets culture in motion, we have seen that access to this motion is not evenly distributed. There are those who rarely move, and others who interact less frequently with flows moving toward them. At this point it is useful to introduce Doreen Massey's (1994) notion of *power geometry*, which foregrounds the articulations of power that restrict movement in a given field, thus politicizing the term "local." Power geometry refers to the uneven distribution of chances for mobility across space. Massey makes clear that things like class, race, gender, sexual preference, age, location, occupation, etc., are among the many factors that restrict the ability to participate in intercontinental movement. Articulations of power that restrict movement can be analyzed empirically (ethnography) or materially. Cosmopolitan ethnography enables one to create a *strategic* account of experience, one that can guide a subsequent, complementary material investigation.

Materialism, as I have described it here, asks us to produce a historical map of power – the radical context – which surrounds and permeates the object in question. But this map of power is not a predetermined entity. It can vary greatly from analysis to analysis. One creates a map of power by linking the cultural object to those forces that shape and affect it. A good map is one that provides the most useful explanation, which opens political possibilities for those who are effected by power – it provides us with a theoretical basis for struggle. Cosmopolitan ethnography is strategic because involvement in the field allows us to make the right connections in the material investigation; by experiencing power we can pinpoint those realms that most affect our lives, and need deeper analysis.

To take a simplified example, sexism in rock is an issue that is often noted. Surely we would all like a more gender-equitable rock world. Criticisms are frequently raised against sexist male rockers and the male-dominated rock production infrastructure. My own experience suggested, however, that there is great demand for women in all aspects of rock music production, but relatively few women are trained to do it. The men rockers I have associated with are often thrilled when women perform typically male roles requiring high skill levels (sound engineer, lead guitarist), but make it clear that competence is the primary issue. Simply, social ideals of femininity dictate that little girls should not be encouraged to practice electric guitar or drums, and tinker with electronic equipment. I would approach the male-dominated rock world by critiquing discourses of competence, professionalism, and sexism from within the rock establishment, as well as those larger social structures that discourage young girls from pursuing technical endeavors requiring high skill levels based on notions of femininity and masculinity. By the time a girl realizes that she too can rock, boys often have a ten-year jump on her. Cosmopolitan ethnography points us towards the actual paths that must be engaged by women rockers. It asks: what are the real constraints and options for women to move in the rock world? Cosmopolitan ethnography allows us to approach the question of gender from the standpoint of lived access to mobility.

The rock production infrastructure can be seen as a powerful mechanism (among others) regulating flows. Record labels, the press, booking agents, bands, management companies, and clubs (not to mention fans) all have a say in deciding who has access to movement within the field. Cosmopolitan ethnography's accounts of the rock world direct the researcher to the structures of power that discipline movement and must be analyzed materially.

In sum, the strength of this method stems from the mutually constitutive nature of cosmopolitan ethnography and materialism. Cosmopolitan ethnography allows the researcher to experience power geometry. This, in turn, directs the researcher to ask pertinent material questions. The material analysis, which creates context by linking economic, ideological, and historical forces, sheds light on the possibilities of everyday life. A materialist ethnography should play the ethnographic account off the material map. We must ask if the material map points us in new ethnographic directions that we didn't originally acknowledge. Do the stories of experience gathered by the cosmopolitan ethnographer reflect the "radical context?" Are the material maps and experiential accounts effective – are they useful? Most importantly, did cosmopolitan ethnography strategically enable us to construct better maps? Using cosmopolitan ethnography and material analysis as mutually constitutive dimensions in a comprehensive cultural studies project might possibly answer the critics of certain strands of cultural studies who feel that the specificity of daily life is being avoided in favor of theory and abstraction, and critics of interpretive work who feel material effectivity is being subsumed in the hermeneutic process. Through a careful analysis of rock experiences across the continuum of success, combined with explanations of the articulations of power that govern this continuum, we can discover further political possibilities for popular music production and consumption.

NOTES

1. It is also my contention that the primacy of the written word in academia has led to significant amounts of rock scholarship that engages in various forms of lyrical analysis. Because these studies rarely consider the manner in which the fan "uses" the *music*, the results tend to be banal or flat-out incorrect. For example, Mohan and Malone (1994) did a content analysis of rock song titles (!) in order to determine if "alternative" music has more instances of socially disruptive terms.

2. See Frith (1981, 1988), Jones (1992), Negus (1992), Breen (1995), and Robinson, Buck, and Cuthbert (1991) for varying accounts of rock's different textual forms in relation to the music industry.

3. Frith (1981) is correct to point out that rock "amateurism" is actually a myth since these amateurs are generally not hobbyists, but rather upwardly mobile careerists with an acute understanding of the rules of the game, the financial potential, and professional acumen. Nevertheless, I use the term interchangeably with "low-level" to distinguish between those who make a living playing music and those who wish they could.

4. I use the term "quasi-professional" because the great majority of people who make their living playing rock music live near the poverty line. There is not much of a rock middle class (some sound engineers, session players, or cult bands can sustain a decent income). Rock is like Brazil – a few very rich and most just scraping by.

5. Of course, there are many unsuccessful major label acts, or newer groups that are "developing" on a major label, but the basic continuum holds true.

6. Malm and Wallis have written several important books and articles (Malm, 1993; Malm and Wallis, 1992; Wallis and Malm, 1993) concerning the global exchange of popular music. These works effectively explore the relationship between music industry conduct, national media policies, and music-making practices. However, the work of Malm and Wallis concerns international cultural diffusion, and is less applicable to the American rock terrain since media policy is significantly more uniform and unobtrusive in the United States than in other countries, and regional American cultures usually share more similarities than differences. The challenge, then, is to understand musical exchange within the United States (the region, along with Britain, usually seen as the source and exporter of popular music).

7. The relationship between cover bands and low-level bands playing original music is not cut and dried. Most "original" bands play a few covers, and cover bands often play a few originals, but the distinction nevertheless remains important since upward mobility is directly tied to notions of originality.

8. There are many positions and approaches that claim to be "global." For a variety of perspectives, see Anzuldúa, 1987; Appadurai, 1990, 1993;

Bhabha, 1994; Clifford, 1992; Gupta and Ferguson, 1993; Harvey, 1989; Jameson, 1984; Lash and Urry, 1994; Massey, 1994; Rosaldo, 1989; Soja, 1989; and Wolf, 1982. My intention is not to provide an overview of the different theories of globalization. Rather, I seek to acknowledge the diversity of work in this area, and present one particular strain which raises issues that directly effects ethnography and cultural studies.

9. Interconnection is slightly different from the previously mentioned situation of a band trying to access global influence, because it implies that culture flows towards people as well as away. Anyone can consume global flows, but only successful people can actually be the flow.

10. It is unclear how Appadurai comes up with these designations, and there is no argument as to why these five flows adequately portray global movement. We can substitute other flows if we feel that his designations are inappropriate labels for the types of movement we notice. For instance, in rock music, the flow of commodities seems like a necessary set of trajectories to trace, especially in relation to flows of people, money, and images.

11. For a fine discussion on the limits of identity politics for political transgression see Deem (1996).

REFERENCES

Anzuldúa, G. 1987. *Borderlands/La Frontera*. San Francisco: Spinsters/Aunt Lute Books.

Appadurai, A. 1990. "Disjuncture and Difference in the Global Cultural Economy." *Public Culture* 2(2): 1–24.

———. 1993. "Patriotism and Its Futures." *Public Culture* 5: 411–29.

Attali, J. 1985. *Noise: The Political Economy of Music*. Minneapolis: University of Minneapolis Press.

Bhabha, H. 1994. *The Location of Culture*. New York: Routledge.

Breen, M. 1995. "The End of the World as We Know It: Popular Music's Cultural Mobility." *Cultural Studies* 9(3): 486–504.

Carducci, J. 1990. *Rock and the Pop Narcotic*. Chicago: Redoubt Press.

Clifford, J. 1992. "Traveling Cultures." In *Cultural Studies*, edited by L. Grossberg, C. Nelson, and P. Treichler, 96–116. New York: Routledge.

Cohen, S. 1991. *Rock Culture in Liverpool*. London: Oxford University Press.

Deem, M. 1996. "From Bobbit to SCUM: Re-memberment, Scatological Rhetorics, and Feminist Strategies in the Contemporary United States." *Public Culture* 8: 511–37.

Deleuze, G. and F. Guatarri. 1987. *A Thousand Plateaus*. Minneapolis: University of Minneapolis Press.

DeRogatis, J. 1996. *Kaleidoscope Eyes: Psychedelic Rock from the '60s to the '90s*. Toronto: Citadel Press.

Finnegan, R. 1989. *Hidden Musicians*. Cambridge: Cambridge University Press.

Frith, S. 1981. *Sound Effects*. New York: Pantheon.

———. 1988. *Music for Pleasure*. New York: Routledge.

Foucault, M. 1972. *The Archeology of Knowledge*. New York: Pantheon.

———. 1977. *Discipline and Punish*. New York: Vintage Books.

———. 1978. *The History of Sexuality, An Introduction: Volume One*. New York: Vintage Books.

Goodwin, A. 1994. Dancing in the Distraction Factory: Music Television and *Popular Culture*. Minneapolis: University of Minnesota Press.

Grossberg, L. 1988. "Wandering Audiences, Nomadic Critics." *Cultural Studies* 2(3). 377–91.

———. 1992. *We Gotta Get Out of This Place*. New York: Routledge.

———. 1995. "Cultural Studies: What's in a Name (One More Time)." *Taboo* 1(1): 1–37.

Gupta, A. and J. Ferguson. 1993. "Beyond Culture: Space, Identity, and the Politics of Difference." *Cultural Anthropology* 6–23.

Hall, S. 1986. "On Articulation and Postmodernism." *Journal of Communication Inquiry* 10(2): 45–60.

Harvey, D. 1989. *The Condition of Postmodernity*. Oxford: Basil Blackwell.

Jameson, F. 1984. "Postmodernism, or the Cultural Logic of Late Capitalism." *The New Left Review* 146: 53–92.

Jones, S. 1992. *Rock Formation*. Newbury Park: Sage.

Kreiger, S. 1991. *Social Science and the Self*. New Brunswick: Rutgers University Press.

Lash, S., and J. Urry. 1994. *Economies of Signs and Space*. London: Sage.

Malm, K. 1993. "Music on the Move: Traditions and the Mass Media." *Journal for the Society for Ethnomusicology* 37(3): 339–52.

Malm, K., and R. Wallis. 1992. *Media Policy and Music Activity*. New York: Routledge.

Massey, D. 1994. *Space, Place and Gender*. Minneapolis: University of Minnesota Press.

Middleton, R. 1990. *Studying Popular Music*. Milton Keynes: Open University Press.

Mohan, A., and J. Malone. 1994. "Popular Music as a 'Social Cement': A Content Analysis of Social Criticism and Alienation in Alternative-Music Song Titles." In *Adolescents and Their Music*, edited by J. Epstein, 251–82. New York: Garland.

Negus, K. 1992. *Producing Pop: Culture and Conflict in the Popular Music Industry*. London: Edward Arnold.

Radway, J. 1988. Reception Study: Ethnography and the Problem of Dispersed Audiences and Nomadic Subjects. *Cultural Studies* 2(3): 359–67.

Robinson, D., E. Buck, and M. Cuthbert. 1991. *Music at the Margins: Popular Music and Global Cultural Diversity*. Newbury Park, CA: Sage.

Rosaldo, R. 1989. *Culture and Truth*. Boston: Beacon Press.

Shank, B. 1994. *Dissonant Identities: The Rock 'n' Roll Scene in Austin, Texas*. Hanover, NH: University Press of New England.

Soja, E. 1989. *Postmodern Geographies: The Reassertion of Space in Critical Social Theory*. New York: Verso.

Wallis, R. and K. Malm. 1984. *Big Sounds from Small Peoples: The Music Industry in Small Countries*. New York: Pendragon Press.

Wolf, E. 1982. *Europe and the People without History*. Berkeley: University of California Press.

14

— 'Everybody Loves Our Town' — Scenes, Spatiality, Migrancy

Mark J. V. Olson

Everybody loves us/Everybody loves our town/That's
why I'm thinking of leaving it/Don't believe in it now.../
It's so overblown.
> –Mudhoney on the state of the Seattle scene,
> in the song "Overblown"

"Right now, there's a new scene being born somewhere," says Jon Pone-
man, founder of the indie label Sub Pop (Azerrad, 1992: 48). But, for
the time being at least, everybody loves *my* town: Chapel Hill, North
Carolina. Increasingly touted as a "hot" indie scene, Chapel Hill is sometimes called "the next Seattle." I must admit that I chose to attend graduate
school at the University of North Carolina at least in part because of the
allure of the emergent Chapel Hill scene. This allure was driven by a desire
to be "where all the action is," and in many ways by the sense that being
there would somehow give me an unmediated experience of the "real" scene.
I believed this would confer upon me a greater degree of authenticity, both
as a fan of such Chapel Hill bands as Superchunk, Spatula, and Ben Folds
Five, *and* as a cultural studies student interested in popular culture.[1]

In many ways, the move from my hometown of Minneapolis to Chapel Hill had started before I actually left, for the trajectory of my investments in the Minneapolis scene had already shifted, redirected toward Chapel Hill and Seattle. Still, my move(ment) has not settled, even though I've already "arrived." For I've found that "being there" didn't necessarily entail participation in nor belonging to the Chapel Hill scene *as such.* This essay arises out of that context, of never really arriving in "Chapel Hill." It is an attempt to map the articulations, both actual and virtual, between music scenes, mobility, authenticity, and the political. In the end, I want to consider how alternative modalities of fandom can signal new forms of political community. Scenes like Chapel Hill possess the ability to move people, mobilizing their investments and their bodies. Such a dynamism points to a model of politics that refuses a distinction between location (being there) and movement (going elsewhere), and instead points to what Paul Carter terms a "migrant perspective": "An authentically migrant perspective would, perhaps, be based on an intuition that the opposition between here and there is itself a cultural construction, a consequence of thinking in terms of fixed entities and defining them oppositionally. It might begin by regarding movement, not as an awkward interval between fixed points of departure and arrival, but as a mode of being in the world. The question would be, then, not how to arrive, but how to move, how to identify convergent and divergent movements" (1992: 101).

SCENES: START RIGHT HERE

Coming to terms with the specificity of scenes is a likely place to begin, yet much of contemporary popular music studies elides such specificity. A survey of recent cultural studies work on popular music reveals a proliferation of writing about the various practices (of resistance, appropriation, empowerment, alliance building, consumption, etc.) enacted by various agents and agencies *within* particular music scenes.[2] However, most of this work takes the notion of a "scene" itself for granted, invoking notions of a "punk rock scene," or a "dance club scene" or the "Seattle scene" as the mere backdrop for what supposedly *really* matters: such as popular resistance on the dance floor, dub practices and identity formation, bricolage in punk subculture, or commodification of the "grunge look."

The term "scene" is usually deployed interchangeably with the notion of a music subculture (i.e., hip-hop culture = hip-hop scene). Or the term references the space in which the practices valorized by a particular cultural studies observer get enacted. A scene is reduced to the mere *scenery* in front of which take place the politics and pleasures of music production and consumption. Rarely is a scene viewed as a singular place in its own right, possessor of its own effective logics, its own reality independent of, yet also affecting, the practices that traverse it. Perhaps this is not surprising, for as Lefebvre notes, "Many people will find it hard to endorse the notion that space has taken on...a sort of reality of its own" (1991: 26).

Will Straw's (1991) essay provides an exemplar of the tendency in popular music cultural studies to elide the specificity of scenes. In his discussion of the North American heavy metal and dance music scenes, Straw defines a music scene as "that cultural space in which a range of musical practices coexist, interacting with each other within a variety of processes of differentiation, and according to widely varying trajectories of change and cross-fertilization" (1991: 373). By defining a scene as a "cultural space," Straw acknowledges its reality as a space distinct from the practices that operate within it. Yet Straw's argument leaves the particular logics and effects specific to scenes-as-cultural-spaces undertheorized. For example, he repeatedly writes of practices and their effects as played out within a musical scene – such as "particular music practices [that] 'work' to produce a sense of community" – but he fails to theorize scenes independent of these practices (Straw, 1991: 373). In other words, Straw's scenes are merely empty vessels within which certain practices interact, but these vessels themselves seemingly have no effect on those practices (and perhaps are not even affected by them). Given this interpretation, it is inaccurate to describe Straw's conception of scenes by using the common metaphor "containers." Containers possess the very powerful effectivity of containment – radical territorialization – but Straw's scenes do not seem to possess any effectivity at all. Instead, perhaps we should think of Straw's scenes as a contourless terrain upon which, or over which, practices operate: an empty, inert blank space. Ultimately, Straw ends up conflating the spatial specificity of a scene with a phenomenological "sense" of community (i.e., solidarity).[3]

In a 1994 essay, Lawrence Grossberg picks up where Straw left off in elaborating the ontology of scenes. Following Straw, Grossberg further distinguishes scenes from the practices that operate within them when he writes of a scene's durability despite the continual reconfiguration of the musical practices operating across it. He writes: "Reinterpreting a recent argument by Will Straw, a scene is characterized by a particular logic which may, in a sense, transcend any particular musical content, thus allowing the scene to continue over time, even as the music changes. This also means that very different musics may exist in very similar scenes" (Grossberg, 1994: 46). Two important insights might be highlighted here: first, scenes are "relatively autonomous." They exist and function, in part, independently of the particular practices that traverse them. Second, extrapolating from Grossberg, this "relative autonomy" of scenes means that one cannot "read off" a particular music (style, genre, sound) from a particular scene (or vice versa). The existence of grunge music in a particular scene does not necessarily mean that the scene can be said to possess the same logics and effectivities as the Seattle scene. Nor, for example, does the difference between Seattle's grunge rock and Nashville's country entail an equivalent degree of difference between the Seattle scene and the Nashville scene. Indeed, they may be quite similar along any number of axes (for example, both deploy similar logics of place-based authenticity; e.g., both are meccas, drawing large crowds of fans for whom "being there" is all-important, etc.).

In his essay, Grossberg then defines a scene as an *apparatus* of music, producing particular configurations of tastes and taste-cultures, and thereby moves beyond Straw's rather "empty" definition.[4] As "apparatuses," scenes are products of a "logic of production/commercialization,…the largely industrial attempt to market music by segmenting it" (Grossberg, 1994: 46). In other words, scenes for Grossberg are marketing and media-constructed entities — their constructed nature need not make them any less real — deployed in the service of the music industry's profit-driven interests. Different scenes are created in the interest of sustaining and extending a market for music industry commodities. As Lefebvre argues, "every society – and hence every mode of production with its subvariants… – produces its own space" (1991: 31).

Popular music studies' focus on the music business often valorizes the transgressive or resistant possibilities of the entertainment itself and elides the profit-driven context from which these possibilities spring. Yet, ultimately, it is important to position the recent proliferation of scene-marketing within a larger shift in the economics of the entertainment business, a shift predicated on the absorbtion of record labels into multimedia conglomerates. These conglomerates produce highly mobile commodities that are marketed across a wide variety of media. As such, the recent attempts to

organize taste through the marketing of scenes can be viewed as one extension of this deterritorializing logic of capital.[5] Grossberg sees the contemporary production of stars as another. He argues that "the primary product
of entertainment is gradually changing: the production of a hit is less important than the production of a star as a marketable commodity. While stars
have long been produced and promoted, their mobility across media and
genres used to be circumscribed by the identity which defined their popularity. These limits have not only disappeared, but it is their absence which
now defines the star. The new star does not need a history. The old model
of a star building an ever-expanding audience while 'paying their dues' is
being replaced by the immediate insertion of a figure into a position of stardom already waiting for them" (1988: 318). Grossberg, writing in 1988, cites
Bruce Willis as just such a highly marketable, highly mobile figure, who
moves easily between singer, spokesperson in commercials, and star of both
television and the silver screen. Other more recent examples come to mind:
Sting, Whitney Houston, Will Smith (a.k.a. The Fresh Prince), David Has-
selhoff, rappers Ice Cube and Queen Latifah, and LL Cool J and Brandi, both
of whom have recently starred in their own sitcoms.

    The logic of scenic production resembles star production (Grossberg,
1992) in two complementary ways. First, scenes, though not displacing the
production of stars, are being produced alongside stars across media to produce markets. The Seattle scene possesses a high degree of what Marcus
Breen (1995) calls "cultural mobility," moving easily into other markets
beyond the scope of the music industry – into film and fashion, especially.[6]
For example, the movie *Singles* was as much a success based on the popularity of the Seattle scene as it was on the basis of the "star-quality" of any of
its primary actors. Or consider the advertising campaign of Best Buy, which
recently promised to provide the next best thing to the Seattle and Boston
scenes by citing the various hang outs that have made such places
renowned. Each of the ads culminates with "Come to Best Buy: It's the *Best*
place to buy music." All the scenes mentioned in the ads lose their geographic specificity and become, quite literally, one place, the place to buy
music. Best Buy, of course.

    Scenes are valuable because they can secure consumption of those com-
modities identified with a particular scene. This is a common marketing
strategy, one that Sub Pop Records has mastered. Says Grant Alden, managing editor of *Rocket:* "[Sub Pop's] strategy has been to create Sub Pop as an

identity...to create trust that if it's on Sub Pop, it's worth owning, even if you've never heard of the band" (Azerrad, 1992: 44). The same works for the marketing of scenes: if it's associated with the Seattle scene, for example, it's worth owning, even if you've never heard of the band (or movie, or style).

Strategies of deterritorialization meet with contestation, however, at the site of the scene. Fans within a particular scene are continuously deploying logics of authenticity and distinction that aim to establish, once and for all, the geographical or historical specificity of the scene. In a manner similar to other national, regional, and local "exclusivist claims to places," scenesters attempt "to fix the meaning of particular spaces, to enclose them, endow them with fixed identities and to claim them for one's own" (Massey, 1994: 4). For example, Jay Faires, president of Chapel Hill's Mammoth Records, distinguishes between the ahistorical Seattle scene of the popular media and its "real" (read: historical) counterpart: "People forget the Seattle scene was around eight or ten years before it broke" (Davies, 1993: I-30). Meanwhile, the logic of capital works in a contrary trajectory, for such historical knowledge works to situate scenes into particular narratives of space-time and therefore hinders a scene's mobility. One effect desired by multimedia industry, then, is to deterritorialize scenes once they are produced, severing them from any origin, historical or geographical, that would hinder their mobility across media and across time.

It is important to resist the authenticating logics deployed in this struggle, relying as they do on an essentialist conception of place. Doreen Massey points out the "lack of basis for any claims for establishing the authentic character of any particular place (whether such claims are used as the grounds for arguing for ethnic [or scenic] exclusivity or for opposing some unwanted development – 'it would be out of place here'). There is, in that sense of a timeless truth of an area, built on somehow internally contained character traits, no authenticity of place"(1994: 121).

However, I also think it is important to note that scenes, once produced, *can* become productive in their own right, and in multiple and sometimes contradictory ways, or at least in ways counter or contrary to the desires of the music industry. As Judith Butler points out, founding moments are not necessarily determinant (1990: 145). A failure to look beyond the production of scenes in the service of capital and into the productivity of scenes themselves ends up reducing the relation of power to the scenic to an instrumental one. Massey (1994) describes the consequences of this functionalist approach to the spatial. According to Massey, such an approach "rob[s] places in a certain measure of their individual specificity" and implies that "in the end they [are] all products of international capital accumulation" (1994: 117).

SCENES: A GEOGRAPHY AND AN ONTOLOGY

Instead of thinking of scenes only as empty receptacles for practices and their effects, or merely as instruments deployed in the service of power, I want to think of a scene as a space qua space within popular culture in general and popular music in particular. In discussing the spatial singularity of scenes and their functions in contemporary culture, I hope to return to the issues I alluded to in the introduction – "being there," movement, authenticity, and belonging – for these terms are integral to understanding scenes not only as places produced but as productive places. In what follows, I propose a preliminary map of scenic place. One hindrance in coming to terms with the scenic revolves around the tendency to conflate scene with community (see, e.g., Thornton, 1996). While a scene may in fact be the mise-en-scène of community, a scene itself is not reducible to relations of solidarity. In other words, it becomes quite easy to slide from the spatial to the social. For example, Massey (1994), from which I draw extensively in this chapter, ultimately – yet quite productively – ends up conflating the spatial with the social.[7] What, then, can be said for the specificity of the spatial scene?

First, a scene has a rather peculiar relation to geography per se. The designation of a scene always entails reference to some geographical marker (most commonly a city, but also a locality or region, a set of dance clubs, or even "the world"), but the place of the scene itself does not necessarily correlate with the boundaries of its geographical referent, for the reach of its effects does not respect geographic borders. Consequently, any theorization of, say, the Seattle scene must mark the relationship between Seattle, the city – a spatially bounded and geographically specific entity – and Seattle, the scene.[8]

I will use three examples to illustrate my point. First, the Motown scene, which has been almost completely disconnected from Detroit the geographical locality (one most likely would not *go there* to find the Motown scene), provides an example of a scenic space that correlates with literally no geographical referent. However, despite being "nowhere," the scene has a presence, real enough to say that certain musical groups "come from" the Motown scene or "populate" it.[9] Second, as I have noted, the Seattle scene provides an example of a scene that exceeds its geographical boundaries; it's almost global in scope, a "new playground for all of us to play in (Spencer, quoted in Bertsch, 1993). In fact, the Seattle scene functions almost imperially, extending its territory over a larger and larger space. Sub Pop Records, one of the agencies in this imperializing mobility, moved to "annex" northeastern Canada into the Seattle scene. "Underscoring [the] conviction that scenes extend beyond their geographical boundaries, Sub Pop records is releasing this spring an album featuring recordings by Sloan, Eric's Trip [both from Halifax, Nova Scotia], and two other New Brunswick-area bands, Jale and Idée du Nord" (Davies, 1993: I-30). The Seattle scene's territory extends from Seattle to Seventh Avenue (Tilsner, 1993) and even into the Netherlands (Bellafante, 1993) and Russia (Orlova, 1993). Finally, the "world music" scene's seeming claim of encompassing the totality of global geography belies, despite its moniker, the quite limited reach of this particular scene's effectivity (and thus its "borders"). Thus, coming to terms with the specificity of any particular scene involves specifying the singular relationship between the particularity of scenic place and geographic location.

Furthermore, scenes can be differentiated according to their distinct temporalities. A scene's temporality can be read two different ways: as the sum total of the temporalities found within it, or as a temporality in its own right. Straw outlines the first when he writes: "Different cultural spaces are marked by the sorts of temporalities to be found within them – by the prominence of activities of canonization, or by the values accruing to novelty and currency, longevity and 'timelessness.' In this respect, the 'logic' of particular musical culture is a function of the way in which value is constructed within them relative to the passing of time" (1991: 374). In other words, many different temporalities are available within a scene, depending upon the particular configuration of musical practices operative within it. So, for example, a scene defined in part by the predominance of classic rock (or folk music, or any variation of "retro-") may be said to contain a different temporality than modern rock or techno scenes.

Rave scenes provide a vivid example of a scene being marked by the various temporalities within it – a collusion of temporalities, all in the same scenic space. In a *Time* magazine report on the rave scene, Guy Garcia (1992) chronicles the different temporalities operative within the rave scene of a New York City nightclub, The Shelter. Raves signal the future (or "phuture") and the futuristic through the techno sound and through the marketing of the experience of the scene as an entering into "Timecapsule One" of "'NASA' (Nocturnal Audio and Sensory Awakening)" (Garcia, 1992: 60). Garcia describes techno as "galvanizing...an intensely synthetic, hyperkinetic form of dance music" that resulted from a "fusion of the futuristic computer-driven sound of European bands like Kraftwerk and the rhythmic possibilities of computer-controlled keyboards" (1992: 60). Though futuristic, raves also signal a return to the past, a return to the more "organic" communities of the 1960s. As one raver described the rave scene, "It's a love circle...It's like a 1960s scene – all the races are together, dancing, having a communal experience. We want to go to Woodstock and rave for a whole week" (Garcia, 1992: 60). Finally, raves also signal simultaneously the end of time (one T-shirt read: "Smile – It's the Apocalypse"), the present and the urgency of investing in the "now" ("There'll be booths where people can get information from groups like ACT-UP and Rock the Vote"), and even the escape from temporality and the ever present banality of life altogether ("It's about forgetting who's going to be President and having a good time") (Garcia, 1992: 60–61).[10] Scenes are thus the site of a temporal dialogism, "an arena where memories of the past" – and, I would add, representations of the 'now' and the future – "serve to critique and change the present" (Lipsitz, 1990: 100).

However helpful, Straw's argument, by focusing on the temporalities coexisting *within* a particular scene, fails to acknowledge that the scene itself has its *own* temporality. In this conceptualization, the temporality of a scene is a function of its popularity. Those scenes that are popular are the most "current" or fully present. Those that are no longer popular are "passé" and those that are on their way to popularity are emergent, the "scenes of tomorrow." Scenes follow a trajectory from "birth" (often ascribed *after* their "discovery" by the media and music critics) through varying degrees of currency (or popularity) and into a decline of variable duration (certain scenes are "out" right now). As Cocks notes: "Athens, Ga., was the regional rage just...well, was it yesterday? And there was Minneapolis only a few years back; before that it was Philadelphia, Detroit, Memphis. These days – these moments – it's Seattle" (1992: 70). However, this trajectory need not be linear or non-reversible. A scene's temporal trajectory can be cyclical, with certain scenes staging a comeback.

Ultimately, the temporality of a scene that is emergent (upcoming) or present ("in") can be read as a marker of its "sensibility," its ability to empower certain musical practices with the capacity to "move" their listeners, and certain bands with the ability to perform them. Scenes that are passé do not – or at least their effectivity is diminished. Ultimately, such distinctions are attributions of value and effectivity assigned by fans to particular scenes. So, for example, to claim that Chapel Hill is the "next Seattle" does not mean that bands like Superchunk have some sort of artistic creativity fostered within the space of Chapel Hill that has the unique ability to move people, and that they then "express" in their music. Instead, this ability to affect people is in a certain manner produced from the relationship between scenic sensibility and its productivity – the relationships between bands, fans, and their location in relation to places such as Chapel Hill.

Yet this temporal logic of comparison between scenes is not entirely constitutive of scenic identity. Obviously, part of a scene's sense of identity and authenticity is defined in opposition to and by its difference from other scenes, by the characterization of these "others" as inauthentic and commodified. Or the scene may be differentiated from more abstract or imagined "others." For example, Susan Thornton describes the import of the distinction made by youth "between the 'hip' world of the dance crowd...and its perpetually absent, denigrated *other* – the 'mainstream'" (1996: 5). Furthermore, as scenes become more and more mainstream, scenes themselves come to be defined as the commodified other to an "authentic" music community. Consider Mudhoney's rant about Seattle, or Vanilla Trainwreck's Greg Elkins, who decries the notion of a North Carolina scene: "We hang out as a people, not as a scene. People outside call it a scene....[One reviewer] wrote about our first album and mentions the 'slow-rock/love rock North Carolina scene.' So somebody lumps us all together and we look at each other and go, 'My God, we're a scene! What are we gonna do?'" (Davies, 1993: I-22). In this sense, "when you know what everybody else is, then you are what they are not" (Hall, 1991: 21). Again, such distinctions map the value and potential efficacy of scenes (this scene moves me, the other cannot). Consequently, it appears that many scenes deploy logics of authenticity that require scenes "to be enclosures, to have boundaries and – therefore most importantly – to establish their identity through negative counterposition with the Other beyond the boundaries" (Massey, 1994: 169).

On the other hand, scenes do have identities independent of their relationships to or differences from other scenes. This identity is not inter-
changeable with any other scene; it is unique in its own geographic particularity, its own historical development, its own temporality, and the
particular configuration of practices operating within it. As one member of
the Martha's Vineyard scene described it, "there are a billion islands in the
world ... but I don't think there any that have the spiritual feeling this place
does" (Morris, 1994: 11). Nowhere else in the world does the Martha's Vineyard scene exist *as such*; it exists as a "singularity." The singularity of scenes,
however, does not imply an insular localism. That is, while the identity of a
scene cannot be reduced to a simple counterposition with an outside (other
scenes or the "mainstream"), notions of singularity do not preclude specifying precise relationships and linkages to and through that outside. Consequently, a "mapping" of the scenic also involves recognizing "relations of
contiguity" and "negotiable proximities," or what Meaghan Morris calls "the
logic of the next" (1988: 41). In other words, how are scenes distributed in
space? How "close" or "far away" are two scenes from each other? How easy
is it to "travel" to those scenes that are contiguous, or at least in close proximity to the scene in which one is located? For example, the Seattle scene,
the Minneapolis scene, the Athens, Georgia, scene and the Chapel Hill
scene, although separated by many miles, are all in close proximity to each
other in terms of scenic geography. Consequently, one can, as a fan, "travel"
between them with relative ease.[11] Travel between other scenes is difficult
at best. For example, there are no easy roads between the Nashville scene
and the techno scene, although the Swedish band, Rednex, has recently
managed to negotiate one by forging its own (although the success of these
trailblazers was marginal). Here, contiguity and proximity mark not the
presence of a border, but rather the directionality and intensity of trajectories and flows. Scenes intermingle, producing relations of mobility.

RECONFIGURING AUTHENTICITY AND FANDOM: SCENES AS PRODUCTIVE SPACES

Scenes do more than just mark the existence of flows; they also produce
them. The ability of scenes to initiate and modify the production of flows
and trajectories, a mobility of investments and bodies, moves us to scenic
productivity – and into the realm of the political. Coming to terms with this

productivity requires a detour through a discussion of the politics of the rock formation. According to Grossberg (1992), the politics of the rock formation have always relied on the operation of a territorializing machine, producing sites of authenticity and attachment that enable and organize affective investments, points of anchoring for youth. For Grossberg, a territorializing machine spatializes the temporal, producing singularities of place; it "transforms events into places and distributes them as other (rather than different) to each other" (forthcoming). Read in this light, popular music provides many of what Stuart Hall describes as "those points of attachment that give the individual some sense of 'place' and position in the world" even if they may not, in actuality, occupy those places, imagined or otherwise (Hall, 1989: 133).

These spaces of authenticity, of affective investment, are constantly being constructed within popular music as *other* to the spaces produced by another territorializing machine, the machine of daily life. Following Lefebvre, "everyday life" refers to a mode of existence structured by the boredom of redundancy and recurrence, a tedious "compound of insignificances" (1984: 24). Everyday life colonizes the spaces of our daily lives by introducing normalized routines and daily rituals – the mundane writ large. This is a common discourse of youth, especially prevalent in Gen X and slacker discourses. Sarah Dunn's *The Official Slacker Handbook* (1994) describes this aversion to everyday life. Dunn writes that *"normal life* is what's alarming. Normal life, when you stop to think about it, is utterly appalling" (1994: 66). Dunn offers the slacker's solution to everyday life: chronic wanderlust. Similarly, rock works to counter everyday life through mobility itself. The territorializing machine of everyday life therefore works in a trajectory contrary to popular music's production of sites of affective investment and authenticity that are characterized by passion, and passionate commitment, fandom, play, and fun. Ultimately, everyday life produces immobility, emplacement, and imprisonment in boredom. The rock formation is always producing (its own) mobility, always trying to differentiate itself from the logic of everyday life, to claim or reclaim authenticity, where authenticity marks difference from the commodified existence that perpetually encroaches. But because each new site of authenticity is always already sliding towards inauthenticity ("Athens, Ga., was the regional rage just....well, was it yesterday?"), popular music must continually produce new sites of authenticity for particular bands to occupy and for fans to invest in, *redefining what constitutes the authentic in the process.*

Traditionally, the measure of authenticity within the rock formation was its sound, or "voice."[12] In other words, it was a distinctive sound or affectively charged voice that served as the criterion of differentiation in the struggle to define "really" authentic rock. However, there is at least some evidence that affective investment in the differences between musics is on the wane; identification with a particular musical genre or distinctive sound no longer matters as much, or in the same way, as it did in the past. Indeed, musical taste no longer seems to be organized according to affiliation with any particular genre; rock's sensibility has changed. When asked what kinds of music they prefer, many people respond in manner similar to Julie Hall, a 23-year-old clerk at TNN: "I'm just as likely to buy the Black Crowes as I am to buy a Travis Tritt tape. I like good music. *I don't care what it is*" (Painton, 1992: 65). Perhaps this itinerancy of fandom can be attributed to the blending and proliferation of musical genres, which thereby diminishes any one genre's capacity to function as a powerful marker of difference and therefore, of authenticity. As Sloop and Herman point out in chapter 15, sampling technologies further illustrate the absurdity of the discreet musical commodity. Where can we locate authenticity in such hybrids as heavy-metal punk, or – my favorite example – the techno-hillbilly-country of bands like Rednex? How can we differentiate between authentic and inauthentic sounds when, as Daniel House of C/Z Records points out, "there used to be just Pearl Jam, and now there are 10 bands who sound just like Pearl Jam," a phenomenon someone once dubbed "Alice in Stone Temple Pearl Jam's Garden" (Davies, 1993: I-22)?

Since differences in sound no longer seem to make any difference, I believe we need to look elsewhere for new sites of authenticity production, literally in/to new places: place-based scenes. Such scenes are the new authenticity machines. If scenes "transform events into places" – and it seems that they do, for they transform individual musical events into the identity of a place – then scenes can be said to function as territorializing machines. Yet the production of place need not imply stasis. Instead, territorializing machines channel and redirect libidinal, affective, and monetary flows. As such, territorializing machines function in a manner similar to de Certeau's discussion of *metaphorai*, or spatial practices: "they traverse and organize places; they select and link them together; they make sentences and itineraries out of them" (1984: 115). They are both *topical*, defining places, and *topological*, deforming lines of trajectory across space (de Certeau, 1984: 129). Following de Certeau, certain scenes "organize walks," inducing certain mobilities that set bands and fans on trajectories of becoming – or, more appropriately, *belonging;* their position on these trajectories determines their authenticity. Place-based scenes produce places where one can presumably live an "authentic" relation to rock in one's daily life.

Authenticity is measured, then, according to the *degree* and *manner* of belonging to a particular scene exhibited by a particular band or fan. Within a scenic logic, what makes Pearl Jam more authentic than any other similar-sounding band is not its authentic sound, but rather the degree to which it belongs to the Seattle scene. In many instances, the manner of "authentic" belonging is temporal: a function of an historical investment in the scene. For example, the Artist Formerly Known as Prince (TAFKAP) maintains his authenticity in the eyes of Minneapolis scenesters by virtue of literally "being on the scene": by maintaining residence in Minneapolis and by consistently rearticulating his affiliation with the scene itself by playing spontaneous concerts in small venues like First Avenue and The Quest. As Cocks pointed out, "of the many differences between Prince and his predecessors (he's shorter, he's a better dancer), one thing stands out: *Prince stuck around.* He's the local boy who's still on the scene" (1990: 121). In sum, Prince belongs more than others because of his emplotment in a particular scenic history. In other words, he is considered more authentic because he has paid his dues over a long period of time within his particular scene.

In Seattle, the existence of a temporal trajectory of "belonging" produces interesting effects. In order to be considered "authentic," bands seem to be revoking and displacing their actual histories and emplotting themselves in those histories deemed more authentic. Geoff Mayfield of *Billboard* discusses this phenomenon: "What I'm hearing now is that bands from L.A. or the Midwest are moving to Seattle and telling record companies, 'Yeah, we grew up here, and this is where we make our music" (Cocks, 1992: 71). A temporal claim is not the only way of "belonging" in a place-based scene, however. The new configuration of fandom produced within a scene seems to point to another – a *spatial* trajectory of belonging.

SPATIALIZED FANS AND POLITICAL MIGRANTS

Recall that the rock formation is always producing lines of flight in reaction to the territorializing machine of everyday life. Rock produces excitement and works to counter everyday life through the production of mobility itself. Consequently, this production of mobility is not without its imagined destination, a utopic space of "true" authenticity, a final redemption from the banality of everyday life. Historically, this destination has been defined temporally, or at least identified with the experience of a particular time – "leisure" time. As both Elton John and the Bay City Rollers assert, lived plenitude had everything to do with Saturday night. We are, after all, "workin' for the weekend."

With the emergence of place-based scenes, however, the trajectory of the lines of flight are redrawn and reoriented toward literally being "somewhere else," toward the imagined full-bodied, robust experiences to be had by being in that "other" place. Ah, what fun could be had, if we could only be "on the scene." As Bertsch (1993) points out, "even if we can't single out actors, we'd at least like to identify where the action takes place." It is as if Seattle or Chapel Hill existed outside of the reach of the territorializing machine of everyday life; thus fans project onto such scenes an imagined lived plenitude and richness to daily life, and move their bodies – quite literally – towards the scene.[13]

Accordingly, place-based scenes have become meccas, and fans are like diasporic pilgrims *on their way there* in hopes of finding their salvation from everyday life. How many so-called Gen Xers have set themselves upon the highway toward Seattle in hopes of finally living the cool, hip, authentic life of the Seattle scenester? Contrary to the temporal modality of scenic belonging that seems to determine a band's authenticity, a fan's authenticity is determined by the positive force of desire, by investments in spatial trajectories or by affiliations with a particular place. Consider Pleasant Gehman's (1992) description of Seattle as a "modern day Mecca…currently to the rock 'n' roll world what Bethlehem was to Christianity." This description does not suggest someone leaving home to find an imagined authenticity, but rather someone displaced from home, trying to get back to where he or she belongs: a diasporic subjectivity on a trajectory toward a topos.[14] Yet the distinction between location and movement breaks down, for this trajectory is itself a topos, literally a "meeting place" of fans (Massey, 1994: 154). Here community (of fans) is predicated not upon *already* being there, upon an arrival, but in terms of a common desire to be there, a common belonging to a trajectory of investment towards a particular place: a movement. A scenic logic of mobilization points to scenes as places "where nobody is, but where everybody belongs," where being is not made a precondition of belonging (Melechi, 1993: 37).

As I have said, however, affective commonality or investment in a particular scene need not be productive of an identity.[15] As Nancy argues, "such a thinking – the thinking of community as essence – is in effect the closure of the political. Such a thinking constitutes closure because it assigns to community a *common being*, whereas community is a matter of something quite different, namely, of existence inasmuch as it is *in* common, but without letting itself be absorbed into a common substance"(1991: xxxviii). In fact, fandom needs to be differentiated from other degrees of investment or involvement in a scene. Grossberg specifies that "fandom is different from…fanaticism, by which I mean an (ideological) identification which involves the production of identity. In fanaticism, the investment in particular cultural practices becomes the dominant structure of one's self-imagination" (1997:6). In fandom, on the other hand, the investment in cultural practices and places is much more itinerant, even flirtatious. Flirtation, as Hebdige has noted, "may, in the long run, be more productive than the white heat of commitment, the passionate and violent divisions and couplings that mark the rapturous ascent of identity politics" (1996). In fandom, identifications and investments with particular scenes are continually shifting, in flux, never forever in place or emplaced. This itinerancy of fandom introduces a migrancy, a continual reorientation toward new sites, new scenes, new homes. "Migrancy…involves a movement in which neither the points of departure nor those of arrival are immutable or certain" (Chambers, 1994: 5). In a sense, then, fans never "go home" for home is always moving elsewhere, reconfigured as a "mobile habitat" (Chambers, 1994: 4).[16]

Given that the Left seems ensnared in what Eve Kosofsky Sedgwick calls the "recalcitrant knots" of identity politics, the promise of the scenic machinery of mobilization lies in its ability to function as a heuristic for imagining new forms of political practice and political community: a migrant politics and a political migrancy, a politics of the "in-between," a perpetual proceeding "from the middle" to an elsewhere (Deleuze and Guattari, 1987: 25). If politics is about moving people from this place to someplace better (and realizing that this project is never to be accomplished once and for all), the political exigencies would seem to be less about who you are than about where you are going. Politics becomes a matter of inducing and structuring mobilities towards meeting places, creating common mobilities or trajectories towards someplace that is imagined as better. Charting the trajectories of mobility produced by music scenes can only be the first step towards such a politics of movement and migrancy. As Audre Lorde points out, "what you chart is already where you've been. But where we are going, there is no chart yet" (quoted in Chambers, 1994: 37). The itinerancy of political investment forces us to abandon the certainty of providing a map to point the way. Instead, perhaps our energies are better invested in the possibility of an ethics. For *"ethos* means to locate oneself in another place. In the endless interplay between *ethos* and *topos* we are forced to move beyond rigid positions and locations," forced to move toward an(other) place, the place of the other (Chambers, 1994: 42).

NOTES

An earlier version of this chapter was presented at the Drake Conference on Popular Music, Des Moines, IA, March 29-30, 1996. I would like to thank Ted Striphas, Larry Grossberg, John Sloop, and Andrew Herman for their help in the development of this piece. And, as always, my gratitude to Melissa for her unfailing support.

1. As such, my desire was driven by the authenticating logics of both the rock formation and the intellectual formation of popular culture cultural studies, an anxiety that my authority as a fan and a scholar could not be had any other way. I was a bit amused that my Chapel Hill address allowed me to accrue a certain degree of cultural capital at the conference in which some of the chapters composing this volume were delivered as papers. Yet one cannot assume that popular music scholars somehow stand outside of the logics of authentication operative in the object of their study. I do, however, want to mark the necessity of challenging, rather than reproducing these logics.

2. See Ross and Rose (1994) for a number of excellent examples.

3. As I point out later in this chapter, the specificity of a scene can often function as the commodified other in *opposition* to "authentic" musical community. Arguably, this was the logic of distinction operative in Mudhoney's disgust of Seattle's rise in popularity.

4. Grossberg (1992) defines an apparatus as alliances or articulations that "actively function to produce structures of power" (397). In this instance, the structure of power is a particular configuration of investments called "taste."

5. The deterritorializing logic of capital and its effects have been mapped by a number of contemporary theorists, most notably Deleuze and Guattari (1983), Harvey (1989), and Grossberg (1992). Aided by the creation of new, more flexible and "efficient" modes of capital accumu-

lation and the increasing interconnection of a global economy, capital seems to reproduce itself through the production of the mobility of capital alone, independent of any particular location or identity that capital occupies. As Grossberg (1992) argues, capital itself is defined "by its mobility, its ability to move across time and space, through different social formations (even noncapitalist ones)....It is capitalism's mobility that is at stake, and the current globalization of capitalism signals its increasing mobility as it moves into and through every social formation" (348). Or, as Deleuze and Guattari (1983) put it: "Capitalism schizophrenizes" (232).

6. "Music is moving rapidly into fresh areas. Likewise, the corporations that own and control the music business are strategically using music to develop new markets for consumer products, while developing new products. I call this *cultural mobility*" (Breen, 1995: 497).

7. In many ways I, too, would fall to prey to the same allegation.

8. I derive this distinction from Ang and Stratton's (1996) discussion vis à vis Australia.

9. The same can be said for "virtual" scenes, which exist empirically only in the complex of computer terminals dispersed in offices and living rooms around the world.

10. This latter experience is probably the most postmodern, in that experiences in the rave scene, often fueled by the synthetic drug, Ecstasy, are commonly described in terms similar to Jameson's (1991) description of the postmodern schizo experience: "a series of pure and unrelated presents in time" (27).

11. See Clifford (1992) and Morris (1988) for insightful and thought-provoking discussions of the problems and possibilities of the notion of "travel" as trope in cultural theory.

12. See Grossberg (1992: 207–8).

13. It is important to point out that this escape from everyday life is never really attainable. Authenticity is always already displaced to a "somewhere else." Even Chapel Hill has been territorialized by everyday life. Cat's Cradle, for example, the bar presumably the epitome of the Chapel Hill scene, is housed in a strip mall next to Pizza Hut and a video rental store – not exactly the environment where all your scenic dreams come true.

14. Such a notion of diasporan pilgrimage is important because it subverts the modern opposition between traveler and tourist (see Clifford, 1992; Morris, 1988).

15. The editors of this book rightly point out in their introduction that "emplacement and emplotment cannot and should not be reduced to the dynamics of language and discourse" (chapter 1). I would add that emplacement and emplotment need not be reduced to a question of identity formation.

16. As Marjorie Garber remarks, "You can't go home again. Why? Because you are home" (quoted in Chambers, 1994: 42).

REFERENCES

Ang, I., and J. Stratton. 1996. "Asianing Australia: Notes toward a Critical Transnationalism in Cultural Studies." *Cultural Studies* 10(1): 16–36.

Azerrad, M. 1992. "Grunge City." *Rolling Stone*, April 16, 43–48.

Bellafante, G. 1993. "Grunge Goes Dutch." *Time*, March 29, 69.

Bertsch, C. 1993. "Making Sense of Seattle." *Bad Subjects* [On-line], 5 (March/April). (http://english-www.hss.cmu.edu/BS/05/bertsch.html).

Breen, M. 1995. "The End of the World As We Know It: Popular Music's Cultural Mobility." *Cultural Studies* 9(3): 486–504.

Butler, J. 1990. *Gender Trouble: Feminism and the Subversion of Identity*. New York: Routledge.

Carter, P. 1992. *Living in a New Coutry: History, Traveling and Language*. London: Faber and Faber.

Chambers, I. 1994. *Migrancy, Culture, Identity*. New York: Routledge.

Clifford, J. 1992. "Traveling Cultures." In *Cultural Studies*, edited by L. Grossberg, C. Nelson, and P. Treichler, 96–111. New York: Routledge.

Cocks, J. 1990. "Still Thriving on Home Turf." *Time*, November 19, 121.

———. 1992. "Seattle's the Real Deal." *Time*, March 23, 70–1.

Davies, B. 1993. "Good Luck, Chapel Hill: Scene Veterans Say 'Don't Believe the Hype.'" *Billboard*, March, I–22, I–30–31.

de Certeau, M. 1984. *The Practice of Everday Life*. Berkeley: University of California Press.

Deleuze, G., and F. Guattari. [1972] 1983. *Anti-Oedipus: Capitalism and Schizophrenia*, translated by R. Hurley, M. Seem, and H.R. Lane. Minneapolis: University of Minnesota Press.

———. [1980] 1987. *A Thousand Plateaus: Capitalism and Schizophrenia*, translated by B. Massumi. Minneapolis: University of Minnesota Press.

Dunn, S. 1994. *The Official Slacker Handbook*. New York: Warner Books.

Garcia, G. 1992. "Tripping the Night Fantastic." *Time*, August 17, 60–1.

Gehman, P. 1992. "Artist of the Year: Nirvana." *Spin*, December.

Grossberg, L. 1988. "'You [Still] Have to Fight for Your Right to Party': Music Television as Billboards of Post-Modern Difference." *Popular Music* 7(3): 315–32.

———. 1992. *We Gotta Get Out of This Place: Popular Conservatism and Postmodern Culture*. New York: Routledge.

———. 1994. "Is Anybody Listening? Does Anybody Care?: On Talking about 'The State of Rock.'" In *Microphone Fiends: Youth Music & Youth Culture*, edited by Λ. Ross and T. Rose, 41–58. New York: Routledge.

———. 1997. *Dancing in Spite of Myself: Essays on Popular Culture*. Durham, NC: Duke University Press.

———. Forthcoming. "Cultural Studies, Modern Logics, and Theories of Globalization." In *Cultural Industries: New Work in Cultural Studies*, edited by A. McRobbie. Manchester, UK: Manchester University Press.

Hall, S. 1989. "The Meaning of New Times." In *New Times: The Changing Face of Politics in the 1990s*, edited by S. Hall and M. Jacques, 116–34. London: Verso.

———. 1991. "The Local and the Global: Globalization and Ethnicity." In *Culture, Globalization and the World-System*, edited by A. D. King, 19–40. London: Macmillan.

Harvey, D. 1989. *The Condition of Postmodernity*. Cambridge, MA: Blackwell.

Hebdige, D. 1996. "On Tumbleweeds and Body Bags: remembering America." In *Longing and Belonging: From the Faraway Nearby* [An International Exhibition curated for the SITE Santa Fe]. Albuquerque: University of New Mexico.

Jameson, F. 1991. *Postmodernism, or The Cultural Logic of Late Capitalism*. Durham, NC: Duke University Press.

Lefebvre, H. [1971] 1984. *Everyday Life in the Modern World*, translated by S. Rabinovitch. New Brunswick, NJ: Transaction.

————. [1974] 1991. *The Production of Space*, translated by D. Nicholson-Smith. Cambridge, MA: Blackwell.

Lipsitz, G. 1990. *Time Passages: Collective Memory and American Popular Culture.* Minneapolis: University of Minnesota Press.

Massey, D. 1994. *Space, Place, and Gender.* Minneapolis, MN: University of Minnesota Press.

Melechi, A. 1993. "The Ecstasy of Disappearance." In *Rave Off: Politics and Deviance in Contemporary Youth Culture*", edited by S. Redhead, 29–40. Aldershot, UK: Avebury.

Morris, E. 1994. "A Music Scene Grows on Martha's Vineyard." *Billboard,* August 13, 11.

Morris, M. 1988. "At Henry Parkes Motel." *Cultural Studies* 2(1): 1–17, 28–47.

Nancy. J.-L. 1991. *The Inoperative Community*, translated by P. Connor, L. Garbus, M. Holland, and S. Sawhney. Minneapolis: University of Minnesota Press.

Orlova, L. 1993. "Grunge: Everything Like in Life." *Moscow News*, November 12, 15.

Painton, P. 1992. "Country Rocks the Boomers." *Time*, March 30, 62–6.

Ross, A., and T. Rose, eds. 1994. *Microphone Fiends: Youth Music & Youth Culture.* New York: Routledge.

Straw, W. 1991. "Systems of Articulation, Logics of Change: Communities and Scenes in Popular Music." *Cultural Studies* 5(3): 368–88.

Tilsner, J. 1993. "From Trash Can Straight to Seventh Avenue." *Business Week,* March 22, 39.

Thornton, S. 1996. *Club Cultures: Music, Media and Subcultural Capital.* Hanover, NH: University Press of New England.

15

Negativland, Out-law Judgments, and the Politics of Cyberspace

John Sloop and Andrew Herman

FOR IMMEDIATE RELEASE JUNE 1 1992:
NEGATIVLAND "U2" ALBUM WILL NOT BE CENSORED!!!!

The Copyright Violation Squad, a division of the Aggressive School of Cultural Workers, Washington Chapter, is called into action once again as the satirical "U2" album by Negativland, loaded with strong social significance, is suppressed by the Entertainment-Military Establishment.

It is obvious by now that the real motive behind banning recordings such as this is not the money these artists are supposedly keeping the "owners" of the work from "legally earning." It is the suppression of a very well-guarded secret: NO ONE can own the Electronic Environment; one can only own the means by which to produce it. The music industry sure would like you to believe they do (money talks...), but really, pay no attention to the man behind the curtain. Works of art that have been praised the world over are now being

banned from existence. Nobody has the right to abolish
ideas, and recorded music is only organized thoughts
and sounds.

Therefore the Copyright Violation Squad makes available a cassette copy of Negativland's "U2". This is only
a temporary solution. The perpetrators of these archaic
notions of censorship must be convinced to reverse
their decisions. The contacts can be found at right. Tell
them they should stop letting their fantasies of control
from getting in the way of cultural expression.

–Posting on the Original
Negativland Web Site (1993)

In Jacques Attali's (1985) *Noise: The Political Economy of Music*, he notes that
in the case of sound as a cultural phenomenon, relations of power are
located in the shifting boundary between "noise" and "music." Specifically, for Attali, music is tamed noise. That is, while music is a structural code
that defines the hegemonic ordering of positions of power and difference
that are located in the aural landscape of sound, noise (sound that falls outside of a dominant musical code) transgresses the dominant ordering of difference. Music provides an affirmation of the dominant ordering of sounds,
of aural pleasure, of contemporary ideology; noise is threatening precisely
because it is not affirmative of contemporary codes.

Of course, as anyone who has listened to unfamiliar sounds long enough
knows, what is noise at one moment can be symphonic the next; what hurts
the ears later pleases them. Indeed, a colloquial history of music would have
to point out the multiple voices that called early rock and roll "noise," that
decried punk as "noise," that heard hip-hop as "not music – just a bunch of
sounds." It is the slippage of music and noise that makes up one of the most
riveting battlegrounds of culture. Moreover, notions of music and noise
could easily be parlayed as metaphors into discussions of all hegemonic and
counterhegemonic discourses in that what was once oppositional becomes
dominant, what was once an illicit shortcut becomes a paved pathway allowing one to legally "walk in the city."[1]

Witness the words of the Copyright Violation Squad, as noted above,
that "recorded music is only organized thoughts and sounds." For the Copy-

right Violation Squad, the Negativland single, a pastiche of various sounds and recordings that was on the losing end of a copyright battle, was "organized noise" or "music" and hence could not be owned by anyone. To those attempting to keep the single from being sold, marketed, or heard on the grounds of copyright violation, the single represented legal "noise" of sorts precisely because it was transgressive of normal legal and cultural codes. The single was "organized sound" rather than noise only for those with the ears, the cultural sensibility, to hear the music.

In this chapter, we will explore the legal case surrounding Negativland's "The Letter 'U' and the Numeral '2'" in order to comment on the transformation of noise into music, both metaphorically and legally. Our discussion will not center on the single itself or its sounds (except to comment on our appreciation for it) but will instead focus on the political and legal battles over music and noise. In particular, we will suggest that the advent of Internet and the World Wide Web have provided spaces, at least temporary ones, in which those who hear "noise" as an alternative music are able to establish alternative systems of judgment and aesthetics. In this case, at least, the legal battle over the status of Negativland's single provided the impetus and space for the establishment of a community that made judgments "outside of the law" (out-law judgment) and enacted those judgments. In effect, because they termed "music" what another community had termed "noise," it was up to them to implement procedures that treated the sounds of Negativland as music rather than noise. We are not simply suggesting that communities have different shared aesthetics – of course they do. In this particular case, we are suggesting that the difference between noise and music provided a battle ground on which questions of legality, aesthetics, and rights were waged.

Finally, we contend that one of the imperative functions of cultural critics is to not only investigate cases like this one, but also to bring these cases to public attention in order to allow them to act as sparks in the social imaginary, sparks that encourage transformations of dominant laws and ideology.[2] Given that we are in a period of growing social and academic conservatism, nothing could be more urgent. Moreover, given that much of this academic conservatism has been placed at the foot of the self-reflectiveness of "post" scholarship,[3] we advance this study as an attempt to work with post assumptions and, working with a set of judgments made in a vernacular community, an attempt to bring the case forth as an example by which transgressive judgments can be made. Hence, we will look materially at how a transgressive judgment was made and carried into practice, and we will then attempt to bring this transgressive judgment to the fore as one possible way to reorganize contemporary dominant understandings of justice and judgment.

You, too?:
The Organic Creation of a Resistant Community[4]

I remember the moment I first heard Negativland's "U2": I was driving home from school one evening, the night air just warm enough to keep the windows of my car rolled down, when the college radio DJ announced that a new Negativland single had arrived that day. From start to finish, I was riveted to the sounds, my driving becoming hazardous as my attention was drawn more and more fully to the radio. I parked my car in my apartment complex's lot and sat listening, feeling confused and elated, as the temporal anchors of my rock and roll biography slipped loose from their moorings. The maniacal voice of an apoplectic Casey Kasem deconstructed my past. Frustrated by the inability of the producer to cue up the correct song dedication in honor of "Snuggles," the recently deceased dog of a fan, Casey exploded, "OK, I wanted a goddamn *concerted effort* to come out of a record that isn't a fucking up-tempo record every time I do a goddamn *death* dedication. It's the last goddamn time, I want somebody to use his *fuckin'* brain not to come out of a record, that is, uhh, that, that's up-tempo an' I gotta talk about a fuckin *dog dyin'!*"

He then turned his wrath upon the newest band of world-historical importance by saying "That's the *letter* U and the *numeral* 2. Is that the way I say it? I dunno how to *say* it…this is bullshit, nobody cares …these guys are from England and who *gives* a shit." Was this the same friendly voice who first introduced me to Elton John and Grand Funk Railroad?, I wondered as Casey and his signature ID derailed off the tracks of radio friendly propriety: "We're counting down the 40 biggest hits in the 50 states. This is American Top 40, right here on the radio you grew up with. Music Radio 138. This is American Top 40. This is American Top 40. This is bullshit, bullshit, bullshit."

And if the sounds of my old Top 40 friend going ballistic were not disconcerting enough, the fragmented voice of Bono vapidly ruminating on the

need for innovation in rock and roll, cut and mixed with the kazoo-led lyrical implosion of "I Still Haven't Found What I'm Looking For," deconstructed my present: "I have kissed honey lips/felt the healing in her fingertips/It
burned like fire/and it reminded cheap, melting plastic/But I haven't found
what I am looking for, I haven't found it...I 'm *lookin'* for it, but I don't even
know where it is. I don't even really know anything anymore. I just don't
really know what to do...Or do I? Maybe I oughta be shot point blank in
the stamper tonight." A song that had been an apotheosis of soulful yearning and rock and roll sincerity now suddenly seemed to me to be typical pop
song pompous sentimentality. I couldn't leave the car, even after the song
was over; in a ten-minute period, the song forced me to reposition myself,
to rethink my relationship with music in particular and in specific. I made a
mental note to buy the single the following day. As was often the case in
graduate school, however, the following day turned into the following week,
and by then, it was too late. When I tried to buy it, the record store clerk
told me that the single had been pulled from distribution and from the airwaves, mumbling something about censorship at the hands of "corporate"
record companies, "corporate" rock stars, and "corporate" deejays. While he
mumbled about censorship, I was simply angry and disappointed that I had
waited too long to purchase it. But then, I could always tape a friend's copy.

However, the story of what had happened legally to the single and to
Negativland is important to how the remainder of this case develops. Negativland is a group of sound artists that gathers together fragments and samples of sounds and images from the mass-mediated aural landscape, mixing
them together in order to provide a parodic collage-critique of contemporary culture. In the case of the "The Letter 'U' and the Numeral '2' " single,
the band compiled studio outtakes from Casey Kasem's "American Top 40,"
various fragments of U2's "I Still Haven't Found What I'm Looking For" as
well as a vocalized parody of the same, interviews with U2 band members,
samples from the MTV Video Music Awards (a production that, in one of
the many ironies of the case, had used samples from one of Negativland's
recordings), and a variety of other sounds. The recording was released by
SST Records in a package that featured the letters "U2" prominently super-
imposed upon an image of the (in)famous American spy plane of the same
name. As we will discuss in more detail below, the cover art purportedly led
some U2 fans to purchase the single assuming that it was a new U2 song.
Within a few week's of the song's release, Island Records and Warner-Chap-
pell Music (respectively, U2's label and music publishing company) filed suit

against both Negativland and SST demanding that they turn over all physical manifestations of the single's sound and image and agree to no longer produce copies of the song. In the end, the judgment of the dominant legal system was draconian: the single and all "legitimate" signs of its existence were removed from circulation and both Negativland and SST were ultimately compelled to pay over $90,000 in legal fees and damages resulting directly and indirectly from the case.[5] By any reckoning, the consequences of the litigation were disastrous for Negativland: their royalties from existing and future recordings were encumbered; their capacity to work as artists, as well as their very livelihood was threatened; and the product of their artistic talents was (to use their own words) "removed from the world" (Negativland, 1995: 245). Yet, paradoxically, this literal disaster provided the conditions for the elaboration of a positive, and distinctively postmodern form of "disastrous" (which literally means to be without stars) outlaw judgment – a judgment made without a guiding star, but which provided an efficacious ground for a cultural practice of resistance that was disseminated and decentered.

Since Island/Warner Chappell first filed suit in November 1991, the case has acquired a good deal of notoriety as an interesting example of copyright (and trademark) infringement in the age of sampling and digital reproduction.[6] Although issues concerning copyright, authorship, and ownership of the cultural commodity do indeed loom large in the case and are crucial to our analysis, they are not our central focus.[7] Rather, our primary concern is with how such cyberspace services as E-mail, newsgroups, and the World Wide Web functioned as decentered, interstitial institutional contexts for the development and practice of postmodern out-law judgment. In this case, a community grew *organically*, in the Gramscian sense of the term, out of the need for an alternative judgment, in a need to make available the "music" of Negativland after the dominant legal system had seen it as a form of "noise."[8]

As we will show, over time, a community constituted itself and not only provided a recording and loose distribution system for the song itself, but it also provided a medium for producing and disseminating a sophisticated oppositional discourse to the dominant legal and economic system that had stopped the "legitimate" release of the song. In short, the case became one in which an alternative community, an out-law community, not only made judgments, but made judgments that were resistant to contemporary domi nant politics and practices. As we work our way through this story, we will use this case to explore the possibilities of cyberspace for resistant judgments, as a site where individuals ("I"s) can bind together to constitute alternative communities on particular issues and to practice their own judgments.

How did this out-law community come together? My own experience in trying to get a copy of single is exemplary. When I finally did attempt to record the CD, I found that none of my circle of friends had purchased it. Hence, I resigned myself to never hearing it again, a none too pleasant thought. Late the next year, however, I not only was listening to it again, but I had been mailed a copy of it from someone I had never met before physically and haven't talked to since. My acquisition of the single was precipitated by my access to, and use of various cyberspace sites, including newsgroups. Given a computer and Net access as a condition of my first faculty position, I discovered the "alt.music.alternative" USENET newsgroup and posted a note requesting information about Negativland's "U2." The response was, for a novice user, overwhelming. Not only did a number of people write back, each offering to record it for me (some off the original, some numerous generations old), but I was flooded with over 30 documents that pertained to the legal and popular culture "case" that resulted in the aftermath of the single's being pulled from distribution. When I finally did choose to have someone make a copy, this person did so without pay – he said it was in the interest of letting the band be heard. I had the song, at last, but I also had much more: documents written by the band in defense of their right of "free speech," the band's description of their practice of pastiche, faxes from Casey Kasem to fans explaining why he did not want to sanction the release of the song, legal transcripts, lawyer's letters, etc. Eventually, I became intrigued with the case as much as I did in the song.

Over the next couple of years, the amount of information, and the availability of the single increased. Not only were the documents from the case regularly posted in full on "alt.music.alternative" but a home page was also established from which one could make links to each of the documents.[9] Moreover, the distribution of the song itself became more systematic when the so-called Copyright Violation Squad made cassette versions of the single available for $7, with any profit given back to the band to help sponsor the Negativland Legal Defense Fund. Later, and to this date, the recording was made available more simply through downloading off the Negativland home page.

In effect, once I posted that one note asking for information about the single, I discovered an entire community of people who were not only constituted by a shared sense of aesthetics but who, without an official organizer, established their own loose "court of judgment" on this case and then provided the means to carry out their judgment. It is not that any of this occurred as the result of a "leader" gathering together opposition troops for battle. Instead, people were drawn together because of their access to the net, and once gathered, set up their own means of justice – the song was not a copyright infringement, and it would be distributed, regardless of the dominant legal system's decisions on the case. Within two years of the single's release it had became easy to access a recording of "U2." Moreover, a Web page was established with the names and numbers of people to contact about the case or a recording of the song, a history of the case, pertinent documents, as well as information about censorship laws and ways of changing laws in the "dominant" legal system. Those who came to the Web page through the music of Negativland were provided with information on how to change legal judgments, on how to use "dominant" tools to transform noise into music.

It is important to note that this was not simply a case of people resisting the law by making a recording illegally for a friend or circle of friends. Instead, a community was constituted around the case by individuals who would in all likelihood never meet in the flesh, and who are constituted "as one" or "as a community" only in and through this case. The various manifestations of cyberspace and its resources created a space in which people with a different sense of justice were able to come together "virtually" on the basis of their concerns. Once together, they established a discourse community that provided them with a hitherto nonexistent sense of identity. The coming together was "organic" in that the existing legal and economic system created the conditions under which individuals who were concerned about the song were forced to gather together, to identify one another.

Without the Net, there of course would have been some distribution of the song among friends and some distribution of the materials from the case. With the Net, however, not only were more individuals invited to become part of this circle (if only because it allowed them the opportunity to overcome geographic boundaries), but the Web sites for materials concerning the Negativland case then became links on other pages dealing with issues of censorship. Hence, someone attempting to resist legal decisions on one matter, say, censorship of a particular type of artistic expression, might find links that would take them to Negativland's case. As a result, the Negativland community set itself and its space up not only as a resistant community with an alternate sense of justice but also, and this is key, in making their judgment, they become part of a larger alternative system of judgment. In a sense, the judgment of the "Negativland" community operates as a precedent in a series of other cases brought before the Web. In order to make a point that a particular case should not be censored, one links to the "Negativland page" and provides a precedent of a case in which a recording was made available. The "You, too?" of Negativland fan to Negativland fan becomes a "You, too?" of like-minded individuals on general matters of free speech, even when those individuals may not share the particular brand of speech.

ARTICULATING NOISE AS MUSIC: NEGATIVLAND'S LEGAL ARGUMENT

Not only did an out-law community develop that deployed a different judgment about the legality of the single, but Negativland themselves attempted to articulate a defense of their actions within the logic of the dominant legal system. It is here, in their explicit encounters with dominant culture, that Negativland was forced to most clearly articulate a logic of aesthetic and artistic "authenticity" that differed from the dominant notion.

The development of an oppositional discourse of authenticity for out-law judgment was messy and contradictory. In the many statements and communiqués produced by Negativland as the case unfolded, one can discern conflicting notions of authenticity, which were invoked as grounds for challenging the dominant law judgment under the umbrella concept of "Fair Use." Fair use, of course, is a provision of the United States Copyright Act of 1976 (Section 107) that allows for the use of copyrighted material without the prior consent of the owner of the copyright, provided that it does not detract from the market value of the material.[10] Over the course of the case, Negativland spent a considerable amount of time and money arguing for a liberalized interpretation of the fair use provision. Indeed, ironically, much of Negativland's argument for liberalized definitions of fair use was affirmed by none other than Justice David Souter in the Supreme Court's decision in the 2 Live Crew/Pretty Woman case.[11] As Negativland's lawyers were to later note, if that decision had been in effect when Island Records initially sued, Negativland would have won the copyright infringement part of the suit hands down.

However, even a liberalized notion of fair use that is legally sanctioned by the courts binds cultural practice to the discourse of dominant law. This is not to say that prevailing juridical definitions of copyright and fair use were immaterial to the case or to the issue of authorship and authenticity in musical production, particularly with respect to sampling and other electronic means of aural (re)production (cf. Sanjek, 1994). Rather, it was Negativland's broader connotation of fair use that is of more interest and pertinence for our analytical purposes.

In their very first public statement after the copyright and trademark judgment was rendered, Negativland called for a "more humane attempt at reasonable discourse about artistic integrity and the artless, humorless legalism that controls corporate music today" (Negativland, 1995: 22). They situated this desire for "reasonable discourse" within the context of the immense disparity in economic and legal power between themselves (and SST) and entertainment corporate behemoths such as Island Records. Faced with the "unyielding intimidation of money and power" of Island Records, and "preferring retreat to total annihilation," Negativland "had no choice but to agree completely" to Island's demands. However, even though they had no choice but to settle the suit, they maintained that the assumptions and logic of the dominant legal judgment could not remain unchallenged. Indicting the restricted symbolic economy of the cultural commodity, and its status as sovereign territory of private property, they argued that

> apparently, Island's sole concern in this act of censorship is their determination to control the marketplace, as if the only reason to make records is to make money....In this culture, the market rules and money *is* power. They own the law, and no one who is still interested in the supremacy of a vital and freewheeling art can afford not challenge this aspect of our decline. It is a telling tribute to this culture corporation's crass obsessions that Island's whole approach to our work automatically assumed its goal was to siphon off their rightful profits. These people lost their ability to appreciate the very nature of what they are selling a long time ago....For the law to claim that this alleged motive [enti-

tlement to profits] is the sole criterion for legal deliberation is to admit that music itself is not to be taken seriously. Culture is more than commerce (Negativland, 1995; 22).

This critique of music as commodity, with its attendant notion of authenticity as property right, was succinctly stated later by Negativland in the "Tenants of Free Appropriation": "No one should be allowed to claim a private control over the creative process itself. This struggle is essentially one of art against business, and ultimately about which one must make way for the other" (Negativland, 1995: 251). In these statements Negativland is invoking one of the central axes of discrimination and differentiation that has long been central to the traditional ideology of authenticity in rock culture. At one end of this axis is the inauthentic mainstream center of the culture industry, which understands music simply as an entertainment commodity. At the other end is the authentic margins of musical artistry, which understands the "very nature" of music as a process of "freewheeling" cultural creativity that is always in excess of commerce.

Although this invocation of an authentic "artistic integrity" that transgresses the "artless, humorless legalism" of corporate sovereignty is one of the grounds upon which out law judgment in this case was developed, it was not the only notion of "authentic" that was deployed. Indeed, by itself, this notion of artistic integrity proved to be a contradictory point of ideological contention between Negativland and SST Records. As we discussed above, this notion of authentic artistry is rooted in the romantic conception of the artist as a centered, singular, and unique creative subject. As appropriators and manipulators of found sound, Negativland, both as individuals and a collective, do not fit the definition of romantic authorship. This was the argument that was used against Negativland by the owner of SST records, Greg Ginn, when Negativland refused to pay the entire costs of the case (they offered to split the costs 50/50). Ginn, who was a founding member of the L.A. punk band Black Flag, accused Negativland in a press release of not being real musicians or a real band because "they have never toured and have only played occasional live shows" (Negativland, 1995: 51). In contrast to "real" authentic marginality and oppositional music of punk, Ginn claimed that Negativland was simply an "upper middle class hobby." He also said that the band members were "paranoid victims of a media cocoon they frequently lampoon" (Negativland, 1995: 52). Ironically, in spite of Ginn's invocation of the "real world" of punk music and ethics as a ground of authenticity (the SST motto was "Corporate Rock Sucks"), he himself eventually sued Negativland for their transgression of his own corporate sovereignty. This transgression, according to the suit, consisted in, of all things, copyright infringement when Negativland published a magazine containing his press releases. Thus, the notion of noncommercial artistic integrity was not sufficient as an effective ground of postmodern out-law judgment.

The ground upon which this judgment was based was constructed around a different notion of artistic integrity and authenticity than that entailed by the romantic notion of creative authorship. This authenticity, as Negativland described it in their second press release, was the "authenticity of copyright infringement and sampling as a legitimate creative technique" (Negativland, 1995: 48). Or, as Negativland was later to call it, this is authenticity of "free appropriation." The construction of an authenticity of appropriation as basis for out-law judgment involved a complex and multilayered analysis of the history of cultural production.

In their very first press release Negativland directly attacked the romantic notion of authorship as the sole criterion of artistic authenticity, and its embodiment in copyright law, by arguing that "the law must educate itself to the fact that ever since monkey's saw or did, *the entire history of art forms has been BASED UPON THEFT*" (Negativland, 1995: 23). In one of the documents about the case most widely circulated in the Web out-law community, "Crosley Bendix Discusses the Copyright Act," Negativland expanded this argument by discussing the development of different forms of popular music and modern art. Folk music, blues, jazz, Dada, surrealism, and pop art have all had "creative theft as their modus operandi" (Negativland, n.d.: 3). Such historical examples of artistic creation through appropriation were so profuse that it "all but forms a tradition of 'natural' law" (Negativland, n.d.: 3).

Second, within this logic and practice of appropriation as creative theft, the artistic process is seen as an "obvious and natural desire to embody or transform existing things as a form of dialog with the material environment" (Negativland, 1995: 150). Accordingly, a rather different standard of artistic authenticity and originality is deployed here. Rather than viewing "originality" as inhering in the singular vision of the individual artist, it inheres in the process of transformation that occurs only within the context of the shared culture of a community. The authenticity of appropriation, whether it be through digital sampling, satirical parody, or audiovisual collage, is therefore decentered and dialogical. Far from being a simple act of piracy or plagiarism, appropriation is a gesture of respectful inspiration, where one uses an original source as a springboard for one's own creativity, thus adding something new to the cultural conversation. Appropriation is also democratic. As Dick Hebdige has described the tactics of appropriation and quotation in the reggae practice of "versioning," "It's a democratic principle because no one has the final say. Everybody has a chance to make a contribution. And no one's version is treated as Holy Writ" (1987: 14).

Finally, for Negativland and the out-law community, it is the democratic nature of appropriation that acquires particular salience as ground for judgment and cultural practice in the postmodern mediascape. As they argue in their "Fair Use" essay that was originally published on the Web, the media environment has become the dominant sphere of everyday life. Therefore, everything that circulates in the mediascape should be understood as always-already in the "public domain" and thus suitable for appropriation. However, the dominant law of copyright and the restricted symbolic economy of the cultural commodity entails "a surrender of the age-old concept of shared culture to the exclusive interests of private owners which has relegated our population to spectator status" (Negativland, 1995: 190). The proliferation of new technologies of "media capture" and electronic reproduction represents an opportunity for people to move from being passive spectators to active participants in cultural production. Moreover, appropriation can serve as a resistive cultural practice, a "tactics of the weak" in Michel de Certeau's (1984) terms, whereby the restricted economy of commodified mass culture is subverted by its intended audience:

> In modern terms, appropriation is about culture jamming – capturing the corporately controlled subjects of the one-way media barrage, reorganizing them to comment upon themselves, and spitting them back into the barrage for cultural consideration. The act of appropriations from this media assault represents a kind of liberation from our status as helpless sponges which is so desired by the advertisers who pay for it all…Appropriation sees media, itself, a telling source and subject, to be captured, rearranged, even mutilated and injected back into the barrage by those who are subjected to it. Appropriators claim the right to create with mirrors. (Negativland, 1995: 196)

And, for Negativland and the out-law community, the right to create with mirrors through appropriation forms the ground, however contingent and tenuous, for a judgment and justice that is extravagant and generous.

Again, we are not simply suggesting that this difference in judgment results from the fact that cyberspace allowed a gathering place, but that it also happened as a result of the epistemological changes brought on by changes in media. Walter Ong (1982) has suggested that print and literacy allowed for the idea of independently owned thoughts (and hence copyright) (78–84) in that these media also allowed for the creation of the "individual." With the slow advent of the changes in consciousness brought on by new electronic media technology, we may be beginning to see the deconstruction of solid individuality and ownership, on a mass cultural level. This case, because it involved a "product" made up of an electronic pastiche, and because a great deal of it took place on the web, may be a prophet to these changes in logic.

In his discussion of cyberspace and hypertext as cultural technologies, Stuart Moulthrop (1994) deploys Deleuze and Guattari's concepts of "smooth" and "striated" space in order to discuss their epistemological politics. For Deleuze and Guattari (1987), "striated space" is a field or territory that is mapped and gridded as a horizontal plane, with the locations and paths between all locations in the territory defined and determined by the *logos* of law and the state. In contrast, "smooth space" is fluid, liminal and multidimensional. It is always in the process of arrangement as territory through principle of *nomos* (as opposed to *logos*), a practice or custom that is unwritten and open-ended. As Moulthrop notes, smooth and striated spaces "exist only in mixture: smooth space is constantly being translated, transversed into a striated space; striated space is constantly being reversed, returned to a smooth space" (1994: 316). What Moulthrop, as well as Deleuze and Guattari, would note in looking at this case is that not only did the space of the Web allow for a community to distribute "noise" that they heard to be music, but that it also allowed for the construction of a new sense of ownership that is nomoetic but that did not harden into the *logos* of dominant law. That is, individuality and ownership do not disappear in an electronic epistemology; they change. We move from a logic of romantic individualism to a logic of pastiche products and pastiche individuality. We're still here and "art objects" still exist; we, and they, are simply made up of already existing pieces.

Moreover, one of the ways that George Landow argues that hypertext might operate as a liminal practice of smooth space is that it allows for the multiplicity of identities and judgments, all existing simultaneously, and not necessarily in conflict with one another (1994: 185–90). The availability of information in cyberspace, the multiplicity of links, and the impulse to take oneself in any chosen "reading" direction (and the lack of a desire to interfere with the readings that others develop), allow cyberspace (as hypertext) to develop into a nomoetic space in which one merges fragments in one's own designs, pulling them together and taking them apart, making hybrids, and being generous enough to allow others the same leisure. As Moulthrop (1994) says of the possibilities of hypertext, "If we can say anything at this point about interactive media and their possibilities for cultural change, it must be that any new culture will be as promiscuous as its texts, always seeking new relations, fresh paralogical permutations of order and chaos" (317).

One of the fascinating aspects of the Negativland case is the way it embodies this promising but rather abstract politics of epistemology. In a pragmatic sense, because of the distribution of materials concerning the case, and because of the availability of the Negativland tape, a different decision was made than that which was predetermined by legal and financial concerns. The Web site provides a space of defiance and distribution that operates between the poles of the smooth and the striated, the nomoetic, and the logocentric – the site is in essence a fragmented record company (fans making copies of tapes for other fans) that illegally uses "legal" communication and distribution processes (Internet, and "snail" mail) to distribute an illegal recording (albeit with tacit approval by the band itself). Hence, "justice" is served pragmatically through the appropriation of services provided by dominant institutions. While such a judgment certainly reifies the "father's tools" (here, the Internet), it is not these tools with which a problem was had; indeed, while these tools have their own ideological problems, here they provided a site for pirate justice.

Given the relative marginality of Negativland,[12] the Web site can be said to have been not just helpful, but almost necessary, for this case of out-law justice. While some friends and acquaintances would have surely made dubs of the single had there not been a web site for discussion, the Web site brought a worldwide community into being by allowing people an identity around which to constitute themselves (e.g., "free speech advocates," "fans of Negativland"). Moreover, numerous people who would not have known someone who owned a copy of the single or who did not care enough to purchase a copy of the song, were given a site to sample the single; the virtual community provides the song with a much greater shelf life than it would have had otherwise. In essence, the Web provided a site for a group of individuals, angered at the decisions of dominant institutions to gather, to constitute a community who made its own judgment, one directly in opposition to that made by SST and Island Records. Theirs was the justice of the out-law, a judgment made in the interests of a community that arose out of a particular need.

The out-law, at least as the decisions of the out-law work on the Web, also acts as a model, an alternative and contingent precedent in an alternative system of law. Because of the various links that are made from different sites on the Internet, the out-laws of the Negativland case not only provide distribution of the song and legal documents to fans but also, in providing a series of documents that show how their sense of justice works, provide a model of judgment for others interested in similar issues. At the Negativland site, one is able to find original reviews of the song from popular press publications, series of legal letters between record companies and legal firms, series of press releases by the band concerning their case, and a Negativland statement on "Fair Use." In some sense, the band provides enough documents to those visiting the site that visitors are in effect invited to gather together fragments in a way similar to Negativland's own practice, "recontextualizing captured fragments to create something entirely new – a psychological impact based on a new juxtaposition of diverse elements, ripped from their usual context, chewed up, and spit out as a new form of hearing" (Negativland, 1995: 23). Those who come to the site are invited to gather together fragments of the case, with the case acting as a model, in order to create a different sense of justice and then to take these arguments forward publicly and change the way that decisions are made in all forums.

Moreover, the case acts as a model of judgment for other communities who make links to the Negativland home page. For example, if one visits the Elvis Presley home page, Andrea Berman, the author of the page, explains that she has been threatened legally by the Presley estate for having a guided tour of Graceland, with pictures and sounds, that Presley Enterprises had not approved.[13] The visitor to the site is invited to make a link that allows him/her to read the letter from the Presley Estate. Arriving at that page, one of the options is to learn more about censorship issues by making a link to the Negativland page. In essence, the Net operates as an alternate set of precedents. When the owner of one page is faced with legal action that it sees as unjust, it can easily cite other cases of out-law justice and invite its community to link with other forms of judgment and justice.

CONCLUSIONS AND CAUTIONS

While in this case, the Web provides a site of resistance, at least one form of resistance, one must be careful not to celebrate the Web as inherently a site of resistance. There are at least two obvious problems with the way Internet operates as a space for judgment and justice: access and discourse. Even if the Web were a utopian space for "free speech" in a Habermasian sense, which it is not, there are still very real economic, class, and cultural barriers to access to the Web. While there are certainly improvements being made to public access, it is also the case that those whose background has more often put them one on one with computer technologies are the ones more likely to use that technology when it is available. Hence, in a very basic sense, the Internet is at best a site of resistance for already privileged peoples.

Second, and perhaps more importantly, one must not forget that those who are interacting on the Web are always already embedded in, and emerging from, the same cultural discourses that exist outside of Internet. Hence, we are not meaning to claim, due to this one case of alternative justice, that the web creates a space for, as Charles Ess attempts to argue, free and separate individuals to get together for community dialogue (1994: 237). Instead, we are acknowledging that the "individuals" who engage in discussion on the Internet are of course only able to have discussions based upon their own positionality as subjects within racist, classist, and sexist cultural discourses. One enters the Internet as a positioned subject, shaped by discourses, institutional practices and lived experiences, and makes judgments as a result of one's basis within these discourses. Moreover, as Martin Rosenberg (1994) notes, even while hypertext in general can lead to a reading of fragments, it "always already" reproduces the very logocentric, geometric patterns that it attempts to subvert (291). While particular sites may provide a space for a struggle over judgment, a space where various fragments can be pulled together in new and different ways, it is also a site for reproduction. One must be careful where one steps and what one praises.

Both the case of Negativland's "U2" and the shape of cyberspace hold important lessons for poststructuralists in search of justice. Judgment and justice are not only, as Aristotle argued, a matter of practical wisdom and of the moment, but are also something to be struggled over by those people who feel they have been wronged and who hold their own sense of judgment, regardless of its contingency, as the correct sense of justice and judgment. That is, the out-law does what is right, not what is contingently right, but what appears to be transcendentally correct. However, in making judgments, one is always rewriting the judgment systems of dominant culture. Cyberspace allows, so to speak, a "hypersense" of the rewriting of the home page of judgment. Hence, when Negativland and its community rejudge the validity and legality of "U2," when they rewrite the laws of censorship, they create a space for rewriting justice, for rethinking judgment. The home-page is never stable, the links never permanently fixed, the sites always changing whether one realizes it or not. In this sense, cyberspace becomes a metaphor for out-law justice, with arguments and changes always in process, with links being made by groups with varying interests, varying desires. In cyberspace, one can never go home again, as home is always contingent upon the experiences of the trip. And with questions of judgment, one cannot find a space that is not shaped and transformed by the out-law judgments that one encounters along the way.

NOTES

1. We are of course playing off of de Certeau's (1984) discussion of "walking in the city" (91–110).
2. The idea of out-law discourse is explored in more theoretical detail in John M. Sloop and Kent A. Ono's (forthcoming) "Out-law Discourse: The Critical Politics of Material Judgment." In their essay, they argue that out-law discourses are the commonsense notions of justice made materially by vernacular communities on matters of right and wrong that are different than, although not necessarily opposed to, those of dominant ideology and dominant institutions. Out-laws are discourses or phrases in dispute; they are not individual actors. While all out-law judgments are not progressive, many can be used, at the discretion of individual critics, to provoke possibilities in the social imaginary for different ways of judging.
3. Dubbed the "crisis of authority" by Grossberg (1992), the crisis is said to be a condition in which those who make "post" assumptions expend

their energies refuting the viability of any essential ground (personal or Archimidean) upon which to make judgments. The academic and political Right, on the other hand, has no need for such persistent self-reflection, and hence its views gain currency as it posts a stable space for authority in a fragmenting world. As Probyn (1993) notes, "As the left continues to attack itself from within, a growing public discourse of 'new traditionalism' actively articulates care and community to the New Right....Transparent as it may seem...the right's reclaiming 'fundamental' values constitutes an appealing platform" (58).

4. The section contains a story told from the perspective of an individual. As far as "true" goes in "true stories," this is a true one. Rather than using such awkward phrases as "One of the two authors...," we will simply write the story from an individual perspective, as if there were only one author.

5. Of the $90,000, not all costs were a direct result of the initial suit by Island/Warner Chappell. SST incurred about $40,000 in costs from the Island suit and subsequently sued Negativland themselves over who was to bear the burden of the costs and other issues relating to Negativland's pursuit of (out)law justice outside the courts. Ultimately, Negativland's loss from both suits came to over $40,000. See Negativland, 1995 (166–7)

6. The case has been widely written about in the music press, as well as discussed in articles in law and other academic journals. Indeed, the notoriety of the case has been in no small measure due to an aggressive guerrilla publicity campaign waged by Negativland on the Internet and other alternative media. Negativland themselves have collected nearly all of the texts produced by and about the case in *Fair Use: The Story of the Letter 'U' and the Numeral '2'* (1995).

7. See Jones (1993) for a brief but useful analysis of the case in terms of authorship and authenticity that is complementary to the one we offer here.

8. Although we are discussing "community" here in a nonproblematic sense as the rhetorical or discursive label under which people constitute themselves as a group, we are well aware of the problematic "anthropomorphic" function of this term, as Whitt and Slack (1994) have recently commented on. We do acknowledge the links that this case, and the Internet in general, have to environmental concerns, even if we are not dealing with them in this chpater.

9. The site address is <http://sunsite.unc.edu/id/negativland>.

10. The status of the "fair use" provision within copyright law is a complex issue and, although it formed an important part of the Negativland case, it is not our primary focus here (for reasons that will be made clear shortly). For detailed discussion of the evolution of fair use as legal doctrine, especially in the context of sampling technology, see Korn (1995), Marcus (1995), and Negativland's own "Copyright, Fair Use and the Law" (1995), all of which can be found in Negativland (1995) as well as hypertext links from Negativland's home page on the World Wide Web.

11. In brief, the 2Live Crew/Pretty Woman case (legally known as Campbell v. Acuff-Rose) involved a parody of the original Roy Orbison song by the rap group 2Live Crew. The court found that the parody was an acceptable fair use under the Copyright Act. The text of Souter's opinion in the case, as well as Negativland's commentary on it, can also be found in Negativland (1995) and, yes, at Negativland's home page.

12. Even while popular on the "alternative" music scene, their recordings were not massive sellers. Indeed, it is very easy to find numerous college students who have never heard of the band or the "U2" single. When they have heard of it, it is likely because they are fans of U2 rather than of Negativland. According to their own estimates, the band's singles usually sell only between 10,000 and 15, 000 copies.

13. The address for the Elvis Presley home page is <http://sunsite.unc.edu/elvis/elvisholm.html>.

REFERENCES

Attali, J. 1985. *Noise: The Political Economy of Music*. Minneapolis: University of Minnesota Press.

de Certeau, M. 1984. *The Practice of Everyday Life*. Berkeley: University of California Press.

Deleuze, G., and F. Guattari. 1987. *A Thousand Plateaus*. Minneapolis: University of Minnesota Press.

Ess, C. 1994. "The Political Computer: Hypertext, Democracy, and Habermas." In *Hyper/text/theory*, edited by G. P. Landow. Baltimore, MD: Johns Hopkins University Press.

Grossberg, L. 1992. *We Gotta Get Out Of This Place: Popular Conservatism and Postmodern Culture*. New York: Routledge.

Jones, S. 1993. "Critical Legal Studies and Popular Music Studies." *Stanford Humanities Review* 3(2) (autumn): 77–90.

Korn, A. 1995. "Renaming That Tune: Audio Collage, Parody and Fair Use." In *Fair Use: The Story of the Letter 'U' and the Numeral '2'*, by Negativland. Concord, CA: Seeland.

Landow, G. P. 1992. *Hypertext: The Convergence of Contemporary Critical Theory and Technology*. Baltimore: Johns Hopkins University Press.

Marcus, J. 1995. "Don't Stop that Funky Beat." In *Fair Use: The Story of the Letter U and the Numeral 2*, by Negativland, 205–12. Concord, CA: Seeland.

Moulthrop, S. 1994. "Rhizome And Resistance: Hypertext and the Dreams of a New Culture." In *Hyper/text/theory*, edited by G. P. Landow, 299–319. Baltimore, MD: Johns Hopkins University Press.

Negativland. 1995. *Fair Use: The Story of the Letter 'U' and the Numeral '2'*. Concord, CA: Seeland.

Ong, W. J. 1982. *Orality and Literacy: The Technologizing of the Word*. New York: Methuen.

Probyn, E. 1993. *Sexing the Self: Gendered Positions in Cultural Studies*. New York: Routledge.

Rosenberg, M. E. 1994. "Physics and Hypertext: Liberation and Complicity in Art and Pedagogy." In *Hyper/text/theory*, edited by G.P. Landow. Baltimore, MD: Johns Hopkins University Press.

Sanjek, D. 1994. "Don't Have to D.J. No More." Sampling and the 'Autonomus' Creator. In *The Construction of Authorship: Textual Appropriation in Law and Literature*, edited by M. Woodmansee and P. Jaszi. Durham: Duke University Press.

Sloop, J. M., and K. A. Ono. 1997. "Out-law Discourse: The Critical Politics of Material Judgment." *Philosophy and Rhetoric*.

Whitt, L., and J. Slack. 1994. "Communities, Environments, and Cultural Studies." *Cultural Studies* 8(1): 5–31.

Index

Flores, G., 213, 216
Fong-Torres, B., 52
Foucault, Michel, 17, 258
Frankfurt school, 4–5, 37
Fraser, N., 86, 87, 89
Freeman, Chris, 105
Fregoso, Rosa Linda, 211, 214
Fried, S., 177
Frieden, Betty, 159
Friend, B., 221–2, 224, 226–7
Frith, Simon, 191–2, 194, 195, 197, 223, 250, 252, 254, 255
Fuchs, Cynthia, 22

Gaines, Donna, 77, 80–1, 87–8, 90, 92–3
Garber, Marjorie, 63
Garcia, Guy, 277
Gasper, Bob, 51
Gates, Henry Louis, Jr., 32–3
Gehman, Pleasant, 283
General Agreement on Tariffs and Trade (GATT), 192
Gingrich, Newt, 181, 198
Ginn, Greg, 301
Gitlin, T., 56, 59–60, 172
Goldberg, David Theo, 207
González, A., 213, 234, 235–6
Goodwin, Andrew, 22–3, 220, 228, 229, 233, 247
Gore, J., 233
Gramsci, Antonio, 5
Green Day, 108–11
Gregory, D., 8
Griffin, S., 163, 165
Griggers, Cathy, 103
Grogan, Emmett, 59

Grossberg, Lawrence, 6–7, 78, 108, 157, 207, 209, 210, 237, 255, 257–8, 271–3, 280, 284
Guattari, F., 21, 220, 238, 258, 284, 304

Hall, S., 206–7, 258, 278, 280
Hanke, Robert, 24
Hanna, Kathleen, 111–14
Havel, Vaclav, 198
heavy metal, 143, 147
Hebdige, D., 4, 5, 104, 157, 284, 303
Herman, Andrew, 25
Herman, J. P., 110–11
Herron, Jerry, 56
Hess, E., 160
hip community, Detroit (1960s), 51–2
hip-hop, aural recycling of, 41; dance mixes as covers, 148; repetition in, 37; tropes in, 40
hipster (Mailer's conception), 66–7
Hiwatt, Susan, 62
Holland, B., 180
Holliday, Billie, 34
Holm-Hudson, Kevin, 133
Hooker, John Lee, 58
House, Daniel, 281
Houston, Whitney, 178
Hunter, Tom, 225
Hurt, John, 32

identity, conception of Mexican American, 213; meaning in music related to, 158; of scenes, 279
industrial music, 40

mapping in understanding of music, 8

Marcus, Greil, 210

Marin, R., 183

markets, for cultural production, 189; for musical production, 189–90; regulation to counter, 191

Marsh, Dave, 49–50, 54–5

Martinez, L. B., 215

masculinity, electric guitar in depiction of, 62–3; performance in rock of, 79–81; in rock, 82–4

Maslin, Janet, 142

Massey, Doreen, 262, 274–5, 278–9

Masters, K., 177

materialism, combined with ethnography, 259–62; opposed to ethnography, 257–9

Mayfield, Geoff, 282

MC5, appropriation of black masculinity by, 57–60, 66; audience of, 52–3, 55; definition from Detroit's racial unrest (1960s), 60; lyrics of, 57; musical development of, 50–2; need for purification, 66; politics of, 48–9, 60, 64–8; song combining race, gender, and technology, 63–4, 71; translation of sensations of, 67–8

media industries, mergers and consolidations, 182–3; music industry as part of, 175

Melechi, A., 283

Mercer, Colin, 6

Middleton, Richard, 33

Miller, Mark C., 182–3

Miller, S., 197

mimesis, 15–16

minstrelsy, black–face, 60–1; New Christy Minstrels, 40

Monk, T. S., 38

Moore, A. F., 167

Moore, D., 236

Moore, Michael, 38

Morley, D., 219, 224

Morris, E., 279

Morris, M., 207, 279

Morthland, John, 209

Moulthrop, Stuart, 304, 305

MTV Europe, 221, 223

MTV Latino, establishing presence and local interest, 225–7; estimated audience and appeal, 221, 224–6; music television, 219–21; regional markets, 227–8

MTV Networks, 221–2, 227

multiculturalism, 207

Muñoz, C., Jr., 211–12

music, See also black music; conjunto music; industrial music; jazz; New Age music; popular music; ritual music; rock music; techno music; tejano music; African American traditions, 32–3; Attali's description, 18–19; as composition, 20; intimacy of, 133; meaning in, 157–8; meaning in British counterculture, 159–62; musical forms used to express counterculture values, 158; of Pansy Division, 109; political centrality of (Attali), 70–1; programmed into machine, 126; as repetition, 20, 42; as representation, 20, 42; as sacrifice, 19–20, 42; as tamed noise, 18–19, 292; time and memory in, 132–3

musical television, MTV Europe, 223–4; MTV Latino, 219–21; programming transnational, 225; programmming for, 228–31

music industry, Big Six entities in corporate regime, 174–5; changing structure of, 175; evolving nature of, 173; new paradigm to analyse, 176–82

Nancy, J.-L., 284

Narcisco Martinez Cultural Arts Center, 216

Nathan, Hans, 31, 33

National Public Radio (NPR), United States, 192

Negativland; availability of U2 song recording, 295–8; identified, 295; interpretation of copyright law and fair use provision, 299–300

Negativland Legal Defense Fund, 297

Negus, Keith, 177

Negus, P., 4

Neville, J., 154

New Age music, 39

noise, amplification to produce, 69–70; Attali's interpretation of, 70; in industrial and techno music, 40; mapping of social space with, 21; music as tamed noise (Attali), 18–19, 292

North American Free Trade Agreement (NAFTA), 192

Nunziata, S., 175

O'Brien, L., 79

O'Grady, T., 161

Olson, Mark, 24–5, 251

Ong, Walter, 19, 304

Orlova, L., 276

Painton, P., 281

Pansy Division, 101, 105–6, 108–12

Passeron, J. C., 199

Patoski, J. N., 206

Peña, M., 212–13

Pérez-Torres, R., 208, 211

politics, of British counterculture, 159; of MC5, 48–9, 60, 64–8

popular music, airplay quotas in Canada, 191; British regulation shaping, 191–2; characteristics of, 248–9; composition, 130; creation and marketing of, 254; cultural form of songs, 7; as cultural technology, 6–7; funding in Netherlands for, 192; lack of U.S. local intervention to support, 196–7; Latin American, 220–1; as producers' and programmers' medium, 130; Rocklist discussion group, 77–8, 81; spatialized analysis of, 8–9; subsidies in Canada for production of, 193–4; support in European countries for production, 194–6; U.S.national policies related to, 192–3; versions of, 138

popular music memory, 131–3